THE CULTURE OF ENTREPRENEURSHIP

A publication of the
Center for Self-Governance

THE CULTURE OF ENTREPRENEURSHIP

Edited by

Brigitte Berger

ICS PRESS
San Francisco, California

This book is a publication of the Center for Self-Governance, dedicated to the study of self-governing institutions. The Center is affiliated with the Institute for Contemporary Studies, a non-partisan, nonprofit public policy research organization. The analyses, conclusions, and opinions expressed in ICS Press publications are those of the authors and not necessarily those of the Institute, or of its officers, directors, or others associated with, or funding, its work.

Inquiries, book orders, and catalog requests should be addressed to ICS Press, 243 Kearny Street, San Francisco, CA 94108. (415) 981-5353. Fax: (415) 986-4878. For book orders and catalog requests call toll free in the contiguous United States: (800) 326-0263. Distributed to the trade by National Book Network, Lanham, Maryland.

Library of Congress Cataloging-in-Publication Data
The Culture of entrepreneurship / edited by Brigitte Berger.
    p. cm.
    Includes bibliographical references and index.
    ISBN 1-55815-159-1 (cloth)
    1. Entrepreneurship. 2. Political culture. I. Berger, Brigitte.
  HB615.C85 1991   305.5'54—dc20   91-33622 CIP

Book design by Herman + Company. Index by Shirley Kessel.

10 9 8 7 6 5 4 3 2 1

Contents

Foreword

This book explores two things that are critical to self-governance: *entrepreneurship* and *culture*.

Why entrepreneurship? From the stalls of a Moroccan open market to the high-tech firms of California's Silicon Valley, entrepreneurship is transforming the globe in ways that many who study the world have yet to grasp. Perhaps they were expecting a different sort of revolution, one in which the chariot of development—whether socialist or capitalist—would be drawn by the state. But as *The Culture of Entrepreneurship* shows, we are now witnessing the rise of an alternative development mechanism. In Latin America and Asia, Eastern Europe and Africa, a bottom-up revolution—what the Peruvian economist Hernando de Soto calls *El Otro Sendero* ("The Other Path")—offers a new world for the dispossessed.

Why culture? The study of entrepreneurship has heretofore been dominated by economists. It is not to denigrate their many achievements to say that when it comes to entrepreneurship, economics doesn't give us the whole picture. Indeed, many economists intentionally ignore what some think is the most important element of entrepreneurship: the influence of social forces such as morals, norms, and values. These form the framework within which individuals can pursue entrepreneurial opportunities. Contrary to what some think, capitalism is not evil or amoral. In its proper form it encourages such virtues as hard work, cooperation, resolve, deferral of gratification, and openness to new thinking.

It is the juncture between entrepreneurship and culture that those who are interested in self-governance find most fascinating. *The Culture of Entrepreneurship* shows that in certain circumstances, entrepreneurship produces *its own* culture. It is important that this be cultivated, not least because it runs counter to the culture of bureaucracy that permeates mature organizations, both public and private. The whole point of entrepreneurship is to get around problems that others find impassable. These barriers are as often institutional as they are technical.

To improve one's lot by making the world work better appears to be a universal aspiration. Given the chance, Brigitte Berger reminds us, "individual entrepreneurs seem almost to emerge out of nowhere in societies without a history of entrepreneurship." *The Culture of Entrepreneurship* is about unleashing that power worldwide.

Robert B. Hawkins, Jr., President
Institute for Contemporary Studies

Preface

The Institute for the Study of Economic Culture at Boston University, founded in 1985, is a research center for the study of the relations between culture and economic processes. From its inception it has been especially concerned with the cultural contexts of entrepreneurship. The chapters in this book were originally prepared for a conference, "The Culture of Entrepreneurship," sponsored by the Institute and held in Indianapolis, Indiana, January 26–27, 1990. *The Culture of Entrepreneurship* brings together contributions to this topic from individuals who have conducted research under Institute auspices with contributions by others, some of them critical of an emphasis on culture. The conference and the preparation of the volume were funded by a grant from the Lilly Endowment. I would like to express my great appreciation to the Endowment, and personally to Gordon St. Angelo, for this indispensable help.

As the topic dictates, the authors of the following papers come from a variety of disciplines and institutions. Brigitte Berger teaches sociology at Boston University. Don Lavoie and Janet Landa are economists at George Mason University and York University (Toronto), respectively. David Martin is a sociologist recently retired from the London School of Economics. The following four authors are all connected with business schools: Gillian Godsell at the University of the Witwatersrand (Johannesburg), Ashis Gupta at the University of Calgary, S. G. Redding at the University of Hong Kong, and Richard Whitley at Manchester Business School. Walter Connor teaches political science at Boston University. The research projects by Martin, Godsell, Gupta, and Redding took place under Institute auspices. The results of the Martin and Redding projects are contained in two recently published books, in much greater detail than could be presented here: David Martin's *Tongues of Fire: The Explosion of Protestantism in Latin America* (Blackwell 1990) and S. G. Redding's *The Spirit of Chinese Capitalism* (de Gruyter 1990).

Peter L. Berger, Director
Institute for the Study
of Economic Culture
Boston University

Brigitte Berger

1

Introduction

This book explores the cultural dimensions of modern entrepreneurship. All of the contributors—economists, anthropologists, sociologists, political scientists, and management experts—have been impressed by the importance of cultural factors at work in entrepreneurship, just as they have been impressed by the culture-producing capacity of the modern entrepreneur himself. The authors are in broad agreement that a fuller appreciation of the many-faceted role of the modern entrepreneur can no longer be achieved within the confines of traditional academic disciplines; and although the authors do not agree on every point, they are in accord that a more comprehensive approach to entrepreneurship must be interdisciplinary, comparative, and, above all, must take culture seriously.

It would be presumptuous here to call for a "paradigm shift" in the study of the modern entrepreneurial phenomenon, but the contributors are persuaded that the existing lacunae on factors of culture in the voluminous literature on entrepreneurship need to be redressed. It is hoped that the interdisciplinary, cross-cultural research outlined in this volume will clarify entrepreneurship and the revolutionary forms of cognition and practice embodied in it. Such a revised understanding of modern entrepreneurship is long overdue. Yet the accumulated data from disparate fields of inquiry strongly suggest that the modern entrepreneur is not only extremely productive economically, but also one of the prime carriers of peculiarly modern modes of cognition and behavior that are fundamental to modern industrial society.

We know that throughout human history most people in most places most of the time have existed in conditions of considerable misery. Only with the rise of capitalism and its productive dynamics was a fundamental improvement in the living standard of the general population engendered in particular societies of the West, slowly expanding through Europe and North America. For generations social scientists have been preoccupied with the identification and analysis of factors responsible for the spectacular transformation of the West. Although scholars and visionary politicians continue to debate the causes of the "great transformation," there can be little doubt that the progressive improvement in the living conditions and general well-being is real. Regardless of the significance of particular material and cultural forces in this transformation process, many, if not most, scholars have for quite some time recognized the Promethean role played by a new breed of entrepreneurs. Analysts of different persuasions tend to agree that the history of the rising capitalist industrial societies of the West and, more recently, of the prospering countries of the Pacific Rim, is to a large degree also the history of the modern entrepreneur. Rising out of a tangled web of demographic, legal, technological, material, ideational, and cultural influences, the modern entrepreneur has emerged as a new social force.

With contemporary social pressures pushing ever larger numbers of people into capitalism's wealth-creating system, its viability depends on the continued vitality and expansion of its productive powers. A substantial body of information available today allows us to make two defensible propositions: first, that the mind-sets of modern entrepreneurs and the coincidence of entrepreneurial principles with the mechanisms of the market appear to be singularly useful in circumventing the stifling forces of bureaucracy that tend to develop in mature industries and organizations, including those of governments;[1] and second, that the recent history of productive innovation and the spread of new services was spearheaded by small-scale entrepreneurs. Inasmuch as it appears modern small-scale entrepreneurship is peculiarly well suited for the development of innovative economic activities, it may well be argued that modern entrepreneurship and the mind-sets peculiar to it hold a unique potential for taking old, established industries in new directions.[2]

At a time when capitalist industrial societies continue to prosper and expand, gradually incorporating other similar economies into their productive dynamics, large portions of the population of third world countries continue to live in stagnant economies and in conditions of unrelieved wretchedness. Despite forty years of effort by the industrial nations of the West to improve the lot of the world's poor through massive capital transfers, global missions, expert interventions, and a multitude of aid programs, it has become increasingly evident in recent years that not much has changed.[3] This stark reality brings into focus the enormous potential modern entrepreneurs hold for the future of their societies. Research conducted in the underdeveloped world today demonstrates that individual entrepreneurs, given the chance, seem almost to emerge out of nowhere in societies without a history of entrepreneurship.[4] Evidence exists that under particular cultural and political constellations entrepreneurs can make substantial contributions to the formation of economically dynamic and politically viable industrial institutions in stagnant economies. It does not come as a surprise then that countries across the globe, in the underdeveloped nations of Africa, Latin America, and Asia, as well as those of economically stagnant Eastern Europe organized under socialism, have begun to invest increasingly great hopes in the transformational power of the modern entrepreneur.

This collection of essays once again brings into focus the very different approaches to the study of entrepreneurship that traditionally have divided the social sciences. Today, as in the past, we can roughly distinguish between two camps, each with its own subdivisions and vanguards: economists, who on the whole are inclined to see entrepreneurship as a variable dependent upon economic factors and largely independent of culture, and scholars from other disciplines, who tend to see entrepreneurship as a variable deeply embedded in culture, both produced by and productive of it at the same time.

Economists, taking as a given the basic motivation to maximize one's gain, postulate that entrepreneurial activities will emerge more or less spontaneously when economic conditions are favorable. Hence the members of this camp—the "mainstream" economists of neoclassical fame—emphasize the pre-eminent importance of the availability of capital, access to markets, labor supply, raw materials, and technology. They formulate their analyses in terms of "economic opportunity conditions" and "economic risk," and their analytical models use a combination of rather narrowly defined, functionally interrelated factors in more or less mechanistic ways. In contrast, anthropologists, historians, psychologists, and sociologists emphasize in varying and often contradictory terms the influence of noneconomic factors such as social norms and beliefs, psychological motivations for achievement, the legitimacy of entrepreneurship, questions of social "marginality," and the "internal fit" between any and all of these in the rise of modern entrepreneurship.

Because mainstream economists with their clearly defined analytical models currently dominate the discussion and are influential in shaping present-day economic policies, the analysis of entrepreneurship in cultural terms has remained elusive. We hear a lot about "the culture of organizations" and how different management styles affect productivity rates, but both the constitutive elements of this organizational culture and its operation remain only vaguely connected to our understanding of society and culture. During the 1960s and 1970s—a period preoccupied with the analysis of all aspects of individual and social life in terms of power relations—analyses of culture received little attention. Only in recent years can we observe a renewed interest in the influence of cultural factors on various aspects of social life, including the economy. This renaissance has been fueled in no small measure by the dazzling rise of the societies of the Pacific Rim: Japan, South Korea, Taiwan, Hong Kong, and Singapore. After exploring exhaustively the relative significance of all sorts of variables, many analysts have concluded that Japanese, Korean, and Chinese cultures, in spite of their vast differences, appear to be particularly well suited to those entrepreneurial activities that traditionally have led to capitalist industrialization.

At the same time, their success stories raise many questions, chief among them why other societies with long traditions of bazaar activities and technical sophistication have failed to develop similarly and why in some areas within existing dynamic industrial societies (such as southern Italy and the inner cities of the United States) individuals and groups remain resistant to manners of life that are obviously in their self-interest. By the same token, recent attempts at perestroika (economic restructuring) in the USSR have shown that individual entrepreneurs cannot perform magic on command and that economically productive forms of modern entrepreneurship cannot be invented overnight. In response to these realities, scholarly attention has begun to refocus on Max Weber's famous attempt to explain the rise of capitalism in terms of early Calvinism's ability to release, harness, and channel modern entrepreneurial energies. But the large body of research that has accumulated since Weber's early formulation also suggests that Weber's pathbreaking cultural analysis of entrepreneurship and economic dynamics is in need of substantial revision. Nonetheless, social scientists like Peter Berger have argued that while Weber may have erred on details, and while the broad strokes of his comparative cultural analyses need empirical substantiation, modification, and, at times, revision, he nonetheless asked the right kind of question. Weber's shortcomings, Berger points out, in no way invalidate a cultural approach to the study of social phenomena, including those of the economy.[5]

These chapters on entrepreneurship should be seen as building blocks forming a conceptual frame for the systematic analysis of the cultural dimensions of modern entrepreneurship, rather than as the finished product itself. Much hard thinking and focused research is needed before an empirically secured and polished theory of the culture of entrepreneurship can be set forth.

The contributors to this book participated in lengthy and often heated discussions of their research during the workshop "The Culture of Entrepreneurship," raising difficult and sometimes even antithetical questions. Differences are of course inevitable among scholars trained to think in different ways; at the same time, their distinct approaches and diverse findings frequently complemented one another in a surprising manner and also illuminated the importance of the cultural dimensions in entrepreneurship instead of diminishing them. Other differences could not be resolved easily and are in need of further exploration. This holds particularly true with regard to a clear and workable definition of the central concept of culture as well as that of entrepreneurship. Because of the centrality of these concepts, a few comments are in order here.

It cannot be our task to inundate the reader with the myriad definitions of culture that have been advanced and discarded by scholars over the years, only to resurface without agreement time and again. Rather than providing a summary of the debate between the two major camps—the more restricted emphasizing symbolic dimensions, and the more inclusive embracing the total way of life of a people—the contributors to this book found an inclusive conceptualization of culture to be of the most utility for their purposes. Culture as understood in the chapters of this volume encompasses the totality of life of distinct groups of people, their interpersonal relations and attitudes as well as their values, beliefs, norms, and cognitive styles. It is important to keep in mind that "culture" is an ideal-typical concept constructed for heuristic purposes and that it rarely exists in pure form in social reality. It should also be emphasized that distinct "manners of life" are not only characteristic of different societies at any given moment in time, but may coexist within a particular society. As many scholars have pointed out, cultures are as varied as nations, ethnic groups, religious sects, occupational groups, companies, and clubs. Indeed, any collection of people whose thinking and practices are distinct from that of others may be said to have a culture. Although some anthropologists oppose formulations that emphasize the uniqueness of particular cultural constellations, the contributions to this volume are united by their search for common constitutive elements of entrepreneurship across cultures and over time. It is hoped that the chapters may help to achieve greater clarity in theoretical formulations that have preoccupied the social sciences for some time. The authors of these chapters are further united in broad agreement that culture itself is not an immutable entity, but is perpetually in the process of birth and rebirth and thereby potentially always open to change. Hence it is important to emphasize that the conceptualization of "the culture of entrepreneurship" in the analytical schemes of the contributors to this book in no way implies that the culture of modern entrepreneurship is closed to groups of people who are lacking in this tradition. Any culture is available to any group at any time, provided external conditions (as well as social values, practices, and norms) permit and encourage new patterns to unfold and take root.

A similar argument has to be made with regard to the conceptualization of the economic activity called entrepreneurship. In the surfeit of books and articles written on the nature and role of the entrepreneur, we find a great variety of propositions about who the entrepreneur is, what he does, and what makes him vital to the economic process.[6] Suffice it to observe that different writers have identified characteristics such as motivation for profit, skepticism, open-mindedness, willingness to take risks, and the ability to innovate (that is, to combine familiar components in new ways rather than invent the components themselves), make purposeful decisions, and persevere in the face of adversity as being essential to entrepreneurship. Empirical evidence suggests that a combination of characteristics appears to be at work; none is insignificant. From a larger historical perspective, however, it can be observed that the shifting emphasis on the supremacy of one entrepreneurial function over another may perhaps reflect the shifting needs of the economy at particular points in history in the mind of particular authors.

With a few notable exceptions, most economic theorists of entrepreneurship share the point of view that entrepreneurial activities are a response to exogenous forces in the market system. Although economists like Schumpeter, the Austrians, neo-Austrians, and their followers have successfully expanded the interpretational schemes of "mainstream" economy to include some social and even cultural factors, virtually all continue to be beholden to the methodological individualism of "Robinson Crusoe economics." If noneconomic factors are taken into consideration, they are typically those pertaining to the political-economic system, while wider questions of society and culture remain largely ignored. Few have tried to enrich their studies from a cross-cultural and historical perspective, and even fewer have attempted to come to grips with the changing nature of cultures and society. Because entrepreneurship is embedded in culture, such dynamics must be incorporated into our studies of it. It is this gap in the research that the contributors to this book seek to redress. For most of them, modern entrepreneurship is a distinctly new variant of a timeless species, created and sustained by culture and creative of it at the same time.

Though emphatic about the importance of cultural factors in entrepreneurship, the authors in this book were unable to agree on a definition of entrepreneurship itself. The many definitions of entrepreneurship gravitated around two conceptualizations: the first tends to identify entrepreneurship with small-business activities and the second with a cluster of behavior patterns and psychological propensities such as innovation, decision making, and risk taking. The authors were dissatisfied with the first because there are many small businesses that are not entrepreneurial and large businesses that are. At the same time, the authors were only too aware of the inherent weakness of the second definition because all of the identified traits can also be found in noneconomic activities and evidence shows that many modern economic activities do not necessarily depend upon such traits.

No book on the culture of entrepreneurship can afford to keep the definition of its central theme in limbo; hence, fully cognizant of the complexities of the question and at the risk of transgressing against the preferences of some of the authors, an ad hoc definition will be proposed that admittedly reflects the editor's own predilection: Entrepreneurship is an innovative and value-adding economic activity. The individual, for example, who takes a few battered vehicles and turns them into a taxi service, thus providing new services, new employment opportunities, and a new source of tax revenues may be considered an entrepreneur. (The example describes the formation of SABTA, the South African Black Taxi Association.)

Progressing from more theoretical expositions to comparative case studies and ending with the search for entrepreneurs, these chapters present the distinct analytical approaches of their writers. From the intellectual perspectives of their own academic discipline, the authors explore the influence of cultural dimensions in their own research on entrepreneurship.

Brigitte Berger's chapter, "The Culture of Modern Entrepreneurship," explores in a general way cultural factors that give rise to a distinctly novel form of entrepreneurship. She presents a first, and tentative, delineation of a cultural approach to entrepreneurship that is capable of accommodating a variety of other approaches as well as questions of the relationship between culture and entrepreneurship in societies that have not yet developed an entrepreneurial tradition. In the hope of stimulating new research in seemingly unconnected areas of inquiry, she proposes that the study of entrepreneurship will profit from using the findings from other research efforts—in social demography, social history, East Asian economies, urban migration in the third world, the new role of the household and women in economic development, and the unjustly ignored research on the role of those "mediating structures" that link micro-level activities to the formation of social institutions on the macro-level of society. Equally important, she argues that the study of entrepreneurship in turn may inform some of the core understandings of these areas of inquiry.

Don Lavoie, in "The Discovery and Interpretation of Profit Opportunities," presents a sophisticated and systematic explication of the creative processes of discovery and interpretation that are integral to entrepreneurship. He argues that "entrepreneurship necessarily takes place within culture, is utterly shaped by culture, and it fundamentally consists in interpreting and influencing culture." In his attempt to substantially modify the Kirznerian theory of entrepreneurial decision making, he takes neo-Austrian conceptualizations of entrepreneurship in new and exciting directions. Lavoie's "interpretative approach" to the inner functions of entrepreneurship not only presents a challenge to the methodological individualism of "mainstream" and "market-process" economics; his phenomenological-hermeneutic frame of analysis appears to hold considerable promise for attempts in economic analysis that seek to link on the micro-level to those on the macro-level of society.

In "Culture and Entrepreneurship in Less-Developed Societies," Janet Landa confirms the cultural embeddedness of ethnic enterprises. Sorting out the viability of various economic approaches for the continued success of ethnically homogeneous middlemen groups such as the Chinese in Southeast Asia, the Indians in East and Central Africa, the Lebanese in West Africa, and the Jews in medieval Europe, she demonstrates how cultural factors both allow a particular group to succeed and reinforce the group's homogeneity. Arguing against "individual actor" approaches basic to "mainstream" economics as well as a variety of alternative models, and citing anthropological and sociological literature, she presents the broad contours of a "trans-action cost–cultural approach" to a theory of ethnically homogeneous middlemen groups. Although some members of the "Culture of Entrepreneurship" workshop took strong exception to Landa's attempts to couch her analysis in the terms of sociobiology, her economic analysis demonstrates convincingly that markets can be organized by culturally specific norms, which pattern behavior as well as economic transactions in ethnically homogeneous groups and do not depend on regulations and laws. Beyond this, her research also suggests that rationally constructed economic systems, regardless of the fine tuning of regulatory controls and diverse legal mechanisms, largely depend on the support of a culture-specific normative order and perhaps cannot function without it.

David Martin, in his pathbreaking "The Economic Fruits of the Spirit," based on research in Latin America and reported in more detail in *Tongues of Fire* (1990), argues that the Protestant spirit held by Max Weber to have been instrumental in the rise of capitalism in the West is today alive and flourishing among segments of the urban poor in Latin America. His conclusion, reminiscent of one of Brigitte Berger's arguments, though altogether independent of it, is that Pentecostal and fundamentalist sects have generated a dynamic process among impoverished groups in the teeming cities of Brazil, Chile, and Guatemala that fosters entrepreneurial activities. Taking issue with a generation of analysts who tended to interpret Latin American conditions and prospects in terms of Western imperialism and economic dependency, Martin argues that the Protestant spirit has "gone native" in parts of Latin America. For what appears to be happening today cannot be understood as an act of cultural imperialism, nor may it be regarded as an isolated phenomenon lacking in consequence. Though reluctant to "activate once again the Weberian debate concerning a collusion between the original spirit of Protestantism and the genesis of capitalism," Martin nonetheless proposes that the Protestant sects in contemporary Latin America function to reform the manner of life of often desperately poor people who have been left out for all too long. He insists that it is too early to say whether this newly emerging entrepreneurial culture has the potential to produce a new form of Latin American capitalism, yet he finds it hard to imagine that it will not hold far-reaching cultural and perhaps even political-economic consequences.

In her carefully researched "Entrepreneurs Embattled," Gillian Godsell tests the economic culture hypothesis of distinct entrepreneurial traditions and constellations for three ethnic groups: Indians, Afrikaners, and urban blacks in South Africa. She finds that both South African urban blacks and Afrikaners are markedly lacking in entrepreneurial traditions, while South African Indians command a deeply rooted entrepreneurial culture of long standing. Hence South African Indians, she argues, embedded in "organic networks" and communities, have been remarkably successful in circumventing the massive legal and political strictures of the politics of apartheid, while the other two groups have had considerably greater difficulty responding to entrepreneurial challenges. Afrikaners, with their historical affinity to land and agriculture, have tended to respond hesitantly and inadequately to the opportunities provided for them, and to this day the Afrikaner entrepreneur operates on his own without the supporting mediating structures of his community. Black small entrepreneurs in the townships and other restrictive settings, on the other hand, labor under a double burden. Neither anchored in a cultural tradition supportive of ethnic entrepreneurship nor encouraged by the political and legal realities of apartheid, the black small entrepreneur is a solitary and beleaguered individual. Godsell's work demonstrates convincingly how factors of culture shape the response to economic challenges and provides us with a deeper appreciation of the problems of the political economy in the postapartheid South Africa of the future.

Ashis Gupta's chapter, "Indian Entrepreneurial Culture," is based on extensive interviews with Indian entrepreneurs in Bengal and Eastern India. "Every Indian," says Gupta, "is an entrepreneur." Throughout a long history with a bewildering variety of factors ranging from geography, religion, cultural traditions, forces of imperialism, the vagaries of the present-day political economy and ideologies, individual Indian entrepreneurs have functioned and prevailed. His explorations of variables intrinsic to business (such as control and decision making) as well as those like family, religion, and nationalism extrinsic to it convey a complex picture that defies easy categorization and raises many questions. Nonetheless, through the analytical prism of entrepreneurship Gupta is able to present a fascinating picture of growth and decay in the West Bengal of today. He demonstrates how the fiercely competitive entrepreneurial subculture of ethnic Mawaris has replaced a once dominant entrepreneurial group of Bengalis, who, over time, have lost their competitive edge. Gupta's research once more demonstrates that even within a quintessentially entrepreneurial society and in the face of a political economy that treats ethnic groups equally, subcultural differences are of considerable significance in economic affairs.

In trying to provide a theoretical context for his research on the phenomenal success of the overseas Chinese of Hong Kong, S. Gordon Redding, in "Culture and Entrepreneurial Behavior among the Overseas Chinese," explores whether his data allow for the construction of an "East Asian model of development" distinct from that of Western industrial capitalism and Soviet bloc industrialization. Mining a rich lode of empirical data on Hong Kong entrepreneurs, Redding proposes that a distinctive "spirit of Chinese capitalism" has been largely responsible for the economic progress of overseas Chinese.[7] The constitutive elements of the overseas Chinese entrepreneurial ethic—and perhaps also the distinctive organizational structure of overseas Chinese businesses in general—Redding argues, are derived from aspects basic to the Chinese family and the Confucian ethic. Arguing for the existence of a distinctive East Asian model of development, Redding confirms the Weberian proposition that there can be "no capitalist development without an entrepreneurial class; no entrepreneurial class without a moral charter; no moral charter without religious premises"; in the case of the overseas Chinese, of course, we see a distinctly non-Protestant ethic at work.

Richard Whitley, in "The Revival of Small Business in Europe," presents a structural argument challenging the general culture bias of this book's other chapters. His summary discussion suggests that "the increasing significance of small businesses in many European countries since the mid 1970s is as much a result in large firms' policies and practices as a consequence of an upsurge in 'entrepreneurship' in Europe." He makes a strong argument that changes in the economic, social and, above all, technical environments have helped create a new type of entrepreneurial dynamic. Although Whitley's findings do not fundamentally undermine the economic culture hypothesis, they nonetheless reveal the need for more systematic analyses of the links between dimensions of structure, individual norms and behaviors, and mediating structures that serve to link the micro-level of society to that of the macro-level on the other.

In the last chapter of the book "The Rocky Road: Entrepreneurship in the Soviet Economy 1986–1989," Walter D. Connor provides a thought-provoking account of a nonentrepreneurial culture trying to create—by government fiat—market dynamics dependent upon entrepreneurial activities. Connor's highly informative report on the Soviet economy reveals a society that lacks the legal, property, and taxation structures necessary for the market to operate and a culture in which public resentment and suspicion of entrepreneurship runs high. Many Soviet citizens, it seems, prefer "shared poverty" to opportunities for achieving individual material wealth. In an afterword written in May 1991, Connor observes that the number of cooperatives—the preferred Soviet "entrepreneurial" mechanisms under perestroika—continues to increase and that most recent public opinion polls indicate a slowly growing public acceptance of the restructuring of the Soviet economy in this manner. It may not be far-fetched to conclude that, in the absence of a supportive entrepreneurial culture at the bottom of society, the Soviet attempt at a fundamental reconstruction of the economy from above may well provide academics of the future with an important opportunity to test empirically the primacy of the structural versus the cultural argument.

Brigitte Berger

2

The Culture of Modern Entrepreneurship

The aim of this chapter is threefold: to identify major cultural factors behind the rise of a distinctly modern form of entrepreneurship, to set forth the contours of a cultural theory of entrepreneurship broad enough to integrate a variety of approaches, and to explore the relationship between culture and entrepreneurship in societies other than the West—including those that have never developed an entrepreneurial tradition. This far-flung exploration draws from research findings from disparate and seemingly unconnected areas of inquiry—social demography, East Asian economies, urban migration in the third world, the roles of households and women in economic development, and the contributions of the mediating structures that link the activities of individuals and small groups on the micro-level of society to the formation of social institutions on the macro-level. Statements as sweeping as the ones developed in this chapter call for considerable caution, of course. Indeed, much of what follows should be understood as a first attempt to provide "building blocks" for a general cultural theory of modern entrepreneurship, rather than a cogent and integrated theory itself.

The Study of Cultural Dimensions in Entrepreneurship

Economists have generally seen entrepreneurship as an effect of a constellation of particular economic conditions, rather than as a cause of their growth. Even economists as broadly based as Albert Hirschman[1] and Alexander Gerschenkron[2] tend to downplay the significance of entrepreneurship, arguing that if economic conditions are not favorable, entrepreneurship will not emerge and societies will remain stagnant. But once economic opportunity conditions are in place, economists argue, entrepreneurs will make their appearance and serve, analogous to an electric system, as a sort of conductor by means of which energy is transmitted from one point to another. In a second analogy, one borrowed from the process of spontaneous combustion, entrepreneurs are seen as catalysts "providing the spark" for economic development. By extension, economic determinists typically see all individual and social expressions, including values, beliefs, and consciousness in general, as functions of external forces among which those of the economy figure prominently.

Such concepts of entrepreneurship, I wish to argue, leave much to be desired. To stay within the analogies just cited, I would propose that culture is the conductor and the entrepreneur is the catalyst. This proposition obviously needs further theoretical and empirical clarification.

Economists often fail to make a theoretical distinction between economic development and modernization. The two concepts, however, just as the two processes, are essentially separate though clearly intertwined phenomena. While economic development is enormously important, it is only one part of the overall process of modernization that includes the transformation of the social, the cultural, and the political sphere along with that of the economy.[3] Social scientists other than economists have generally recognized that while an industrial system can be superimposed on nonindustrial cultures, the system will remain alien and thus cannot take root. It will not flourish unless concomitant, perhaps even prior, changes have occurred in the institutional structures of a given society as well as in the consciousness of its individuals.

A few empirical examples may serve to illustrate what is at issue here: "mana"—the celebrated magic force in the form of oil—has in no way helped to speed up cultural modernization either in Arab countries or in Nigeria. Lack of oil and raw materials, in contrast, has not prevented the rapid transformation of Japan, Hong Kong, and South Korea in the past, nor does it prevent Thailand or Sri Lanka from modernizing today. By the same token, recent studies on the efforts of governments to improve literacy rates in selected countries have not revealed any relationship between expenditures in instruction and the speed with which literacy rates rise.[4]

Examples such as these suggest that modernization cannot be understood primarily as a product of economic mechanisms and material wealth simply as a result of improved living conditions. Rather, modernization demands to be considered as an independent social variable, which more often than not precedes economic development. Social demography is particularly instructive here. The findings of the Cambridge social demographers around Peter Laslett, Alan MacFarlane, and Anthony Wrigley may serve as points of reference. On the basis of exhaustive research on the social history of England before and during the "great transformation," these scholars along with the *annalistes* in France and social historians on the European continent have not only thrown many of the dogmas long held by scholars into question but also, most significantly, have shown that the Industrial Revolution in the West was an *effect* rather than a *cause* of changes in people's patterns of behaving and ways of thinking. Alan MacFarlane's recent *The Culture of Capitalism* (1987) has made a particularly important contribution to this argument. Detailed, often minute studies of specific population groups at particular moments in time provide an inkling about the complexities of a process in which cultural and economic factors work in tandem. In observing the degree of their interpenetration, one is tempted to argue that culture and economy are "twin-born," the one being a reflection of the other in more ways than one.

A historical case study may serve as an illustration. Few are better suited for the demonstration of the ways in which cultural and economic factors interact than Rudolf Braun's study of the demographic transition of the Swiss Canton of Zurich at the turn of the eighteenth century.[5] The transition itself was fueled by the inner dynamics of the "proto-industrial household," a type of household that best applies to that segment of rural artisans and peasants engaged in the cottage work system of "putting out" typically connected to the emergent textile industry of that period. Braun's historical description provides us with unique opportunities to glean the interactive relationship between family-rooted patterns of behavior, values, beliefs, and thought on the one hand, and a new type of productive activity that became available at that time. Out of a peculiar constellation of individual preferences and a value system that emphasized new patterns of individuation (such as individual drive, self-regulation, and autonomy), coupled with economically instrumental habits of work and savings, a new general culture emerged that served the advancement of families and individuals alike.

On the *individual level* the putting-out system provided for the first time opportunities for individualized courtship, marriage, and the creation of one's own domestic sphere. Moreover, the formation of a proto-industrial household was the desired way of life for many. Since it was available to anyone who cared to take it up, it was potentially democratic. The new patterns of behavior and work emerging in this fashion from a household-centered form of production rendered tangible results relatively quickly and came to serve as a model to be emulated by many. It may be of some importance to note that the newly emerging way of life did not appeal to those embedded in the traditional structures of peasant life and land ownership; rather, the proto-industrial household became the "preferred option" of the poor, the underprivileged classes, the marginal and roving segment of the population at that time. On the *structural level,* this type of household production fostered a new structure of consciousness and practices which, when put into action on a large scale, were precisely those that served as necessary preambles to the industrial revolution.

Examples such as this indicate that the birth of modern industrial culture is rooted in the values and practices of many small domestic groups. It is here that modern society found its anchor and its engine.

It would, of course, be foolish to deny that external factors of production and technology as well as those of law and politics had no influence on this process. In their masterful *Rise of the Western World: A New Economic History,* Douglass North and Robert Thomas have detailed many of these external factors.[6] Yet Rudolf Braun's prescient conclusion to his demographic transition study is important to remember: it was "not industrialization that altered the customs and usages of matrimony, industrialization simply provided a large segment of the rural population the material possibility of starting new ways."[7] These new ways, we may add, were motivated and carried by strong sentiments of familism.

By the same token, the influence of the Protestant ethic so central to Max Weber's brilliant theory of modernization is also important. Subsequent materials—including memoirs, novels, and pamphlets depicting life of this period—underline the influence of Protestant sectarianism that provided a moral charter for the emerging industrial culture in Protestant Europe. In going through extensive historical records, one is frequently tempted to argue that an "elective affinity" (the term is Weber's) must have existed between the "proto-industrial" household and the Protestant ethic. The question that suggests itself here is whether perhaps the Protestant ethic itself could emerge only from within the type of household just described, a question that Weber ignored. From a broader perspective one could plausibly argue that because it made sense and supplied meaning to many, the Protestant ethic became firmly ensconced in this type of household. Once it was accepted by many, the Protestant ethic in turn reinforced mind-sets, behavior patterns, and productive styles that had their origin in a new kind of familism.

Together, familistic sentiments, the Protestant ethic, and new forms of production required and emphasized hard work, frugality, individual accountability, and reliability, as well as habits of self-regulation and personal drive. They fostered cognitive modes of rational calculation, of doing things for their instrumental utility, and of rationally balancing defendable risk against mere adventurism.

Thus it is legitimate to argue that these mind-sets born out of an interpenetration of familial sentiments, ethical maxims, and productive activities had to be in place before entrepreneurism could emerge on a large scale. A first attempt that links the "manner of life" of a newly rising lower-middle stratum in the Calvinist areas of the low countries, England, Scotland, and Switzerland to later developments and that identifies this manner of life as the catalyst for the transition to industrial capitalism was attempted by Gianfranco Poggi in a recent essay.[8] Although much more detailed research on the social origin of entrepreneurs in the nineteenth century is necessary, evidence already available permits us to argue that modern entrepreneurship is rooted in the values and practices of many small groups in provincial communities.[9]

Building Blocks for a Theory of the Culture of Modern Entrepreneurship

In what follows, I wish to argue that the modern entrepreneur is a derivation of the *homo economicus* of economic literature. Because modern entrepreneurs were the product of ideational and material constellations novel in history and produced cultural forms able to revolutionize the world, they embody, we could argue, a new species of entrepreneurship altogether. Entrepreneurial activities flourished in earlier periods, of course, along with traditional entrepreneurs. Today we know much about artisans and merchants in prehistoric times, in antiquity, and in the traditional bazaar economies of the Mediterranean, Asian, and Near Eastern worlds. No doubt capital, sometimes even a great amount of it, was amassed by some—the merchant princes of Renaissance Italy, for example. Yet, taken together, these traditional entrepreneurial activities neither led to the formation of capital among the population at large nor made for economic growth in general. Commentators as far apart as Adam Ferguson and Fernand Braudel have depicted a propensity toward economic activities among the majority of medieval capitalists in almost identical terms. The traditional capitalist's mentality rested on the dictum "A profit is a profit, however it is acquired."[10] Work attitudes were easygoing, and life revolved around holidays and the enjoyment of the "good things in life," often manifested in conspicuous consumption. The richer traditional capitalists invested in all forms of business activities, including moneylending, tax farming, and colonial adventures, while the majority of small merchants, traders, and artisans appeared to have been content with making a comfortable profit that allowed them and their families to reproduce the material standards of living to which they had become accustomed. To quote a more contemporary summary of the traditional entrepreneur's cast of mind: "An attitude of resignation, involving underconsumption of goods and services combined with overconsumption of leisure . . . seems to have been the 'natural' attitude of man in most societies over long stretches of history."[11]

We cannot doubt that something happened during the seventeenth and eighteenth centuries in Europe that dramatically changed what the Dutch historian Jan Romein called "the common human condition." Much of this change has to do with the rise of capitalism, the emergence of science and technology and its spread into further aspects of individual and social life, and the formation of new modes of living and thinking, first in small groups and gradually in the population at large. How precisely these various sets of factors interacted remains a subject of considerable debate even among analysts who take cultural explanations seriously.

The Weberian Proposition

Among the various explanations of the rise of the modern world, that undertaken by Max Weber in his brilliant *The Protestant Ethic and the Spirit of Capitalism* may serve as the best available foil for a first attempt to identify the constitutive elements of the culture of modern entrepreneurship.[12] Weber, in arguing that the Protestant ethic provided "a necessary though not sufficient precondition" for the rise of capitalism, sought to link profound historical transformations to fundamental shifts in individual motivations, behavior, and cognition. Early Calvinism's double doctrines of individual "vocation" and "salvation" released and harnessed new entrepreneurial energies. No good would be served in recapitulating the various steps of the Weberian argument here, nor can we enter into the many disputes this thesis has provoked. Those who wish to inform themselves on the current status of the debate will do well to consult Gordon Marshall's *In Search of the Spirit of Capitalism* and Gianfranco Poggi's *Calvinism and the Calvinist Spirit: Max Weber's Protestant Ethic* as well as Alan MacFarlane's already mentioned book.[13] For the purposes of our argument here I shall simply summarize the main elements of this shift in individual behavior.

Of singular importance is the shift in the attitude toward work. Under the influence of Calvinism, Weber argues, work was transformed from a technique for survival and crude profit making into a tool for "salvation" by and for the individual. In this shift, individuals became dislodged from their embeddedness in family and kinship and received a new autonomy. While the activity of work was "sacrilized," it became secularized and eventually developed into an end in itself. Interpersonal relations in all spheres of life, but particularly in those relating to trade and commerce, were transformed as well. Because Calvinism's stern commands required absolute honesty in all dealings and enjoined individuals to keep their promises, it created a basis for individual responsibility and the opportunity for trust outside the immediate family to emerge. The individual, furthermore, was required to give account daily to God on everything he or she did. This demand profoundly influenced the world of business and perhaps was even responsible for new methods of accounting. Historians of sentiments like Norbert Elias have located here the source of the modern "bookkeeping" mentality that was to leave an indelible imprint on the modern psyche.[14]

In addition, new patterns of individual behavior, stressing diligence, reliability, fidelity, and responsibility in all matters emerged, reinforced by mechanisms of what today we would call "peer pressures." Because individuals were expected to live up to the demands of their exacting and relentless God, daily and continually, a new element of application and strife entered their lives. This constant living up to expectations gradually took on its own autonomous dynamic.

As for society itself, in emphasizing Calvinism's "innerworldly asceticism," Weber shows how the command to lead a life of simplicity and frugality led to the amassment of capital, just as he shows how early Calvinists, unable to tolerate the psychological pressures created by the uncertainty over their salvation after death, began to "cheat" on their God: prosperity in *this life* was interpreted as a signal of such salvation. And again secularized and vulgarized in the course of time, worldly success and prosperity came to be accepted broadly as signs of individual worth.

In this way, in the "innerworldly asceticism" of early Calvinist "communities of saints," a way of life was born that added up to the methodical self-regulation that Weber found so well-adapted to the requirements of modern "rational" capitalism. As an "unintended by-product" of this manner of life, capital grew on a large scale for the first time in history. Since individuals were not permitted to indulge in the luxuries capital could buy, they were bound to invest and reinvest it perpetually. The consequences of this new moral system, Weber argues, made possible the "qualitative transformation and the quantitative expansion" of an entirely new manner of life, which, in turn, gave form and meaning to the development of modern capitalism.

The Effect of Weber's Theory on the Social Sciences

Among those social scientists committed to a cultural analysis of the entrepreneurial phenomenon, those by psychologists deserve our attention briefly, if only to demonstrate the necessity for separating psychological factors of entrepreneurship from those of culture. A substantial body of research in the tradition of David McClelland has been able to identify psychological factors undergirding entrepreneurship.[15] I have no quarrel with this type of research. Let it be stipulated that different individuals possess drive and motivation in different degrees. Most likely these differences result from a complex process of socialization in which psychological, even genetic, factors interact in a variety of ways with those of family and social class. But it is important to keep in mind that it requires cultural conditions to give form and direction to individual potentials. In one type of culture, individuals measuring high on the entrepreneurial motivation scale may become successful businessmen, and in another type, they may invent a new twist in the ritual of shamanism. In either case, to return to our earlier analogy, it is culture that serves as the conductor, and the entrepreneur is the catalyst.

Others researching the significance of cultural factors in entrepreneurship have insisted on the importance of the legitimacy of entrepreneurship. For instance, Joseph Schumpeter, P. Kilby, and Peter Marris and Anthony Somerset discuss the need for a hospitable social climate for entrepreneurship to unfold.[16] In the minds of some, Alexander Gerschenkron for instance, elites can effect such a climate, while others like Talcott Parsons and Neil Smelser, Fred W. Riggs, and Everett Hagen write about the influence of role expectations and values and norms in general in the formation of a social climate legitimating entrepreneurship.[17] These cultural factors, one would assume, can all be significant in creating an entrepreneurial culture. For the sake of intellectual integrity, however, I have to report that historical research demonstrates that entrepreneurship has emerged even in the absence of such legitimacy.

Equally inconclusive is the evidence of research on marginality, in which two opposing views confront each other. On the one hand, some like Everett Hagen, point out that entrepreneurs tend to be recruited from individuals and groups (religious, ethnic, migrant, second sons, and others) at the periphery of societies historically lacking an entrepreneurial tradition. On the other hand, others argue that in societies where entrepreneurship is a mainstream, if not a preferred form of economic activity, marginal groups, such as racial and ethnic minorities in the United States or urban migrants to the slums of third world cities, are denied entrepreneurial opportunities. No matter how one manipulates the empirical evidence, the fact remains that not all marginal groups become entrepreneurial in the first type of society. In the second type of society, like the United States, not all minorities fail to take a foothold in entrepreneurial activities, as the case of Chinese, Greek, and Asian immigrants clearly shows.

Toward an Integrated Theory of the Culture of Modern Entrepreneurship

In addition to the research just discussed, additional factors have recently been explored by those who seek a cultural explanation of entrepreneurship, such as the role of nationalist ideologies or the importance for entrepreneurs to gain power or control over resources and facilities. Obviously, many of these factors can and do play a role in the formation of entrepreneurship, and an empirically grounded cultural theory of modern entrepreneurship will have to sort out the validity of these claims individually. The approach developed in this chapter, however, insists that any analysis of individual cases of entrepreneurship—whether now located in history or in the contemporary world, in underdeveloped or in advanced industrial societies—must take into account the interpenetration of ideational and nonideational factors, including those of the economy, technology, and the polity.

Moreover, the cultural approach delineated here in its general contours is broader than common usage suggests. It encompasses all the shared ways of thinking, believing, understanding, and feeling as well as those of work practices, consumption, and social interaction in general. Slowly and incrementally the elements that constitute a new manner of life become habituated, routinized, and eventually institutionalized, provided political realities permit them to unfold. In addition, the force of ideas must be powerful enough to enable individuals and groups to transcend the limitations of frequently stifling traditions and other obstacles in an often hostile world.

This kind of cultural approach to entrepreneurship, I would suggest, is capable of showing how economic growth develops from the "bottom up," not from the "top down." The process is fueled by the efforts of individuals and their groups to achieve a variety of goals, among which economic profit and self-advancement compete with others. Moreover, in this fashion ordinary individuals in their everyday activities, in their habits, practices, and ideas, create the basis for other distinctly modern institutions to emerge that may mediate between them and the distant, large-scale structures of society. Institutions of democratic capitalist societies—as expressed in law, education, the class structure, and the like—are usually seen as "functionally" related and interdependent. This, I think, is quite correct as far as it goes. What is frequently ignored, however, is that all institutions have common sources and continue to depend on the same constitutive forces that made for their rise in the first place. Frequently overlooked as well are questions relating to the rootedness of all modern institutions in a particular moral system—questions that have occupied philosophically inclined observers since Alexis de Tocqueville. Indeed, today questions of this sort are asked by a number of scholars who seek to relate the rise of East Asian capitalism to the Confucian ethic.

On a different plane of analysis, we attribute the abiding power of Weber's explanatory scheme to his ability to show how the expansion of what he called the "instrumental rationality" characteristic of the modern entrepreneurial phenomenon also impelled the formation of distinctly modern institutions in all spheres of life, the public as well as the private. The degree to which the forces of rationalization responsible for dislodging individuals from their embeddedness in nature, religion, and tradition continue to shape contemporary and future developments is the study of some current researchers, particularly those influenced by Hansfried Kellner.[18] Closely related to this approach, Peter Berger, Brigitte Berger, and Hansfried Kellner in *The Homeless Mind: Modernization and Consciousness* sought to identify elements of cognitive style that distinguish modern consciousness, including those typical of economic activity.[19] In their view, modern consciousness has a pronounced propensity to combine and recombine empirically accessible components incessantly and relate them to entrepreneurial activities. In this way an interpretational scheme can be developed that understands the modern entrepreneur propelled by a mind-set peculiar to him to combine and recombine various elements of his activities for the achievement of rationally calculated ends including interaction patterns intersubjectively derived. Thus it is theoretically possible to comprehend modern entrepreneurial activities both as sources and as carriers of types of "instrumental rationality," which are part and parcel of the modern economy and its growth.

The Culture of Entrepreneurship in Non-Western Societies

With evidence for a cultural approach to entrepreneurship derived from a historically related series of cases from West European societies as a basis for induction alone, one can have precious little confidence that one's findings can be generalized. Hence it becomes necessary to test the validity of the cultural basis of entrepreneurship on other cultures as well. The centrality of the Chinese entrepreneurial familism in Hong Kong's spectacular economic success in recent decades seems appropriate for this purpose. According to conventional social science thinking, familism and economic development are antipathetic. Clark Kerr and his associates, for instance, hold that the "extended family tends to dilute individual incentives to work, save and invest,"[20] and Edward Banfield in his fascinating study of a southern Italian community in the 1950s coined the term "amoral familism" to explain this community's failure to modernize and develop economically."[21] With regard to Chinese familism itself, the opinions of many contemporary scholars echo Max Weber's famous phrase "the sib fetters of the economy," referring to classical China, though recent research, particularly that by Maurice Freedman has called some of their claims into question.[22] Be this as it may, such negative evaluations of the consequences of Chinese familism for economic development have been accepted by Chinese elites throughout the twentieth century. Communist as well as noncommunist Chinese elites were convinced that the core values of the Chinese family—revolving around family solidarity, patrilineal descent and ancestor worship, patriarchal authority, and filial piety (xiao) requiring "obedience to the father and allegiance and loyalty to the emperor"—were profoundly antimodern. The communist regime under Mao in particular, undertook draconian measures to smash the kinship-oriented structure of traditional Chinese society, with devastating consequences, as we now know.

In turning to the empirical realities that have emerged in the Chinese societies of the Pacific Rim in recent decades, one becomes once more aware of the sobering fact that social life follows neither theoretical abstractions nor political agenda. Gilbert Wong, S.K. Lau, and Gordon Redding, among others, have cogently argued that an economically dynamic ethos, dubbed by Wong "entrepreneurial familism," is directly responsible for Hong Kong's extraordinary rise to success. A brief summary of Gilbert (Sin-Lun) Wong's fascinating findings based on years of research may illustrate what this "entrepreneurial familism" entails.[23]

Hong Kong's Entrepreneurial Familism
The ethos of Hong Kong's "entrepreneurial familism" involves the jia, the family, as the basic unit of production, of saving, and of economic competition. It provides the impetus for innovation and

the support for risk taking. It is an ethos that is by no means confined to the richer segment of the population who already own family firms, but it permeates the whole of society. Where there is little physical capital to be developed, heads of less well-off families can still marshal the limited *jia* resources and try to cultivate human capital for collective advancement. Janet Salaff, in her study of twenty-eight middle- and working-class Hong Kong families, for instance, found that all the working daughters contributed major portions of their income to the budget of their families. Once these families had acquired the basic material necessities (such as adequate quarters and essential consumer durables), "more resources were invariably channeled into the education of younger sons and daughters." Salaff concludes that "each family thus appears to improve its position in life by means of combining income of wage earning members."[24] With families serving as bankers, as Gordon Redding and Gilbert Wong have shown, banks play a minor role in the building up of Hong Kong's businesses.

Wong tries to trace the relationship between the core values of the traditional Chinese family and Hong Kong's newly burgeoning entrepreneurial familism. For instance, the widespread ideal of Hong Kong Chinese to become one's own boss, to be an independent entrepreneur, may be related to the inheritance pattern of the past that recognized brothers as independent and equal claimants to the family estate. While the popular desire to strike out on one's own makes for an abundant supply of entrepreneurs in Hong Kong, it also produces a shortage of dedicated managers and dependable executives in the corporate world.

Hong Kong's famed paternalistic management style may be traced to the traditional Chinese family as well. The pronounced autocracy of the father-headed family firm is widely held to be responsible for the uncommon adaptability and maneuverability of Hong Kong enterprises. Today, as in the past, this pattern is rarely resented, as it is perceived to add to the fortune of the family as a whole. In any case, each family member holds equal share in the family's assets. The fierce competition one encounters in Hong Kong at every turn is similarly held to be a legacy of the past. While in the past competition was between families, today it is between firms. The continuation of the classical Chinese competition between families, Wong stresses, makes for the interesting phenomenon that contemporary family firms in Hong Kong—just as their counterparts in history—rarely endure over time. As a result, there is a rarity of oligopolistic groupings and monopolistic ventures that could prevent other individual enterprises from moving up. With few institutional barriers to upward and downward movements along the social ladder, family fortunes appear to rise and fall in quick succession, and the socioeconomic order appears, in Hugh Baker's apt image, "like a seething cauldron, with families bubbling to the top only to burst and sink back to the bottom."[25] Researchers agree in general that a particular family firm does not last longer than approximately two and a half to three generations.

Thus, I think it possible to argue that the case of Hong Kong's "entrepreneurial familism" clearly refutes those who see traditional family culture and sib relationships as an obstacle to economic development. To the contrary, it appears that the main problem of the Chinese family is not economic inertia, but "excessive competition."

Beyond this, the foregoing considerations provide us with some clues about the importance of political factors in the development of an entrepreneurial culture. Gilbert Wong, again, argues cogently not only that the Chinese family is an economically active force today but also that it had the potential in the past. In former times, however, this potential was checked by a state preoccupied with efforts to balance economic, environmental, and ecological factors. Contemporary analysts have judged these efforts to be misguided, as they locked a whole society into a "high level equilibrium trap." Once such external pressures were removed, the inner dynamics of the Chinese family were unleashed. This insight gains further credence when one compares the case of Hong Kong and other ethnic Chinese overseas communities, on the one hand, with the case of the People's Republic of China, on the other.

The importance of political factors in the development of entrepreneurship needs some further comment. For some time development experts have had a propensity to argue that if latecomers to development, such as China, want to succeed today, they must centralize economic and political decisions in the hands of the government. That is to say, in the contemporary situation, the planning, initiation, and execution of economic activities aiming for development must issue from a strong and unified central government. In the postwar economic race among various Chinese communities, the People's Republic of China most closely followed this prescription, relying almost exclusively on a tight network of political cadres for the planning and execution of virtually all aspects of economic and political life. In the process, the economic dynamics of its some 100 million potentially entrepreneurial families were muzzled, and it is China that most conspicuously lags behind today.

On the basis of studies like these, we may conclude that, contrary to the opinions of many social scientists and experts working in the field, modernization and development do not take place in a society as a whole but through the web of diversified collective social life and in the microcosms of families and communities that compose it. It is here, and not at the planning boards, that the syntheses productive of change occur. Conversely, we become aware of the harsh possibility that hopes for modernization and development can be destroyed and lost if the elements necessary for such a transformation harden or fade away. Under adverse conditions those potentials available in any society at any point in time may become subverted, and their dynamism will be turned on an inward, if not a destructive, path.

The Culture of Entrepreneurship in Less-Developed Countries

During the past forty years the preindustrial three-quarters of the world have witnessed an urban explosion thus far unknown to human history. With growth rates estimated as high as 5–8 percent a year, many third world cities have doubled their population every ten to fifteen years in past decades. The inability of third world governments to keep pace with these monumental demographic shifts is well known. Societies whose degree of development is already the lowest have been unable to absorb a seemingly unending flood of migrants into the economy and the existing structures of urban society. Third world governments, regardless of their ideological tilt and the organization of their economies, have been largely hostile to these migrants in equal measure. Consequently, the urban poor have been forced into the economic and social underground. Unwanted and unaided, lacking in resources and skills, these poorest of the world's poor have been thrown back upon their ingenuity.

What is less well appreciated in much of the literature on third world urban explosion is the fact that the inhabitants of the *barrios* and *favellas* of Latin America, the shanty towns of Africa, and the steaming cities of Asia have prevailed against all the odds, despite being left to their own devices. Even an only casual visitor to the third world cannot fail to be impressed with the energy and resilience of the poor in the cities. But more, in their efforts to survive, they have engendered new patterns of socioeconomic and political interaction and have established rudimentary social structures that hold considerable potential for the future. Almost totally ignored in the literature on development and modernization is the possibility that here too exists a rugged dynamism at the bottom of society, which may provide the social, economic, and political foundation for a more prosperous future.

At the center of these major transformations stand family, household, and entrepreneurship, strongly reminiscent of the situation described in the two other cases in this chapter. Knowledgeable analysts of contemporary Chilean and Peruvian events, for instance, argue that a dynamic potential already exists at the bottom of these societies, waiting to be unleashed. Hernando de Soto, for instance, in his ground-breaking *The Other Path,* based on detailed studies among Lima's urban migrants and squatters, makes a strong case for the recognition of the economic potential of this vast segment of the population.[26] Similar data from across the world suggest that under specific conditions, the as yet uncharted economic and social activities of the urban migrants to third world cities may provide the "engine" for their society's transformation.

I will pass over the failures and foibles of researchers who have made the entrepreneurial potential of the urban poor in the third world invisible. In two more recent books, *Third World Proletariat?* and *Slums of Hope?*[27] the social anthropologist Peter Lloyd has tried to sort out the many contradictory claims swirling around the poor of third world cities. In addition, many migration studies conducted during the past decade have begun slowly but surely to demolish one myth after another. Fresh evidence on cooperation and mutual trust among the urban poor, for instance, discredits notions of a pervasive "marginality" fashionable until very recently. Such findings, incidentally, appear to hold for cultural settings as different as Rio de Janeiro, Mexico City, Lima, Nairobi, Bombay, and Calcutta. This evidence strongly suggests that among urban squatters, there are fewer family breakdowns, less frustration, less apathy, more optimism, and considerably higher aspirations than commonly assumed, along with more economic movement than expected. Lisa Peattie summarized the unwritten rule of squatter existence in these words: "Work hard, save money, outwit the state, vote conservatively if possible, but always in your own economic self-interest, educate your children for their future and as old age insurance for yourself."[28]

Cecilia Mariz and David Martin have explored the role of fundamentalist religion in the socioeconomic progress of the urban poor in Latin America.[29] Their findings support, by and large, Weberian propositions about the consequence of a new social ethic in the making in these parts of the world. In the emergent "new manner of life" in more and more communities, Protestant fundamentalism appears to play a major role. By extension, this demanding new ethic also seems instrumental in inculcating self-regulatory disciplines and aspirations congenial to the emergence of entrepreneurial capitalism.

By the late 1980s up to 70 percent of the urban labor force in some third world countries had become engaged in the "informal" or "underground" sector of the economy, which, more often than not, is based in the household. A brief summary of the typical survival techniques of the third world urban poor may be informative and adumbrate how, at the intersection of family, household, and productive activities, a promising new ethos is developing.

The Culture-Building Potential of Small-Scale Entrepreneurs in Third World Cities

Small-scale entrepreneurial activities in the informal sector are anchored in the family and household. Family labor is used to its fullest extent: young children run errands, "mind the shop," check that loading and unloading are being carried on. Older relatives may sit for long hours guarding and selling small quantities of goods that are a surplus to the main enterprise. Bryand Roberts in *Cities of Peasants* warns us against assuming too quickly that the individual engaged in what appears to be almost profitless activities is an isolated economic unit: "Small-scale market sellers, people offering to wash cars and so on, often appear to make little or no income and, in surveys of poverty, are classed among the desperately poor. They are undoubtedly poor, but it is important to examine the household and not the individual as a unit of economic enterprise."[30]

Many of the small-scale entrepreneurs engaged in the "penny capitalism" of the household economy are women. The women often supply the entrepreneurial skills, the hard labor, the stamina, and the unwavering desire for creating a stable basis for the survival and the advancement of their families. While men in third world cities are always on the lookout for employment in the "formal economy," they have the household economy, engineered by women, to fall back upon. Given the economic realities of the third world, such a fallback position is needed all too frequently.

Policy makers and economists alike have paid scant attention in their models to the vital economic role of women and their contributions to the economies of these parts of the world. To be sure, economists like Michael Todaro and Gary Becker have tried to develop models measuring factors pertaining to the household. What they have failed to recognize, however, is that the economic activities of women in the third world are not so much driven by "rational actor" factors as by values relating to family and family life, which frequently may not be so rational in economic terms. It is one of the great merits of the new research on women in development to have tried to fill this lacuna. Yet feminists too have failed to apprehend the family connection in all of this. Like economists, their focus has been on the isolated autonomous woman and her contribution and place in the economy. But an autonomous woman, who coolly and rationally is concerned only with her own self-interests, is a phenomenon unknown in the third world.

Whether we like it not, in the third world, regardless of culture or geographical location, family life is writ large, particularly for the poor. Women, and increasingly men too, are well aware that only collaboration among all members of a family guarantees a modicum of success. Noncollaboration condemns individuals to live on the margin. In those instances where women have banished their husbands from the household, they have done so only when the husbands have become a burden and stumbling block to a family's advancement.

Instead of choosing "women's liberation" in the Western sense, third world women are primarily concerned with the "domestication of men," for they know such a domestication alone makes their own and their family's progress possible. Research like that conducted by Cecilia Mariz and David Martin in Latin America undergirds the importance of a new domestic ethic, religiously informed and reinforced, in the attempt of often desperately poor people to escape their lot.

A Preamble to Industrialization

Let us now return to the central theme of this chapter, which revolves around the cultural embeddedness of the modern type of entrepreneurship so instrumental in the creation of industrial society. Evidence like the analysis above supports the argument that values and economic practices now present in parts of the urban third world may serve as a preamble to industrialization. Future research may well demonstrate the validity of Arthur Cole's theory of the stages of entrepreneurship, progressing from the empirical to the rational and finally to the cognitive.[31] In this example, as in the other illustrations used in this chapter, a distinctly modern consciousness arises at the intersection of familial sentiments and work, which, when vitalized by a particular ethical system, may produce the formation of an economically and politically sustainable modern culture. Culture so constituted may, in turn, shape subsequent developments in the economy, the polity, and society at large.

The brief sketch of some of the cultural factors active in small-scale entrepreneurship in the urban third world illustrates as well community and institution building in action. For industrial culture to become rooted, as we know, a great variety of institutions congenial to and supportive of it must be potentially available. Small-scale entrepreneurship—in contrast to employment in low-skilled work in factories and mining—appears to be particularly suitable, I would argue, for the construction of such institutions, albeit rudimentary ones. To flourish, small-scale entrepreneurs are compelled to develop all sorts of technical and social skills. The social skills that they are forced to nurture are distinctly modern, rational-instrumental patterns of interaction on several levels. Chief among them are those relating to commercial activities: interaction networks have to be constructed between entrepreneurs and suppliers, between sellers and customers, between entrepreneurs and other actors on the local as well as on the more distant scene. In this way the entrepreneur not only creates and re-creates institutional structures but becomes constitutive of them. Propelled by the need to adapt to the demands of a modern economy, which can no longer be understood in terms of local needs alone, the individual entrepreneur is eager for information on larger issues of technology, economy, and politics. The entrepreneurial mind-set transcends the confines of family and tradition, opening individuals up to modern styles of consciousness and securing them a place in modern industrial society.

As for family life and the household, in consequence of entrepreneurial activities, new and pronouncedly modern forms of interaction are engendered among members of the same "production team," husband, wife, and children, which may serve, in Bernard Rosen's words, as the "industrial connection" in less-developed societies.[32] The characteristically modern interaction pattern that emerges, then, is one decidedly different from that of families embedded in traditional kinship structures. A whole body of literature exists today on the "internal fit" between the nuclear family of father, mother, and their children and the requirements of modern industrial society.[33] In fact, those societies with a nuclear family system in place may well have a comparative cultural advantage in the processes leading to modernization and economic development.

In concluding it is important to realize from a sociological perspective that every human community is a web of shared meanings. If these meanings become institutionalized, a spontaneous process of culture building is engendered. Slowly and incrementally, networks of interaction become habituated, routinized, and institutionalized. The necessary skills are nurtured continually. Interaction, participation, and community-building activities develop into taken-for-granted modes. Under congenial political conditions all these aspects lead, at one and the same time to the formation of a distinctly modern culture as well as to the formation of new modes of production. These modernized institutions, in turn, will affect the likelihood and the rate of a society's development, including the building of factories and a dynamic economy.

Don Lavoie

3

The Discovery and Interpretation of Profit Opportunities: Culture and the Kirznerian Entrepreneur

It is beginning to be evident that the vast literature on growth and development conceals a yawning gap. This void refers to an understanding of the role of the entrepreneur in economic development, both at the theoretical level and at the level of past and prospective economic history. . . .

In the literature dealing more narrowly with growth models, this hiatus is almost complete and is hardly surprising in view of its predominant concern with macroeconomic relationships. In contrast, the literature dealing with development proper gives some attention to entrepreneurship, although little effort has been devoted to formulating a clear theoretical understanding of the entrepreneurial role.

—Israel Kirzner, *Perception, Opportunity, and Profit*

There is an increasing recognition that to understand economic development we need an adequate theory of entrepreneurship. The entrepreneur is the driving force of economic change, bringing innovation, creativity, and coordination to the economy. Centrally planned economies are widely thought to have failed, at least in part, because they left little scope for the entrepreneurial process. In the field of economic development, attention is shifting from attempts to engineer economic improvements from the top down to attempts to design institutions that enable entrepreneurship to flourish and produce development from the bottom up. A theory of entrepreneurship should help us identify the conditions—economic, political, legal, and cultural—that enhance decentralized developmental processes.[1]

Social scientists in general, and economists in particular, often refer to entrepreneurship in a manner that suggests that culture has little to do with it. Indeed, mainstream social science has, with the notable exception of anthropology, largely ignored culture not only as it might pertain to entrepreneurship but also as it might pertain to any other aspect of society. Political scientists, sociologists, and economists typically depict the social process as a causal mechanism, rather than as a means of establishing meaningful human discourse and understanding.[2] The methodological task of the social scientist is understood to be discerning regularities in objective patterns of change but not coming to terms with what these changes mean to human agents or how this meaning contributes to the causes of change. Social scientists see culture in general as a matter for the humanities, not for the social sciences.

To the extent that social scientific research on entrepreneurship takes culture into account at all, such research usually seeks only to identify those cultural groups whose individual members have greater than average entrepreneurial traits. Entrepreneurship is in this case being treated as a psychological attribute of individual people. It is the distribution of individual psychological traits within populations categorized by culture, rather than features of the culture as a whole, that are being examined. We all know, for example, that the overseas Chinese are very entrepreneurial, but we do not seem to know much about *why* they are. To be sure, even finding such culturally specific patterns is an important contribution, because the patterns may suggest possibilities for answering the "why" question. The social sciences, however, do not appear to be making much progress on that crucial explanatory front. In the social sciences, culture is little more than an aggregative classification for grouping individuals, not a substantive theoretical notion in its own right.

For the purposes of this chapter, culture is to be understood broadly as the complex of meanings that allows us to comprehend human action: it is the background context that renders purposeful action intelligible. Culture is the language in which past events are interpreted, future circumstances are anticipated, and plans of action are formulated. Although not a language in the sense of a static set of words and grammatical rules, culture is a discourse. This view has been most eloquently articulated in Hans-Georg Gadamer's philosophy of hermeneutics. Language, in this view, is a continually evolving conversation, an open-ended communicative process. As such it is a complex phenomenon in its own right, which, if it is to be taken seriously, requires explicit theoretical attention by the social scientist.[3]

Unfortunately, the scholars in the humanities who seem to have taken culture more seriously have had little to say about its processual nature. One reason the cultural side of entrepreneurship has been neglected is that anthropologists, who have examined culture more thoroughly than anyone else have generally restricted themselves to statics rather than dynamics. Researchers have concentrated on getting a snapshot of a cultural pattern already in place, rather than understanding the circumstances that bring about change. Neither the ways culture shapes developments in economic, political, or social institutions, nor the ways those institutions influence culture, nor the ways culture reshapes itself, leading to different cultural patterns in the future, have been as well researched as the various cultural "stills" have been. In other words, the study of the relationship between culture and entrepreneurship demands working with both meaning and economic change, whereas the way disciplinary divisions have evolved, few researchers are capable of handling both categories together.[4]

Perhaps more than other social scientists, economists have failed to leave room for meaning and have not done well with change either. Even though some economists claim to study causal change, their methodological approach tends to neglect the radical change generally thought to be involved in entrepreneurship. Change usually appears in economists' models only as deterministic tendencies toward a fixed equilibrium, like the movements of a clockwork mechanism, not as a truly creative process. Thus economists usually explain entrepreneurial action as maximizing an objective function according to given constraints. To act entrepreneurially is simply to take advantage of concrete profit opportunities neglected by others. Success is a matter of who takes the initiative, of who is alert and exploits the gains that are "out there" to be found in the objective situation. Profit opportunities are conceived as quantitative facts that are strictly dictated by the measurable discrepancy between costs and revenues. Culture, in this view, merely shapes what kinds of goods the society happens to prefer, the subjective meaning that goods have to people, not the objective economic circumstances and causal processes with which economic science is concerned. Culture is seen to pertain to the underlying conditions that precede the economic process that entrepreneurship propels, not to the process itself.

This chapter clarifies some aspects of the entrepreneurial process and argues that culture has everything to do with it. Entrepreneurship necessarily takes place within culture, it is utterly shaped by culture, and it fundamentally consists in interpreting and influencing culture. Consequently, the social scientist can understand it only if he is willing to immerse himself in the cultural context in which the entrepreneurial process occurs.

The purpose here is not to develop a whole theory of entrepreneurship as a cultural process, but to sketch some of the main elements such a theory would need.[5] Two properties of entrepreneurship that need to be accounted for better are connoted by the notions of "discovery" and "interpretation." Discovery suggests an element of radical change, a surprising find, an unanticipated break with past patterns. In discussions of economic development, entrepreneurship entails a capacity to introduce new products, new production methods, new marketing strategies—in general, things not already contained in the previous stiuation. Entrepreneurship should include genuine novelty and creativity and should not be rendered as a mechanical search for pre-existing profit opportunities.

Interpretation suggests the point that the profit opportunities entrepreneurs discover are not a matter of objective observations of quantities, but a matter of perspectival interpretation, a discerning of the intersubjective meaning of a qualitative situation. Profits are not measured; they are "read." Entrepreneurship, I argue, is primarily a cultural process. The seeing of profit opportunities is a matter of cultural interpretation. And like any other interpretation, this reading of profit opportunities necessarily takes place within a larger context of meaning, against a background of discursive practices, a culture. That is to say, entrepreneurship is not so much the achievement of the isolated maverick who finds objective profits others overlooked as it is of the culturally embedded participant who picks up the gist of a conversation.

The words "discovery" and "interpretation" also have connotations that pull in opposite, undesirable directions, which I would like to try to avoid partly by taking them together. To some people "discovery" suggests that the thing to be discovered is already there before the discovery process begins, that the process merely "uncovers" something latent in the objective circumstances. And to many, "interpretation" suggests an arbitrariness, as in the phrase "that is just a matter of interpretation." I believe that proper theory of entrepreneurship needs to steer between the rigid objectivism of seeing all change as latent in previous circumstances and the flaccid relativism of seeing change as utterly arbitrary. The objectivistic extreme, toward which most mainstream economics tends, reduces change to mere mechanistic dynamics. The relativistic extreme, toward which some leading critics of mainstream economics are thought to tend, seems to make change unintelligible. What is needed is a theory of entrepreneurial change that makes it intelligible without reducing it to predetermined mechanism.

One school of economics, the so-called market-process or Austrian school, has partially overcome these difficulties. Its critique of mainstream economics can serve as a useful point of departure for my own discussion. The work of Ludwig von Mises, Friedrich A. Hayek, and others provides a promising alternative to mainstream economics for both aspects of entrepreneurship the mainstream has neglected. In von Mises's insistence on the principle he calls "subjectivism," meaning is made central to economic theorizing.[6] In Hayek's notion of "spontaneous order" the idea of radical change is incorporated into a theory of nondeterministic evolutionary processes, and in his latest book he applies this spontaneous order approach to culture.[7] Here, I believe, are the building blocks for a substantive theory of the cultural dimension of entrepreneurship.

Of all the contributors to the market-process school, Israel Kirzner has undoubtedly had the most to say about the nature of entrepreneurship. His work elaborates on the interpretive aspect of von Mises as well as the discovery aspect of Hayek and is especially helpful in connecting them together. Although I believe his work is the best in economics on the subject, I argue that as it stands it does not adequately account for culture.

Maximizing and the Kirznerian Critique

A market consisting exclusively of economizing, maximizing individuals does not generate the market process we seek to understand. For the market process to emerge, we require in addition an element which is itself not comprehensible

within the narrow conceptual limits of economizing behavior. This element in the market . . . is best identified as entrepreneurship.
    —Israel Kirzner, *Competition and Entrepreneurship*

Building on the strengths of his mentors, von Mises and Hayek, Kirzner expands on the implications of their economics for entrepreneurial processes. Under the influence of von Mises's methodological principle of subjectivism, Kirzner's theory emphasizes the importance of the interpretive perspective of the human actor. Action is meaningful only in relation to the purposes, plans, and expectations of the actor. The actor's objective circumstances are not important in themselves, but the specific opportunities and constraints he perceives are. Action, Kirzner says, is not a direct confrontation with objective reality itself but always takes place within an interpretive framework.[8]

Under the influence of Hayek's work on spontaneous order, Kirzner's theory stresses entrepreneurial competition as a discovery procedure, not a predetermined mechanism. The competitive process works through a continuous, multidirectional, and rivalrous tugging and pulling of separate minds and actions, thereby generating an overall order greater than can be comprehended by its participating individuals. In this sense, the process is recognized to be a radically social one, fundamentally dependent on the free interplay of the individuals but not reducible to them. The function of such competition is to disclose information that cannot be obtained in any other way.[9]

Kirzner locates the difficulty mainstream economics faces in its fundamental notion of individual choice as a matter of "maximizing." The favorite theoretical device of economists is the idea of the maximization of a given goal subject to given constraints. Scarce means are described as being deliberately deployed to yield a maximum in regard to predetermined ends.

Mainstream economics typically deploys the maximizing idea on two levels, the individual choice level, where what is maximized is called utility, and the market level, where what is maximized is wealth. For the individual, his preferences, objective opportunities, and constraints are taken as the inputs, and the analysis focuses on the individual's choice as a solution to this maximization problem (this is sometimes called the economics of Robinson Crusoe). Economists contend that this mental experiment provides a general theory of human action, which can serve as a basis for looking at the specific properties of action within market contexts. Human action in general can be interpreted as attempts by individuals to exchange one state of affairs for another, whether they are making exchanges with nature or with one another. The innovative aspect of action can then be theoretically isolated as individual entrepreneurship. "Psychic profit" is the name economists give to the perceived gain the entrepreneur reaps when he exploits an opportunity.

Such individual mental experiments of Robinson Crusoe economics are then combined into a "market experiment," where the hypothetical choices of the various individuals are the inputs and an equilibrium solution, a pattern of mutually compatible choices, is taken as the output.[10] Parallel to psychic profit on the individual level is money profit on the market level. In this way the analysis focuses in turn on the way preferences interact with objective circumstances to yield individual choices and then on the way these choices interact with one another to yield a social outcome.[11]

Kirzner's theory also proceeds on these two levels, so that he identifies what he calls Crusoe entrepreneurship as an aspect of individual choice that eludes the maximizing framework, and what he calls market entrepreneurship as an aspect of social situations that eludes equilibrium analysis. The difficulty at the individual level, Kirzner argues, is not with the maximizing notion itself but with the crucial questions it begs when it takes goals and constraints as given. Human action encompasses more than the mechanical performance of maximization exercises within given choice frameworks; there is also the process by which actors develop those frameworks. Likewise, the problem with treating the interplay of choices in the marketplace as an attempt to find an equilibrium solution involving complete mutual coordination is not, Kirzner says, a problem with the equilibrium concept itself. The difficulty is that equilibrium analysis leaves out the process by which a degree of mutual coordination is achieved. Mainstream economics, according to Kirzner, is not so much wrong as simply incomplete, and on both the individual and the market levels it needs to add a theory of entrepreneurship.[12]

Economists' fondness for maximizing and equilibrium lead them to try to subsume entrepreneurship under these concepts. When Crusoe, for example, makes the entrepreneurial discovery of how to use vine to produce a fishnet, mainstream economics treats it as a deliberate allocation of his scarce attention to the discovery of hitherto unknown

production processes. In a broader social context, the arbitrage entrepreneur who discovers an opportunity to buy low in one market and
sell high in another is treated as allocating his entrepreneurial attention to this discovery. Entrepreneurship, then, is a scarce resource like
any other, which needs to be deployed economically.

Kirzner argues that the attempt to treat entrepreneurship just like
any other scarce resource is a mistake. He suggests the idea of "alertness" to new opportunities as something that cannot be subsumed
within a given maximizing problem. To treat the discovery of an
arbitrage opportunity as itself a maximizing problem presupposes that
the opportunity was already within the entrepreneur's choice framework, in which case it was not in need of discovery in the first place.
As Kirzner puts it, entrepreneurial alertness "is not an ingredient to
be deployed in decision making; it is rather something in which the
decision itself is embedded and without which it would be unthink-
able." He goes on to say:

> If an entrepreneur's discovery of a lucrative arbitrage opportunity
> galvanizes him into immediate action to capture the perceived gain,
> it will not do to describe the situation as one in which the entrepreneur
> has "decided" to use his alertness to capture this gain. He has not
> "deployed" his hunch for a specific purpose; rather, his hunch has
> propelled him to make his entrepreneurial purchase and sale. The
> entrepreneur never sees his hunches as potential inputs about which
> he must decide whether they are to be used.[13]

Thus Kirzner argues that there is something primordial about entrepreneurial discovery, something that involves the creation of a choice
framework, so that it cannot be treated as itself a consequence of
maximizing within that framework. Important policy implications
follow from the primordial nature of entrepreneurial discovery. If
discovery is not simply a scarce resource that can be rationally allocated
to predefined goals, then policies designed to enhance entrepreneurship need to recognize that fact. As Kirzner has pointed out, discovery
cannot be centrally engineered; it can only be cultivated by setting in
place conditions in which the decentralized, entrepreneurial process
can be expected to flourish.[14]

The approach to discovery Kirzner defends explicitly strives to steer
between the two hazards I referred to above as objectivism and
relativism. Kirzner takes T. W. Schultz, the famous development

economist, as an example of the extreme that makes the entrepreneur's action purely responsive to prior circumstances, leaving no room for true novelty. He takes G. L. S. Shackle, the great critic of mainstream economics, as an example of the other extreme, which makes the entrepreneur's action purely initiatory, leaving no room for any intelligible systematic connectedness with the previous circumstances:

> The one view sees the entrepreneur as responding systematically and frictionlessly to the conditions of the market, with pure entrepreneurial profit the smoothly corresponding reward that these market conditions require and make possible. From this perspective entrepreneurship is "called forth" systematically, if not quite predictably, by these market conditions. . . . The second view sees entrepreneurship not as *responding to* external market conditions, but as independently and spontaneously *injecting* new elements *into* those conditions, in a manner totally unpredictable from and wholly undetermined by existing circumstances.[15]

The hazards have, I believe, been appropriately identified by Kirzner here, even if we may not completely agree with his interpretations of Schultz and Shackle. Navigating between the hazards is particularly difficult because of the prevailing notions in economics about causal explanation. To many economists, explanations that are not fully mechanistic are necessarily unintelligible.[16] Indeed, in the next section I suggest that Kirzner's theory has not completely avoided these hazards. The general approach to intelligible causation arising from the modern market-process school does, I think, offer a way to avoid these hazards by making room for what I have called the discovery and interpretation aspects of entrepreneurship.

To me, the greatest strength of Kirzner's contribution lies not only in making room for discovery and interpretation, but in linking them together. According to mainstream economics, individual choice takes place within a given interpretation of opportunities and constraints. Discovery for Kirzner necessitates the transcending of the prior interpretive framework and the emergence of a new one. Thus, Crusoe interprets his world in a fundamentally different way after he discovers the possibility of producing fishnet out of vine. Where before he had seen vine only as an obstacle, as something to avoid getting tangled up in, he now sees it as an opportunity to make psychic profits. As phenomenological philosophers put the point, we do not see an objective thing; we always see something *as* a certain kind of thing. The vine seen as an obstacle is a radically different kind of thing from the vine seen as a possible fishnet. "Seeing," then, is itself interpreting.

Similarly, in the social context the arbitrageur interprets the world in a fundamentally different way after he has discovered the price discrepancy others had overlooked. The alert arbitrageur sees prices others consider of no particular interest as an opportunity to make money profits. According to Kirzner's subjectivist approach, then, human action has to be understood as something that is interpreted from a particular perspective. Discovery amounts to a shift in such perspectives, a fundamental change in the way the opportunities and constraints are seen.

Limitations of Kirzner's Theory of the Entrepreneur

Although maximizing is . . . a part of market process theory, it is not the fundamental notion. Human action is. Human action is partly guided by maximizing, but it is also guided by other mental processes. Alertness, creativity, and judgment also influence what we do. The primary importance of action to economic theory is that it sets in motion a market process.
                    —Jack High, *"Alertness and Judgment"*

If Kirzner benefits from the strengths of his teachers, von Mises and Hayek, he has also inherited some of their apparent shortcomings. Although Hayek's contribution points toward a nonmechanistic rendering of discovery processes, most of his work in economics ties the process to the notion of equilibrium, which appears to keep it within a mechanistic framework.[17] Whereas mainstream economics is preoccupied with states of equilibrium, Hayek sometimes seems to be only drawing attention to the systematic tendencies by which equilibrium is achieved. As Hayek's own later work on spontaneous order shows, though, this equilibration approach fundamentally depends on a strict distinction between the data, usually said to be tastes and resources, and the entrepreneurial process, which systematically pushes the economy toward the equilibrium. Changes in the data, which are thought to exhibit no systematic patterns, are disequilibrating, in the sense that they redefine the equilibrium toward which the economy tends. Only in his more recent work—and primarily in the context of law and culture as spontaneous orders, rather than in the context of economic questions—has Hayek decisively moved beyond the equilibrium style of thinking. This more recent work understands sponta-neous orders as open-ended and genuinely creative evolutionary processes, rather than mechanisms that focus on a predetermined end state.[18]

Kirzner has not been willing to follow some of Hayek's extensions of spontaneous order theory to nonmarket phenomena, clinging to Hayek's earlier position that entrepreneurship is a strictly equilibrating process. Discovery, for Kirzner, brings about a systematic tendency toward an equilibrium, even though long before that equilibrium is reached, the data are bound to change, impelling the market away from that equilibrium. Even when talking specifically about grasping future opportunities, Kirzner insists on treating them as equilibrating, as in some sense finding their way toward a pre-existing equilibrium. Although this is an attempt to deal with radical change, talking about grasping opportunities that are already "out there" obscures the genuinely creative element of entrepreneurship. Despite his warning that Schultz's approach reduces entrepreneurial action to a purely responsive role, Kirzner's theory also seems to treat the entrepreneur's action as something "called forth" by prior circumstances. Entrepreneur-ship appears to be a passive reaction to the equilibrium dictated by the data. A number of critics have charged that Kirzner's theory falls into the very problem he has identified in mainstream economics, ultimately leaving no room for genuine novelty, for truly creative change.[19]

Although von Mises's economics leans more toward an interpretive orientation than can be found in mainstream economics, von Mises was not willing or able to go all the way to a fully interpretive approach. Kirzner too seems unwilling to commit himself fully to an interpre-tive economics. Part of the difficulty, I believe, is their use of the Robinson Crusoe starting point, an issue to which I will return briefly at the conclusion. Much of the problem with Kirzner's theory of the entrepreneur, however, stems from his unfortunate selection of illustra-tive examples, which seriously distorts his rendering of the interpretive dimension. Although the subjectivism Kirzner inherits from von Mises is perhaps reconcilable with a fully interpretive orientation to entrepre-neurship, the examples consistently undercut his argument.

The example par excellence of Kirzner's theory is the pure arbitrageur who simply notices a profit opportunity. By making this special case stand for entrepreneurship in general, Kirzner makes alert-ness the "essence" of entrepreneurial action. The theory has come under criticism by other market-process economists on the grounds that alertness in itself is insufficient to cover all the aspects of entrepreneurship that maximizing leaves out. As Jack High argues, creativity and judgment are also involved in entrepreneurship.[20] I would add only that a crucial component of judgment and creativity is interpretation. The arbitrageur immediately "sees" the chance to buy low and sell high. The case is misleading in that the interpretation is trivial and has already taken place. Kirzner likens the arbitrageur's discovery of profit to finding a twenty-dollar bill on the beach. This example reinforces the impression of profit that one gets from mainstream economics, that it is an objective "find" that does not require interpretation. Most acts of entrepreneurship are not like an isolated individual finding things on beaches; they require efforts of the creative imagination, skillful judgments of future cost and revenue possibilities, and an ability to read the significance of complex social situations.

The Kirznerian entrepreneur "sees" psychic or money profits—he notices them—but he does not seem to have to read them. He uncovers unambiguous opportunities to improve his situation that others have simply failed to notice, as if fixed collections of things called profits were lying around and certain individuals were just more alert than others in finding them. Being more alert seems to be simply a matter of opening one's eyes to see what is right there under one's nose. I would argue that if entrepreneurship is like vision, though, it is like human vision, which does not see merely patches of color but meaningful things. Like visual perception, it involves focusing on an object *as* a certain sort of thing, seeing it against a background. The profit opportunities the entrepreneur discovers are not directly copied off reality in itself; they are interpreted from a point of view.

Kirzner insists that, in spite of economists' propensity to assign every choice a cost, the discovery of profit opportunities is "costless." He stresses the primordial nature of entrepreneurship by pointing out that an entrepreneur does not *deliberately* set aside a known alternative when he notices a new opportunity. Ex ante, of course, there is no alternative being purposely set aside in the act of noticing something, but surely ex post there will be things that remain unnoticed because attention was directed one way rather than another. Kirzner sometimes seems to be denying even this second, ex-post sense of cost to alertness, making entrepreneurship appear more mysterious than it needs to be. Alertness seems to be some kind of general-purpose attentiveness that is "switched on or off," as Kirzner likes to say, or at best is a unidimensional quantity, such that there can be more or less of it, and more is always better. The only opportunity cost of not opening one's eyes, after all, is leaving them closed. The only "opportunity" forgone by opening one's eyes is seeing nothing at all.

I do not see why alertness has to appear to be an exception to the economist's principle that costs accrue to any action, that there are necessarily opportunities forgone. Being alert in any one respect implies that one is not being alert in some other respects. Asking one question is passing over the asking of an infinite number of others. The suggestion that alertness has a directedness about it indicates that it is a matter not so much of seeing what is under one's nose as it is of looking or listening for certain kinds of things. This systematic directedness of the discovery process makes some potential opportunities more likely to be found by certain sorts of alertness. In principle, it is conceivable within Kirzner's approach that someone could be perfectly alert—could see "all the opportunities there are"—even though Kirzner does not believe anybody actually achieves this degree of alertness. Since the very act of paying attention to one aspect of reality inherently involves removing attention from other aspects, however, it makes no sense, even in principle, for someone to be alert to everything. Alertness is multidimensional. It is misleading to treat it like an on/off switch or to say there is simply more or less of it. There are qualitatively diverse ways of being alert.

While Kirzner shows that entrepreneurship involves the displacement of an old framework by a new one, he confines this change to the situation where something under one's nose that was previously ignored gets noticed. In the trivial examples Kirzner uses, profit opportunities are implicitly treated as atomistic—that is, finding a new opportunity need not have any effect on the entrepreneur's understanding of the old opportunities he had already found. But a shift of interpretive framework can bring about a more fundamental change than simply adding to a stock of things that have been noticed. An interpretive framework can change in a far more profound manner: all the old opportunities will suddenly look different, indeed may no longer be considered opportunities at all, when a new one is found. And of course the circumstances one has been alert to in the past help determine the kinds of situations one will be apt to notice in the future. That is, profit opportunities are not independent atoms but connected parts of a whole perspective on the world. And the perspective is in turn an evolving part of a continuing cultural tradition, constantly being reappropriated to new situations.

The way Kirzner renders the idea of alertness leaves inexplicable the systematic process by which one means/ends framework gets replaced by another. It appears to be an arbitrary matter why some things get noticed before others. In this respect his theory comes dangerously close to the hazard he associates with Shackle, cutting change off from any systematic connection to its history. Taking culture more seriously would allow Kirzner's theory to make the process by which perspectives change more intelligible.

Profit opportunities are not so much like road signs to which we assign an automatic meaning as they are like difficult texts in need of a sustained effort of interpretation. Entrepreneurship is not only a matter of opening one's eyes, of switching on one's attentiveness; it requires directing one's gaze.[21] When an entrepreneur sees things others have overlooked, it is not just that he opened his eyes while they had theirs closed. He is reading selected aspects of a complex situation others have not read. And this raises the question of what gives a predirectedness to the entrepreneur's vision, of why he is apt to read some things and not others. I submit that the answer to this question is culture.

Crusoe Economics, Cartesian Philosophy, and Hermeneutics

> *In learning the language, the child absorbs a way of thinking and of expressing his thoughts that is predetermined by the language, and so he receives a stamp that he can scarcely remove from his life. The language opens up the way for a person exchanging thoughts with all those who use it; he can influence them and receive influence from them.*
> —Ludwig von Mises, *Nation, State, and Economy*

> *It is less accurate to suppose that thinking man creates and controls his cultural evolution than it is to say that culture, and evolution, created his reason. . . . So far as scientific explanation is concerned, it was not what we know as mind that developed civilization, let alone directed its evolution, but rather mind and civilization which developed or evolved concurrently. What we call mind is not something that the individual is born with, as he is born with his brain, or something that the brain produces, but something that his genetic equipment . . . helps him to acquire, as he grows up, from his family and*

adult fellows by absorbing the results of a tradition that is not genetically transmitted. . . . Shaped by the environment in which individuals grow up, mind in turn conditions the preservation, development, richness, and variety of traditions on which individuals draw. By being transmitted largely through families, mind preserves a multiplicity of concurrent streams into which each newcomer to the community can delve. It may well be asked whether an individual who did not have the opportunity to tap such a cultural tradition could be said even to have a mind.
—Friedrich A. Hayek, *The Fatal Conceit*

I suggest that the reason why the economic theory of entrepreneurship—even when at its best as in the contributions of Kirzner—has not gotten very far in elucidating the cultural dimension is traceable to its Crusoe economics orientation. Economics has based itself more than it realizes on the case of Robinson Crusoe, a fictional, isolated individual confronting the natural world, and has essentially "added in" Friday, to try to make the analysis into social theory.[22] Choice in general, and thus entrepreneurial choice in particular, is first studied on what is thought to be the more basic Crusoe level and only then complicated by the introduction of other choosing individuals. This analytical procedure has, I believe, led to a failure to grasp fully the radically social element of the human mind and thus of choice.

Questioning the foundational role of Robinson Crusoe is no minor quibble with contemporary economics. Economic theorizing, both in its mainstream and in its market-process variations, usually considers microeconomics the basis of the rest of economics and treats the choice situation of the isolated individual as the basis of microeconomics. The cherished principle economists call "methodological individualism" is in question here.[23] If this principle claims only that the social whole has no purposes but is a complex resulting from the choices of its participating individuals, then the principle is unobjectionable. To most economists, however, methodological individualism seems to mean more than that. It is generally interpreted as demanding an analytical privileging of the study of the individual over the study of society. It seems to insist that Crusoe, the theoretical construct of an isolated individual, must come first to serve as the foundation of the analysis of markets. As Kirzner put it at the beginning of his book on price theory, "Society consists of individual human beings."[24] We need to make sense of the single individual's actions before we can make sense of the way such actions interact in society. The isolated individual becomes the analytical framework for studying human action in general, of which action in regard to market institutions is then taken as a special case.

When the analysis starts from Crusoe, a special difficulty seems to face the agent when other agents are introduced, since now what he needs to know about includes not only external and observable facts of the natural world but also the contents of the other agents' minds. In the theory of entrepreneurship this presents itself as the problem of how the entrepreneur can come to "read the minds" of his potential customers, whether they are consumers or producers, and provide what they will want. It is one thing for Crusoe to see a new use for vine, where he has to anticipate only his own wants, but it is a substantially more difficult thing for him to figure out what Friday will want. Something seems highly mysterious, from this perspective, about the entrepreneur's ability to look into the contents of other minds.

This procedure of starting with the individual mind, which is presumed to be a self-contained, unproblematic entity, and then moving on to address the problem of "Other Minds," has been the mainstream approach in philosophy ever since Descartes. It has come under powerful criticism by a number of contemporary philosophical schools, from which economics could learn a great deal.[25] Among the most interesting critics of Cartesian philosophy is Hans-Georg Gadamer, who shows that the mind is already social before it is rational and thus that a whole variety of special difficulties with the analysis of interpersonal communication prove to be pseudo-problems. The individual agent, Gadamer argues, is already operating within a linguistic process even when he is confronting nature. He is already, as it were, reading other people's minds when he thinks about uses of vine or when he thinks about anything whatsoever. Human beings should have no special difficulty reading the minds of others, since our linguistic practices are tapping into a shared culture all the time.

As the epigraphs by von Mises and Hayek suggest, the market-process school has at least partially glimpsed the main thrust of this critique of Cartesian thinking. The fact that the mind thinks in language, which it acquires in the process of enculturation, makes "the mind" a profoundly social entity. Although Kirzner is right when he declares that society consists of individual human beings, it is also true that individuals consist of society. They are not isolated, self-contained things but interdependent parts of an integral process of cultural dynamics. All understanding of the natural world is already social understanding, embedded in and meaningful only in relation to culture. The methodological priority given to the rational choice of individual minds implicitly treats them as if they could exist in isolated, cultureless, languageless brains.

The peculiarly cultureless "agent" of Crusoe economics is an odd construction to use as a basis for human action in general. Choice theory is constructed as if it does not matter whether the mind operates with a social language or not. The Crusoes of economics, unlike the character from Defoe's novel, need know nothing of language. They simply apply means to ends. All the minds we have experience with, though, can conceive of means and ends only through their language, that is, through their ability to tap into the cultural process. If economics aspires to be about human action as we know it, it should take language and cultural transmission seriously. As von Mises put it, we need to "consider what immense significance language has for thinking and for the expression of thought, for social relations, and for all activities of life."[26]

Economists may say in their own defense that economic analysis only begins with this strange, cultureless, Crusoe character and that it then moves on to the theory of markets, where it specifically takes up the mutual influences of individuals on one another. But where one starts can have important influences on the way one moves on. Not enough seems to change when the analysis moves from the individual experiment to the market experiment. The market seems to be populated with many Crusoes, each devoid of culture and communicating with one another only by price "signals."

The entrepreneur is typically pictured as a loner bucking the crowd, a maverick who sees things differently from everybody else. This view contains an element of truth, of course, in that the entrepreneur comes upon a new reading of his situation that may be qualitatively different from the readings others have been able to make. But his ability to read new things into a situation is not primarily due to his separateness from others but, indeed, to his higher degree of sensitivity to what others are looking for. The really successful entrepreneurs we know are not unusually separate from others; on the contrary, they are especially well plugged into the culture. What gives them the ability to sense what their customers will want is not some kind of mysterious alertness that gets "switched on" but their capacity to read the conversations of mankind. They can pick up the sense of where their fellows in the culture stand, what values they adhere to, what purposes they pursue, what they consider beautiful, and what they deem profane.

Different entrepreneurial acts are the readings of, and contributions to, different conversations. The successful supplier of consumer goods listens to the discourse of the consuming public, senses what they will be likely to find attractive and what they will not, and is thereby more persuasive in getting them to try new products. The successful venture capitalist listens to the concerns of the banking community and thereby enhances his ability to persuade the loan officer to make an invest-ment. The successful supplier of innovative industrial inputs listens to the technological conversations of his potential customers, exploits his skill in anticipating their specific requirements, and thereby gains an ability to persuade them to explore hitherto ignored technological possibilities. The successful employer listens to the discourse of existing and potential employees and tries to shape an attractive work environ-ment that will persuade new workers to come and old ones to stay. What makes entrepreneurs successful is their ability to join conversa-tional processes and nudge them in new directions.

Conversational processes about production and consumption plans existed in human societies before the evolution of market processes and provided the foundation on which primordial elements of markets began to evolve. The process by which direct exchange evolved out of reciprocal gift giving and by which money evolved out of exchange must have been a discursive process. Advanced market institutions such as contract law, the price system, accounting conventions, banking methods, and so forth are emergent properties of the process of cultural evolution. A modern market is still a discursive process, but now one in which the participants are able to use not only spoken and written words but also prices, advertising, stock markets, and other media of communication.

Perhaps, then, a better starting point than Crusoe from which to proceed to the analysis of markets would be the premarket communica-tive process of language and cultural transmission. Rather than con-sider the interactions of individuals in a market context as funda-mentally analogous to Crusoe's isolated actions, we might consider market forms of interaction as fundamentally analogous to linguistic interaction. In particular, Gadamer's theory of language might be a promising place to start. Gadamer's challenging argument—that it is not so much we who speak language as language that speaks us—underscores the point that the process by which we comprehend our world takes place on the social level. If we appreciate the way language constitutes the basis of all understanding, it seems clear that the communicative processes involved in market institutions are emergent extensions of the linguistic process. What existed historically before the emergence of markets was not Robinson Crusoe but processes of cultural evolution in which interacting human beings participated. Markets can be viewed as offshoots of, and complements to, the process of cultural dynamics.[27]

Gadamer's work on the way tradition is "appropriated" is, I believe, an approach to cultural change that can steer between the hazards Kirzner warns against. It makes change intelligible as something that grows out of history; yet it permits radical, nonmechanistic change. I think the theory of entrepreneurship could more fully account for the discovery and interpretation aspects of economic change if it were built on the hermeneutical theory of language and culture.

Janet T. Landa

4

Culture and Entrepreneurship in Less-Developed Countries: Ethnic Trading Networks as Economic Organizations

In this chapter I will focus specifically on the relationship between culture and ethnic middleman entrepreneurship in less-developed countries (LDCs). Ethnically homogeneous middleman groups (EHMGs) have played significant roles in cross-cultural trade throughout history.[1] Some of these EHMGs, such as the Jews in medieval Europe, have persisted over long periods of time; others, in present-day LDCs—the Chinese in Southeast Asia, the Indians in East and Central Africa, the Lebanese in West Africa—have relatively shorter histories. What accounts for the success and persistence of these EHMGs? Does culture play a role?[2]

Economists have paid little attention to this area, relegating the study of culture and of ethnic middleman entrepreneurship to sister disciplines of sociology, anthropology, and marketing theory. In recent years, however, there has appeared a small but growing body of economic literature on the determinants of ethnic group differences in labor markets and in entrepreneurial roles. William Darity and Rhonda Williams, for example, have criticized contemporary economic theory (new-classical and Austrian theory) for attempting to bury the idea that market discrimination explains racial wage differentials or differences in general pecuniary accomplishments across ethnic groups under competitive conditions.[3] Referring specifically to the Austrian view of competition associated with the work of Israel Kirzner,[4] Darity and Williams argued that according to that view, discriminatory wage differentials could not be maintained because a "latent reservoir of alert entrepreneurs presumably would seize the profit opportunities generated by the discriminatory wage, drive discriminating employers from the market, and erode the wage differentials."[5] Darity and Williams also criticized what they call the "new" cultural variant of human capital theory—associated especially with the work of Thomas Sowell[6] and of Barry Chiswick[7]—which proposes cultural explanations for differences in economic achievements across distinct racial and ethnic groups:

> If one accepts the position that cultural differences are significant determinants of ethnic and racial inequality, then one must explain why cultural differences salient for success are persistent. This persistence is impossible to maintain if one believes the market system is imbued with an Austrian process of competition. Sowell,[8] for one, seems to have in mind exactly such a view of competition.[9]

Darity and Williams further argued that the inadequacies of the cultural explanations are compounded by their inadequacies in explaining the experiences of specific ethnic groups. In searching for an adequate theory of ethnic success, they suggested the notion of Marxist competition, which they believe can be reconciled with the existence of market discrimination as a persistent source of difference in racial and ethnic group achievements:

> The evolutionary nature of Marxist competition simply means that competition gives rise to monopolies. . . . Marxist capitalist winners consolidate and concentrate; they can exclude losers and consolidate their positions for long stretches of time. Austrian competition's winning entrepreneur cannot, in contrast, *permanently* maintain barriers to preserve his position.[10] According to the Austrian view, barriers will eventually be torn down by newer contestants.
>   We extend Marxist competition to labor powers. Workers also concentrate and consolidate, particularly by ethnicity or race. . . . Specific ethnic and racial groups could gain control and dominance of particular occupational or labor powers. . . . Pursuit of this line of inquiry necessitates investigation of the concrete economic and historical conditions confronted by specific ethnic and racial groups.[11]

In this chapter, I shall argue that both the Austrian and Marxist notions of competition are inadequate to explain the emergence and persistence of certain EHMGs in LDCs, such as the Chinese in Southeast Asia, the Indians in East and Central Africa, the Lebanese in West Africa, and the Jews in medieval Europe and elsewhere. I shall present an alternative economic theory that takes account of the relationship of culture to ethnic middleman entrepreneurial success and also responds to Darity and Williams's criticism of the work of Sowell.

My theory is based on the concepts of transaction costs from transaction cost economics, which is part of the New Institutional Economics, N-entrepreneurship or entrepreneurial gap-filling function, cultural norms as an ethnic-specific asset, and "group competition"[12] from modern evolutionary theory. It is an empirically grounded theory and is based on examining the empirical realities of the social structures and cultural values of specific ethnic trading groups and the historical-institutional contexts in which these groups are embedded.[13]

Economic Man, Culture, and the Ethnic Group

The concept of the isolated, individual, rational "economic man" *(Homo Oeconomicus)* is at the heart of economics. The economic man carefully weighs benefits and costs before arriving at a rational choice.[14] Before man can make rational choices, however, he must be socialized or enculturated. The role of culture or socializing forces in influencing an individual's rational choice has been generally ignored by economists, with the notable exception of Hayek. Hayek is keenly aware of the relationship between the transmission of tradition and culture largely through the family and the "thinking man" (see Don Lavoie's chapter in this volume). Recently Nobel Laureate Herbert Simon also emphasized the importance of rational man as a "socially dependent creature":

> Human beings are not the independent Leibnitzian monads conjured up by libertarian theory. Society is not something imposed on them; it provides the matrix in which they survive and mature and act on the environment. The society, including but not limited to the family, provides not only nutrient, shelter, and safety during childhood and youth, but also knowledge and skills that are needed for expert, hence fit, adult performance. Society has enormous power, enduring through a person's lifetime, to enhance or reduce fitness.[15]

Cultural anthropologists, on the other hand, have always insisted on the importance of culture in influencing an individual's behavior.

Clifford Geertz, for example, argues that men without culture are "unworkable monstrosities" with

> few useful instincts, fewer recognizable sentiments, and no intellect: mental basket cases. . . . To supply the additional information necessary to be able to act, we were forced, in turn, to rely more heavily on cultural resources—the accumulated fund of significant symbols. Such symbols are thus not mere expressions, instrumentalities, or correlates of our biological, psychological, and social existence; they are prerequisites of it. Without men, no culture, certainly; but equally, and more significantly, without culture, no men.
>
> We are, in sum, incomplete or unfinished animals who complete ourselves through culture—and not through culture in general but through highly particular forms of it: Dobuan and Javanese, Hopi and Italian, upper-class and lower-class, academic and commercial.[16]

The link between man and specific forms of culture is further clarified by anthropologist Fredrik Barth via the concept of "ethnic units" or "ethnic groups":

> Practically all anthropological reasoning rests on the premise that cultural variation is discontinuous: that there are aggregates of people who essentially share a common culture, and interconnected differences that distinguish each such discrete culture from all others. Since culture is nothing but a way to describe human behavior, it would follow that there are discrete groups of people, i.e., ethnic units, to correspond to each culture.[17]

But what precisely is an ethnic unit? What is the cultural content of an ethnic group?

An ethnic group, according to A. P. Royce can be defined in terms of the following six characteristics:[18]

1. The group shares common origins, such as national origins, or common descent.

2. Group members share fundamental cultural values.

3. The group relates to other ethnic groups in a broader system of social relations.

4. Ethnic groups are larger than kin or locality groups and transcend face-to-face interaction.

5. Different meanings for ethnic categories pertain both in different social settings and for different individuals.

6. Ethnic categories are emblematic, having names and group identity.

The first characteristic points to the ethnic group as a biological or racial group, with members of the same group identified by distinguishable, objective physical characteristics.

Among the characteristics listed above, anthropologists have traditionally given central importance to the second characteristic—the connection between ethnic groups and culture. So important is this feature that Barth calls an ethnic group a "cultural-bearing unit."[19] He divides the cultural contents of ethnic groups into two kinds: the overt signals or symbols of identity—what anthropologists term "cultural diacritica"—such as language, religion, rituals, dress style, food preferences that people look for and exhibit to show identity; and the underlying values, ethics, or standards of morality shared by group members. Of particular importance to Barth is the concept of the ethnic *boundary*:

> . . . the ethnic boundary canalizes social life—it entails a frequently quite complex organization of behavior and social relations. The identification of another person as a fellow member of an ethnic group implies a sharing of criteria for evaluation and judgment. It thus entails the assumption that the two are fundamentally "playing the same game". . . . On the other hand, a dichotomization of others as strangers, as members of another ethnic group, implies a recognition of limitations or shared understandings, differences in criteria for judgment of value and performance, and a restriction of interaction to sectors of assumed common understanding and mutual interest.[20]

Barth's emphasis on the dependence of the self on the values and ethics of one's own ethnic group is spelled out in greater detail by biologist Lewis Thomas. Speaking of the individual, "myself," Thomas says:

> The original root was *se* or *seu,* simply the pronouns of the third person, and most of the descendant words, except "self" itself, were constructed to allude to other, somehow connected people; "sibs" and "gossips," relatives and close acquaintances, came from *seu. Se* was also used to indicate something outside or apart, hence words like "separate," "secret" or "segregate." From an extended root *swedh*

it moved into Greek as *ethnos,* meaning people of one's own sort, and *ethos,* meaning the customs of such people. "Ethics" means the behavior of people like one's self, one's own ethics.[21]

There is thus a clear link between the self, the ethnic group, and the ethics of the group; the self is inescapably socialized or enculturated. The self, embedded in an ethnic group, belongs to a "moral community" of people like one's self; the self is "culture-bound."[22]

The third characteristic points to the existence of smaller groups within the wider ethnic group. Anthropologist Marshall Sahlins, for example, sees the individual, Ego, as embedded in ever-widening concentric circles of groupings: the family, the lineage, the village, and finally the tribal/ethnic group.[23] Ego is seen as interacting with individuals in ever-widening social spheres in which kinship/social distance increase as Ego moves out from the center to the boundary of the ethnic group. As social distance increases, mutual aid and reciprocity between Ego and his cooperating partner decrease. Across the ethnic/tribal boundary, Ego expects "negative reciprocity" from interaction with outsiders.[24] Sahlins's model of kinship/social distance and reciprocity describes the phenomenon of nepotism and ethnocentrism in social or economic transactions: A person will always favor close kin over more distant kin, and will favor fellow ethnics over outsiders. Pierre Van den Berghe goes even further to include the sociobiologists' emphasis of kin selection and reciprocal altruism in the nonhuman world as promoting inclusive fitness of the individual. He regards ethnicity as "kin selection" and the ethnic group ("ethny") as representing the outer limits of that

> inbred group of near or distant kinsmen whom one knows as intimates and whom therefore one can trust. One intuitively expects fellow ethnics to behave at least somewhat benevolently toward one because of kin selection, reinforced by reciprocity. The shared genes predispose toward beneficence; the daily interdependence reinforces that kin selection. Fellow ethnics are, in the deepest sense, "our people."[25]

Ethnocentrism, the identification of "us, the insiders whom we trust" and the discrimination against "them, the outsiders, whom we distrust" is an inherent feature of all ethnic groups. Not all ethnic groups are equally ethnocentric, however; some are more ethnocentric than others because they are more effective at enforcing the values and norms of the group.

The fourth characteristic emphasizes the fact that ethnic identity emerges only in the context of interethnic contact situations. Barth, in particular, emphasizes the point that "ethnic distinctions do not depend on an absence of social interaction and acceptance, but are quite to the contrary often the very foundations on which embracing social systems are built."[26]

The fifth characteristic emphasizes situational use of ethnicity, which, according to Royce,[27] implies that identities can be manipulated to suit situations:

> (1) individuals can choose, within certain constraints, between a variety of identities; (2) individuals will maximize the options available to them and will use ethnic identity if they perceive an advantage in so doing; (3) that individuals have to contend, in this process, with other individuals engaged in the same process whose interests and perceptions may be quite different. In other words, the use of ethnic identity is fluid and flexible.[28]

The sixth characteristic focuses on the fact that ethnic groups have names that serve as powerful symbols of identity. In fact, the ethnic group constitutes the outer boundaries in which discrimination and identification of "us" and "them" are based.

To the six characteristics defining an ethnic group, we should add a seventh, namely that ethnic groups are "cultural transmission units" in that the cultural traits of ethnic groups are treated as a group inheritance that is transmitted most often, but not exclusively, through family upbringing. Here the link is once again between ethnic groups and culture, but in this case the concept of culture is defined as "the transmission from one generation to the next, via teaching and imitation, of knowledge, values, and other factors that influence behavior."[29] The various characteristics of an ethnic group will be important in the development of our theory of the emergence and persistence of EHMGs and ethnic trading boundaries.

Rules, Institutions, and Transaction Costs

An essential feature of an ethnic group, as already pointed out, is that members share the same ethics and play by the same rules.

This fact is important for understanding the concept of rules as institutions. What precisely are rules? Rules, according to political scientist Elinor Ostrom,

> refer to prescriptions commonly known and used by a set of participants to order repetitive, interdependent relationships. Prescriptions refer to which actions (or states of the world) are *required, prohibited,* or *permitted.* Rules are the result of implicit or explicit efforts by a set of individuals to achieve order and predictability within defined situations by: (1) creating positions (e.g., members, convener, agent, etc.); (2) stating how participants enter or leave positions; (3) stating which actions participants in these positions are required, permitted, or forbidden to take; and (4) stating which outcome participants are required, permitted, or forbidden to affect.[30]

In short, all rules contain prescriptions that require, forbid, or permit some action or outcome and these rules are monitored and enforced.[31] All ethnic groups have such rules, but it must be emphasized that some ethnic groups are more efficient in enforcing in-group norms than are other ethnic groups. The ethnic groups that have emerged to dominate middleman roles, such as the Chinese in Southeast Asia, the Indians in East and Central Africa, the Jews in Jerba and in Antwerp, all have strict codes that are strongly enforced.[32]

The study of institutions is at the heart of transaction cost economics, which is part of the New Institutional Economics.[33] Institutions emerge in order to economize on transaction costs. Transaction costs include the search for trading partners, costs of contract negotiation, and enforcement. Oliver E. Williamson has identified three alternative economic institutions or modes of economic organization of developed capitalist economies for coordinating the actions of interdependent firms: the market via contracts, the vertically integrated firm, and relational contracting (ongoing long-term contractual relations). Central to Williamson's work is the behavioral assumption that "some individuals are opportunistic some of the time and that differential trustworthiness is rarely, transparent ex-ante. As a consequence, ex-ante screening efforts are made and ex-post safeguards are created.[34] Opportunism is defined as "self-seeking with guile," of which breach of contract is an example. Williamson argues that vertical integration and long-term relational contracts can be viewed as governance structures, alternative to market contracting, to protect parties from opportunism, thereby economizing on the costs of contract enforcement.

Kenneth Arrow has identified yet another way society constrains opportunistic behavior: codes of behavior and ethics that establish trust between two parties who share the same code. The existence of trust economizes on transaction costs. Without trust, transaction costs may be so high as to lead markets to go out of existence.[35]

In LDCs, the existence of mutual trust among trading partners is manifested in the clublike institutional arrangement of the ethnically homogeneous middleman entrepreneurial groups which emerge to economize on the costs of enforcing contracts. (More will be said on this topic shortly.)

Entrepreneurship, Imperfect Markets, and Gap-Filling Functions

Entrepreneurship is often considered a fourth factor of production or input, along with land, labor, and capital. There is, however, no general agreement of the defining characteristics or functions of an entrepreneur. For example, Frank Knight emphasized the uncertainty-bearing function of entrepreneurs; Joseph Schumpeter emphasized the innovation function; Israel Kirzner emphasized the arbitrageur-entrepreneur function as one of possessing the subjective capacity to perceive and seize opportunities from arbitrage arising from the existence of price differentials.[36] (See also Lavoie in this volume.) Because of the lack of consensus regarding the definition of an entrepreneur, the concept of entrepreneurship remains elusive and has been compared to the creature known as the "heffalump."[37]

It is clear, however, that the concept of the entrepreneur as defined by Knight, Schumpeter, and Kirzner is applicable to *developed* Western economies. Since LDCs differ significantly from developed Western economies, it may be expected that the entrepreneurial role in LDCs will also differ. William Glade has provided a useful general framework for analyzing the emergence and growth of entrepreneurship in LDCs.[38] A theory of entrepreneurial formation, he says, must examine the role of opportunity structure, the exogenously determined structural or environmental factors such as technological change, population shifts, shifts in demand, which determine the demand side of entrepreneurship; and the conditions for opportunity appropriation. Given an objective structure of opportunity, what are the factors determining who will perceive and appropriate the opportunities for themselves? Glade suggests that the ability to exploit new opportunities will depend on all key inputs and not just the conventional categories such as land, labor, and capital. Information networks, political connections, "transaction security arrangements," and capital-mobilizing mechanisms may also be key inputs critical to the emergence of entrepreneurship.

Harvey Leibenstein's theory of N-entrepreneurship provides another view of the importance of nonconventional inputs for the emergence of entrepreneurs in LDCs. He defines N-entrepreneurship as

> the activities necessary to operate or carry on an enterprise where not all the markets are well established or clearly defined and/or in which the relevant parts of the production function are not completely known. In both cases, the entrepreneur coordinates activities that involve different markets; he is an intermarket operator. But in the case of N-entrepreneurship not all markets exist or operate perfectly and the entrepreneur, if he is to be successful, must fill in for the market deficiencies. . . . As we have defined the entrepreneur he is an individual or group of individuals with four major characteristics: he connects different markets, he is capable of making up for market deficiencies (gap-filling), he is an "input-completer," and he creates or expands time-binding input-transforming entities (i.e., firms).[39]

The greater prevalence of incomplete and imperfect markets gives rise to the significance of N-entrepreneurship, which includes the capacity to reduce risks and uncertainties associated with imperfect markets. Nathaniel Leff suggests that, given the greater risks and uncertainties in LDCs,

> entrepreneurship in LDCs is likely to involve more than psychological capacity for perceiving new economic opportunities and entering them with an aggressive investment policy. The special conditions affecting risk and uncertainty, and the need to open new channels for factor mobilization and product supply are likely to impose additional requirements.[40]

Leff pointed to the role of the "Group" type of industrial organization, a large-scale firm somewhat similar to the Japanese *zaibatsu* and the American conglomerate, that "invests and produces in several product lines that involve vertical integration or other economic and technological complementarities. Much of the private and domestically owned advanced sector in the LDCs is in fact organized in the Group pattern of industrial organization."[41] His Group overcomes many of the market imperfections in LDCs by mobilizing capital and information and by reducing uncertainty surrounding investment and production decisions.

In this chapter, I focus on the middleman N-entrepreneurial "gap-filling" role of coping with the problem of *contract* uncertainty in LDCs where the legal framework for contract enforcement is not well developed. Specifically, I focus on the middleman-entrepreneur's capacity for creating EHMGs and personalistic exchange networks for economizing on costs of enforcing contracts, a problem ignored in entrepreneurial theory as well as in development economics. The EHMGs are unlike Leff's Group form of organization in that they do not involve vertical integration between firms, but are *decentralized trading networks* among independent marketing firms linked by particularistic ties.

EHMGs and Personalistic Trading Networks as Efficient Economic Organizations: A Transaction Cost Approach

I have elsewhere presented my theory of the emergence of the EHMG[42] and also generalized the theory.[43] What follows is a summary of aspects of my theory of the origins of the EHMG.

Under conditions of contract uncertainty in LDCs, traders must cope with the problem of opportunism arising from breach of contract. Traders, operating at the individual microlevel, are aware that they are not isolated individuals but are embedded in larger macro-units or social structures—the family, the clan, the ethnic group—with rules to constrain members' behavior. The rational "embedded economic man," operating under conditions of contract uncertainty, will not indiscriminately enter into impersonal exchange relations randomly with anonymous traders. When Ego chooses his trading partners, he will choose to enter into exchange relations with those whom he can trust. Ego thus will favor kin over nonkin, close kin over distant kin, and fellow ethnics over outsiders because the closer the degree of social distance the greater the degree of trust; the greater the degree of trust the lower the transaction costs of protecting contracts.

The capacity for self-conscious reflection on the part of individual traders enables each trader to deliberately create Ego-centered particularistic trading networks to cope with the problem of opportunism in LDCs. For some traders, the Ego-centered trading network will become truncated at the ethnic/religious boundary: The trader will not transact across that boundary when the costs of contract enforcement with outsiders are perceived to be greater than the benefits of trading with outsiders. For other traders who must cross the ethnic/religious boundary to have access to the source of supply, the relevant comparison is between the costs of enforcing contracts with outsiders, including the use of cash, and the opportunity costs of excluding outsiders. Given an interdependent marketing network, the structural effect of many individual middlemen's rational choices of trustworthy traders is the emergence of an EHMG/particularistic trading network with norms of behavior constraining middleman behavior. The structural effects of the rational choices of many traders in creating the macrophenomena of EHMGs may not be fully understood by the traders, however. Norms of behavior embedded in the EHMG emerge from an "invisible-hand process" akin to the Austrian notion of spontaneous emergence of order. Since the EHMG is itself part of a larger ethnic group with its tradition and cultural norms already in existence, norms of behavior embedded in the EHMG are seen as *emergent* macrophenomena in a highly complex, multitiered system.

The emergence of the EHMG economizes on transaction costs of protecting contracts of members in such networks in several ways: mutual trust between contracting parties economizes on the costs of enforcing contracts; kinship and ethnic status/identity, because they indicate the degree of social distance, transmit low-cost signals of the degree of trustworthiness or reputation of a potential contracting party, thus economizing on information costs; mutual trust between pairs of traders, in a chain-linked middlemen system, gives rise to transitive trust, which reduces the need to search for the reputation of indirect partners in the chain; and the existence of a dense information network arising from the existence of mutual aid associations or caste organizations in which EHMGs are embedded economizes on the information costs of directly acquiring information on the reputation of a potential partner. Because of these economizing features of ethnic trading networks operating in LDCs, such networks may be considered clublike institutional arrangements or economic organizations, alternatives to

Williamson's three modes of economic organization found in highly developed Western capitalist economies. The particularistic kinship/ethnic trading networks are the dominant form of economic organization found in non-Western LDCs. As such, particularistic trading networks may be considered a fourth kind of economic organizacion in which relational contracting takes place between traders linked by particularistic ties of mutual trust. Alternatively, the EHMG may be considered to be an *intermediate* form of economic organization, lying *between* markets (contracts) and hierarchies (the vertically integrated firm). They are an efficient form of economic organization that emerged for the protection of contracts, given the conditions of contract uncertainty and the historical-institutional context in which these ethnic middlemen-entrepreneurs operate.

EHMGs as "Cultural-Bearing Units": Ethnic-Specific Assets, Symbols of Identity, and "Passing"

Once an EHMG has emerged, what factors account for the persistence of ethnic trading boundaries? I shall argue that the role of the EHMGs as "cultural-bearing units" is one of the important factors contributing to the persistence of the EHMG.

Every trader who belongs to the same ethnic group benefits from belonging to the group because of the existence of shared ethics or cultural norms that function to reduce transaction costs of protecting contracts. Because of this fact, cultural norms embedded in an ethnic group may be considered to be local public goods/assets[44] or "social capital."[45] Since cultural norms of behavior are specific to particular ethnic groups, these norms may also be considered as *ethnic-specific assets*. The importance of ethnic-specific assets is that the identity of individuals matters under conditions of contract uncertainty because traders prefer to transact with insiders rather than outsiders. It is in this context that symbols of individual and group identity—such as names, clan names, dietary rules, language, and religion—play an important signaling function in transmitting nonprice information on the identity of potential partners.[46] This also explains the rationale of ethnic signaling, in which Chinese and Jewish merchants, for example, engage in "situational ethnicity," that is, the strategic use of an ethnic identity to fit particular situations.[47] Chinese traders tend to emphasize Chinese identity when interacting with Chinese creditors.[48] Similarly, Jews in Jerba, Tunisia,[49] and the Jews involved in the diamond trade in Antwerp[50] constantly use clothing, physiognomic indicators, and other symbols of identity to facilitate interaction with each other. The importance of group cultural norms in lowering transaction costs of members of the group also explains the kind of identity manipulation that sociologists and anthropologists call "passing"—masquerading as someone else to improve status. Observe the following phenomena:

Changing surname. An individual who wishes to pass into another clan can change his surname to gain access to trading networks dominated by other clans. Some of the Indians in Central and East Africa bearing the surname of Koli tried to masquerade as the Patels, who successfully dominated middleman roles.[51] Changing names, however, may not be an effective strategy if the trading community has numerous interlocking voluntary associations and dense informational networks that can easily uncover the real identity of those who try to pass via a change of surname. This form of passing or identity switching is rarely used by the overseas Chinese in Southeast Asia, for example, since the Chinese communities there are highly organized. This might also explain why some Kolis are able to pass as Patels because voluntary organizations are not so important in the Indian trading communities in East and Central Africa.

Religious conversion. In order to pass as a member of another religious group, an individual may resort to conversion; however, there are costs to this tactic. For a Malay to convert to a Chinese way of life, for instance, he not only has to invest in speaking the Chinese language, but he also has to eat pork, and both involve high psychological-adjustment costs for him.

Assimilation. Because ethnicity involves immutable physical characteristics, it is very costly for a person from a different ethnic group to switch ethnic identities. Within certain limits, a person may alter physical features by plastic surgery, hair straightening or frizzing, or wearing contact lenses to change eye color.[52] In the long run, the strategy of assimilation through intermarriage allows the children of mixed marriages a greater chance to attain better status through switching ethnic identities. "Switching an identity is sometimes a two-generation process."[53] Because the costs of ethnic identity switching are so prohibitive, both in the short and long run, ethnicity imposes an effective barrier for those attempting to pass as insiders.

A major reason accounting for the persistence of ethnic trading boundaries, then, is the role of the EHMGs as "cultural-bearing units": not only do insiders use symbols of identity to facilitate economic interaction among themselves, but they also establish cultural and racial barriers to exclude outsiders from participation in the "morality community" of homogeneous middleman networks. These barriers to entry create differential costs of passing for outsiders, with ethnicity the most effective barrier. The EHMGs as "cultural-transmission units" further contribute to the persistence of ethnic trading boundaries.

EHMGs as "Cultural-Transmission Units": Private Provision of Public Goods and Family Learning

Another important consequence of the existence of group-specific norms, viewed as ethnic-specific capital assets, is that the capital-asset feature of cultural norms necessitates its maintenance and its transmission to future generations. Since group-specific norms are local public goods, there is the familiar free-rider problem associated with the private voluntary provision of public goods. Unless there are selective rewards, no individual will have the incentive to voluntarily contribute to the provision of public goods.[54] Chinese and Jewish merchant communities have, however, overcome the traditional free-rider problem by providing such incentives; for example, wealthy Chinese merchants frequently donate large sums of money to establish schools, scholarships, hospitals, or graveyards for members of their own community.[55] This is not pure altruism, but it does contain elements of mutual aid and reciprocity as well as self-interest. Successful merchants often are themselves the beneficiaries of mutual aid that enabled them to be successful in the first place. The large donations may represent a return gift for some of the benefits received from members of the same community. The voluntary charitable contributions may also represent pure self-interest in that the contributions further enhance personal reputations and prestige within the community. It is through the learning of cultural values at school and at home that group values are preserved and transmitted to the members of the next generation. Ethnic groups are efficient, low-cost "cultural-transmission units."

In further developing a theory of the EHMG with respect to transmission of cultural values through the family, I draw on the insightful work of Robert Boyd and Peter Richerson.[56] These authors argue that conventional sociobiological theory cannot explain the great diversity of human behavior among ethnic groups—even though genetic differences between such groups are relatively trivial—or the fact that much of human social behavior is culturally acquired. What is needed, they argue, is an extension of conventional sociobiological theory to include cultural transmission of behavior. Their model, which includes both genetic and cultural transmission of behavior, is called a "dual inheritance theory" of genes and culture. In this theory, the concept of culture is crucial and is defined

> quite broadly as the transmission of the determinants of behavior from individual to individual, and thus from generation to generation, by social learning, imitation or some other similar process. From our point of view, the essence of culture is that it constitutes a second, supplementary system of inheritance.[57]

The relative success in cultural transmission—defined as the inheritance of determinants of behavior—depends on parents teaching their children and relatives and individuals learning from or imitating the behavior of others, such as teachers, priests, or "big men." It is social learning that causes the communication of cultural traits directly from individual to individual, so that culture is a "population-level phenomenon."[58] Cultural inheritance is important in the evolution of human behavior because of the costs of learning. If individuals have to discover the optimal local adaptive behavior by trial-and-error methods, and such methods involve significant costs, selection will provide short-cuts to learning. Cultural inheritance is adaptive precisely because it is such a shortcut. Individuals, embedded in a cultural population, can learn to adapt to local conditions with a much smaller investment in learning compared to what is required in an acultural population.[59] Social learning can occur as a result of "direct bias," that is, trial-and-error learning, which can be costly. Where "decision-making costs are likely to be especially high for many common choices that have low 'trialability'—whom to marry, what occupation to choose, what major capital investments to make, whether to convert to another religion, and so forth,"[60] adoption of the following two rules-of-thumb methods for acquiring culture can be efficient: "frequency-dependent bias," copying or imitating the everyday behavior of others ("In Rome, do as the Romans do"); and "indirect bias," imitating those who appear to be notably successful in a particular habitat. These methods for acquiring culture can substitute for costly trial-and-error learning. Crucial to Boyd and Richerson's theory is the idea that the individual is responsive to learning and to imitation, an idea not unlike Hayek's emphasis of the crucial role of tradition's being transmitted to the individual via family and community.

The idea that an individual is responsive to learning and to imitation can be captured in Herbert Simon's concept of "docility." Discussing markets and organization, Simon defines the trait as follows:

> To be docile is to be tractable, manageable, and above all teachable. . . . Docile people are disposed to accept instruction and instructions from the social environment they depend on. They tend to adapt their behavior to norms and pressures of the society. . . . From an evolutionary standpoint, having a considerable measure of docility is not altruism, but enlightened selfishness.[61]

Boyd and Richerson's theory can be used to develop a concept of the EHMG as a cultural-transmission unit, via family learning, that helps the EHMG to persist over time. The present members of the EHMG share the same cultural values, including rules of the game, but they will all eventually die and be replaced by new members. What is the process by which new members acquire the culture of the older generation of middlemen? Since many of the family firms of the deceased middlemen will be passed on to sons, social learning of the culture of the middleman group takes place through docility and "frequency-dependent bias"—sons copying the behavior of their fathers—without the need for costly trial-and-error learning. The next generation can also copy those middleman-entrepreneurs who are especially successful and have emerged to assume roles as leaders and philanthropists in their own ethnic community. Since the enculturation process of social learning also goes on in the wider ethnic community of which the EHMG is a subgroup, new members of the ethnic group will also inherit the cultural values of the group. The rules of the game and other cultural values governing members of the present generation of middlemen, then, will be transmitted via social learning from one generation to the next. Since these cultural rules of the game are local public goods, they are maintained and preserved over time at low cost. Because of this, ethnocentrism of members of the EHMG is reinforced; those who are already in the middleman group will continue to prefer to choose new trading partners from the younger generation of the same ethnic group. The cultural boundaries of middleman trading networks thus persist over time and cannot be eroded by "Austrian competition." The phenomenon of the EHMG is a manifestation of successful "group competition" of one ethnic group against other ethnic groups for middleman-entrepreneur roles.

Group Competition, Group Loyalty, and Identification

The EHMG, as pointed out earlier, is an efficient institutional arrangement for the protection of contracts in LDCs. The concept of efficiency, as Jack Hirshleifer has pointed out, should be defined relative to the boundaries of the group:

> On all levels of life organisms have found it profitable to come together in patterns of cooperative association. But such cooperation is always secondary and contingent, in at least two respects: (1) in-group cooperation is only a means for more effectively and ruthlessly competing against outsiders, and (2) even within the group there will not be perfect parallelism of interests, hence cooperation must generally be supported by sanctions. . . .
> Efficiency, in this interpretation, is meaningful only as a measure of group strength or advantage relative to competing groups in the struggle for life and resources. . . . A totally universalistic measure of efficiency is pointless; we must draw the line somewhere, at the boundary of "us" and "them."[62]

Recently, Herbert Simon has also made a similar argument drawn from modern evolutionary theory. He argues that if a group (a family, a company, a city, a nation, or the local baseball team) that is in competition with other groups has a culture that contributes greatly to the fitness of the group, it could survive at the expense of other groups if individual members are docile and accept the contents of their culture. Simon emphasizes the importance of organizational/group identification and loyalty, ignored in the New Institutional Economics, which overcomes opportunistic behavior.[63]

Viewed from an evolutionary perspective, Hirshleifer's concept of group competition, ignored in conventional economics literature, is crucial to our explanation of the success and persistence of EHMGs. The very success of the foreign, ethnically homogeneous trading groups in LDCs in appropriating middleman roles for themselves attests to the usefulness of the concept of group competition. In the ruthless, competitive interethnic struggle for profit opportunities, in-group members with efficient social structures for the enforcement of cultural norms of behavior have a competitive advantage over other groups in appropriating and maintaining middleman-entrepreneur roles for themselves.

Conclusion

Many EHMGs in LDCs—including the Chinese in Southeast Asia, the Indians in East and Central Africa, the Lebanese in West Africa—have persisted for long periods of time. What accounts for their emergence and persistence? Central to my theory of their emergence is the notion that in LDCs where the legal infrastructure is not well developed for the enforcement of contracts, middlemen must take on the additional "gap-filling" entrepreneurial function of coping with the problem of contract uncertainty. Ethnic groups with efficient social structures for the enforcement of cultural norms of behavior that facilitate mutual aid and cooperation among members will have a differential *group* advantage over other ethnic groups to create personalistic exchange networks based on mutual trust, and hence appropriate middleman-entrepreneur roles for themselves. The existence of an ethnic-specific asset, in the form of cultural norms of mutual aid among members of an EHMG, economizes on the transaction costs of protecting contracts. EHMGs/ethnic trading networks are thus an *efficient* form of economic organization in LDCs, as an alternative to formal contract law and the vertically integrated firm.

To maintain middleman-entrepreneur roles, it is essential for these EHMGs to function as "cultural-bearing units." Members use symbols of group identity to facilitate interaction among members of the group, and to make it costly for outsiders to enter these ethnic trading networks. In addition, EHMGs function as "cultural-transmission units" because wealthy members of the EHMG provide certain local public goods, including education, to fellow members; and because group cultural values are transmitted to future generations of the ethnic group via family teaching. Cultural differences important for EHMGs' success persist over time because the market system in LDCs is imbued with a process of group competition in which once an ethnic group has emerged in middleman roles, the in-group will erect cultural and racial barriers to exclude outsiders—and these barriers will last as long as the opportunity for profit-making is present.

The "Austrian theory" of competition and entrepreneurship, as developed by Israel Kirzner,[64] cannot explain the phenomenon of EHMGs. If subjective perception of profit opportunities is essential for the emergence of entrepreneurship, then one would expect entrepreneurs to be *randomly* distributed among the general population, which is clearly not the case with the EHMGs. Although it is undoubtedly true that the subjective ability to perceive price differentials is essential for Kirzner's entrepreneur to reap profits from arbitrage, it is unsatisfactory to leave the entire arbitrage theory of profit depending solely on the subjective capacity of different economic agents in the market to perceive and seize profit opportunities. In order for the arbitrageur-entrepreneur to appropriate profits, contracts of buying and reselling must be enforced. Kirzner's theory of competition and entrepreneurship implicitly assumes the presence of markets with well-developed legal infrastructure for the enforcement of contracts. Given these assumptions, Kirzner's entrepreneurs' profit expectations always materialize because breach of contract is ruled out in his theory.[65] Kirznerian entrepreneurs do not face the transaction costs of contract uncertainty, hence the need to particularize exchange relations and establish cultural and racial barriers to trade. Kirzner's theory is thus incomplete for an understanding of the emergence of EHMGs because it implicitly assumes zero transaction costs of contract enforcement for the appropriation of profits. Darity and Williams' notion of Marxist competition is also inadequate in explaining why certain ethnic groups emerge to dominate specific occupational roles, since they have not explained how Marxist competition led certain ethnic groups to dominate specific occupational roles in the first place.

My transaction cost-cultural approach to a theory of EHMGs, on the other hand, can explain why certain ethnic groups emerge to dominate middleman roles and why cultural differences needed for middleman-entrepreneur success are persistent.[66] Moreover, my theory, which views competition as group competition, can also be reconciled with the existence of market discrimination as a persistent source of differences in ethnic group achievement.

David Martin

5

The Economic Fruits of the Spirit

The appearance of some forty to fifty million Protestants on the southern bank of the Rio Grande del Norte was not bargained for in the prognostications of sociologists. According to the sociological world-view, Protestantism had done its work as one of the midwives of science, democracy, individualism, and economic initiative, but it had now been peacefully retired and was fit only to fade away into secular humanism. In any case, the specific combination of science, democracy, individualism, and economic initiative was a kind of incidental sideshow in the overall scheme of human and social development, associated with the United States and the peculiar conditions of its emergence. However apparently powerful and successful, the American model of man and of society was a unique case. As other societies felt the pull of social evolution, they would enter upon an organic, collectivist, and probably Marxist future. Certainly in Latin America, social development would ensure a passage from Catholicism to secular collectivism without any reversion or diversion to Protestantism, except maybe in a few back street chapels harboring the passive and inconsequential consumers of religious opiates.

The Source of Protestant Appeal

Insofar as assumptions of this kind have dominated the mind-set of sociologists, the undoubted appearance of Protestants in large numbers in many parts of Latin America, especially in Brazil, Chile, and

Guatemala, has to be viewed as a temporary excrescence brought about by the improper exercise of American power and influence. Yet it is not necessary to believe that American power and influence are invariably ranged on the side of the angels to find this explanation implausible. No doubt American power and prosperity are attractive to many impoverished Latin Americans, and no doubt many of them are exposed to the seductions of evangelistic media financed wholly or in part by Americans. But equally there is a massive counter-propaganda which defines Protestantism as an alien intrusion, and this counter-propaganda can rely on reserves of anti-gringo sentiment. The idea that the current expansion of Protestantism is largely the result of external stimulation simply cannot be sustained. Rather, the dynamics of Latin American culture have generated the Protestant expansion. Although many of the seeds may have been dropped from external sources, the growth is indigenous. Nothing increases a hundredfold without fertile soil.

Indeed, one of the conditions of success and expansion is that Protestantism should "go native" and become incarnate in the forms of Latin American culture. Conversion most frequently occurs by families and villages and by neighborhood networks, rather than by single individuals, and that indicates how Protestantism works in the Latin American mode. When a Protestant church sets up a network of patronage, seeking patrons and dispensing favors, it has adapted itself in some degree to its environment. The authoritative style of the pastorate illustrates the same process. A faith seeking to convert and to change must itself undergo change and conversion.

If, however, we reject the idea that the expansion of Protestantism is an intruding and artificial emanation of American hegemony, and if we recognize that being a Protestant is nowadays just an alternative way of being a Latin American, it is still appropriate once again to invoke the classic problematic of Protestantism and apply that to the new Latin American context. Does Protestantism nurture a novel sense of selfhood and personal responsibility issuing in improved conditions of life? Does it foster educational ambition, literacy, and economic initiative? Does it, together no doubt with other factors, help bring about a culture of sobriety and disciplined endeavor, of striving and saving, likely to ease the advent of capitalism? Is it, in short, the sort of reform of manners which provided the ambience of Methodism in eighteenth-century England and ran *pari passu* with the Industrial

Revolution? (After all, the Pentecostalism which provides the main thrust of contemporary Protestant expansion in Latin America is a clear lineal descendant through recent North American forbears of eighteenth-century Methodism.)

The Protestant Ethic

To redeploy this problematic is not straightforwardly to activate once again the Weberian debate concerning a collusion between the original spirit of Protestantism and the genesis of capitalism. Pentecostals in contemporary Latin America are no more in a position to captain large enterprises than were the colliers and fisher folk, artisans and journeymen converted by Wesley and his followers. Indeed, the personal and economic resources of Latin American Pentecostals are arguably even more exiguous than those of eighteenth-century English Methodists. The question currently posed, then, is whether or not the reform of manners, the shifts of psychic disposition, and the modes of religious solidarity now emerging in Latin America simultaneously ease the lot of those involved and prepare the path of capitalist organization.

It may be that the adoption of personal discipline and temperance, together with a sense of individual worth, of new horizons and possibilities, can help even in the dire conditions of the Latin American poor. Perhaps mutual assistance among the brethren, the acquisition of skills in organization and speaking, the extension of credit to those known to be under the disciplines of a common faith can in combination make some marginal improvement on life chances or at least provide some protection against economic vicissitude. After all, it makes intuitive sense to suppose that disciplined people roped together and animated by a common purpose stand a better chance of survival and advancement than those fatalistically exposed to chaos and disorganization. What, then, is the evidence?

The evidence is contradictory, in part suggesting that Protestants do make some discernible headway relative to their Catholic compeers, in part suggesting that there is little difference between the two groups. Before surveying some of this evidence there is, however, a preliminary point to be made. This concerns the distinction between the first onset of Protestantism in Latin America, which was minor and largely alien in organization, and the current onset, which is massive and largely indigenous. The first onset was associated with "historic" Protestants, in particular Baptists and Presbyterians. There is little doubt that it brought into being a number of Protestant subcultures equipped with educational, welfare, and even medical facilities, and that these sub-cultures secured social advancement and the fruits of the economic spirit. The current onset is largely associated with Pentecostals, though there are also many faith missions, as well as Adventists, Mormons, and Jehovah's Witnesses. The conflict of evidence concerns the current onset and is particularly ambiguous with regard to the Pentecostals.[1]

Pentecostals

The evidence presented by Cecilia Mariz and Cornelia Butler Flora exemplifies the kind of negative conclusions which some researchers have come to with regard to Pentecostals. Cornelia Butler Flora conducted research among Pentecostals in Colombia at an early stage in the overall process of conversion, and argued that there was no perceptible connection between conversion and improved personal circumstances. According to her, Pentecostals had no sense of enhanced personal capacities. At the same time, she found them capable of altering their pattern of consumption and reintegrating the family. And they were to be found in particular among the self-employed and those employed by small enterprises.

Cecilia Mariz undertook small-scale research in Brazil, comparing the life histories of people in Pentecostal groups, Spiritist groups, and Catholic-based communities. She concluded that all three groups enhanced the capacity of their members for survival, but in different ways. The base communities had a political and charitable outreach directed toward the whole community, and in that they followed a traditional breadth of Catholic concern. They constituted an option *for* the poor. The Pentecostal groups, by contrast, constituted an option *of* the poor. Their ambit of concern was restricted to the brethren. Many had been sick or alcoholic. Cecilia Mariz did not find any noticeable economic improvement among them except among those who became pastors, but she did note the effects brought about by enhanced health, by abstinence, and by spiritual calm, on the family budget. She concluded that Pentecostals probably enlarge their capacity to *cope* with poverty. Both the base community and Pentecostal group encourage verbal self-expression, the one in the form of debate and the other in the form of preaching and proselytizing.

What these two researchers show is consonant with a considerable body of evidence. Pentecostals are found relatively more often in occupations which already possess some element of personal self-determination, however lowly and intermittent the actual employment may be. They acquire certain skills through their experience in the group, they alter their patterns of consumption, they build up family solidarity, they help each other, and they cope better with the vicissitudes of life. (Parenthetically it is important to underline the way in which they build up family solidarity. They simultaneously pull out of the wider net of obligations and firm up the innermost familial ties, thus conforming to the picture we have of the proto-industrial family as indicated by Brigitte Berger in her chapter in this volume.)

The characteristics just mentioned, even if not exclusive to Pentecostals, would at least seem to be helpful in the struggle for survival, even though neither Cecilia Mariz nor Cornelia Butler Flora discerns any capacity for economic improvement greater than that experienced by non-Protestant compeers.

The Social Cyclotron

But, other elements must be taken into account. One is that many people enter Pentecostal groups and leave them for others (or simply leave them altogether) in a highly volatile manner. The whole social cyclotron is being speeded up, and the Pentecostal atoms are volatile parts of an increasingly volatile universe. However, this does not mean that movement between Pentecostal groups, or even movement in and eventually out, fails to leave a mark. Moreover, the movement in and the movement out may occur over a generation. If a mother, say, in one generation acquires certain ways of acting, these may easily become part of a continuing family tradition. Let us suppose that she alters patterns of family consumption and entertains ambitions for the literacy of her children. It is reasonable to suppose that those patterns and ambitions bear their economic fruit one or two generations later. The fruits of the economic spirit ripen over time, those in whom they are eventually discernible are not necessarily in the same religious body as their forbears.

Clearly, it is very difficult to draw firm conclusions about the relative advantages of adopting Protestantism and joining a Protestant group just by making comparisons between members of such a group and nonmembers. This comparison is particularly problematic when the group concerned makes a specific appeal to those who are distressed, sick, or in some way partially incapacitated. The group may offer advantages to some of its members, while for others it may merely restore them to something approaching normality.

The point about the advancement achieved by pastors and leaders is worth elaboration. Presumably, those Pentecostals who become leaders have superior abilities in the milieu from which they came. Although they have lacked the conventional means of educational and economic improvement, they have nevertheless advanced to the leadership of an autonomous network of believers. In running a religious organization, they have become a kind of moral entrepreneur. In this role they acquire modest economic resources, as well as connections, contacts, and even international vistas denied to others. They are therefore an emergent stratum of some significance, and moreover one which offers a model to fellow believers for emulation.

The Religious Marketplace

People in this fraternity of moral and religious entrepreneurs are in competition one with another and have converted the whole religious field into a competitive arena. The effects of religious innovation are by no means confined to the innovators themselves but also affect the established religions through the impact of competition. The style of the established priest has to alter to cope with the competition of the preacher. Religious bodies bid for popularity and adjust themselves to the market. Peter Berger has elaborated on the significance of different "lines" in the religious market, more particularly with respect to ecumenism, but in the present context it is important to recognize that religious pluralism can run supportively in relation to both political and economic pluralism.

If the pastors are the leading edge of an entrepreneurial religious culture offering a style to other believers for emulation, so too the more successful churches offer themselves and their style for emulation. Given that salvation is offered to all without account taken of social standing, there follows a process of social mixing within churches. The poorer feel pleased to mix with the somewhat better off. They may even travel some distance to church to share in a particular social atmosphere. In this manner, they by degrees acquire certain habits and assumptions, as well as connections, which stand them in good stead, especially when it comes to employment. The activities of a large, lively, and well-run church will attract people whose meager resources are supplemented by their participation and by all kinds of social learning. Indeed, some of the main churches in the large cities like Bogotá and Mexico City are hives of activity in which a wide variety of skills, including business administration on occasion, may be acquired.

It is worth inserting here a reference to the modest evidence available concerning Mormons and Adventists. Although some 70 percent of contemporary Protestant expansion concerns Pentecostals there is nevertheless a notable advance of Mormonism, and Adventist missions have been active and often successful for generations. So far as Adventists are concerned, they frequently create a complete subculture equipped with medical and educational facilities and acquire a personal discipline, especially in matters of hygiene, which backs up those facilities. They are thus well placed to take up such opportunities as may occur. So far as the Mormons are concerned they integrate believers into an international network which is orientated toward the United States. More than any other group Mormons inculcate the norms of middle-class America and are said to be easily recognizable by their businesslike American clothes and address. Pilgrimages by bus to Utah encourage converts to admire and seek the advantages of an American life style. Moreover, those who accept the faith also adopt an abstemious regimen of health and submit to a code of cleanliness and home improvement. Even if this orientation to America is not sustained to the extent that it once was, nevertheless becoming a Mormon clearly involves participation in a distinctive environment and a severing of previous ties. David Clawson's interesting study of Mormons in a Nealtican community in Central Mexico provides some localized evidence of their readiness for leadership, their desire to read, and their eagerness for economic innovation and cooperation.[2] Of course, Mormonism is only marginally a form of mainstream Protestantism, but its ethos emerged out of an American Protestant context, which it continues to reflect.

Returning to mainstream Protestant activity in Latin America, we need to understand the variety of contexts from which converts are drawn and the different styles of ministry and social organization to which they may be introduced. Jean-Pierre Bastian, writing of Mexico, emphasizes in particular the difference between the activities of numerous small Protestant groups found in rural areas and the bureaucratically organized networks operating in the larger cities.[3]

Comparisons of Protestants with Catholics

The variety of context and milieu from which converts are drawn makes any broad comparisons of the economic situation of Protestants with Catholics problematic. Some studies, for example, show that a group displaced by the advent of a money economy and reduced from poverty to total destitution may be attracted to Protestantism as a hope of last resort. When that occurs, the task of the sociologist is to locate which element or elements in their new faith may help them best to survive dire circumstances.

It may well be, as some studies indicate, that the converts simply begin to look beyond their local situation, make contacts in the towns or other areas of possible employment, and proceed to pass along a helpful network of fellow believers. Other studies may show that in a particular area most people are quite closely bound together into hierarchies and into horizontal bonds and that Catholicism is deeply implicated in these hierarchies and bonds. In such a situation those who become Protestant are likely to be people with some modest independence. In a rural area a smallish group of semi-independent agricultural workers may wish to establish a space in which to exercise social autonomy: Protestantism offers them a comprehensive exit from the status quo. Once within a Protestant group, they are freed from all the social links, costs, and obligations of the fiesta and godparenthood. In a township those working as porters or minor salespeople or stonemasons or nightwatchmen may find attraction in the warmth and solidarity of an evangelistic meeting. Moreover, when the big revivalistic campaigns or local rallies come round, they gain some sense of collective power, confidence, and visibility, as people who at last are literally starting to count. They are, in short, engaging in a form of mobilization, sending out the message that they are *there*, even though that message is peaceable and unthreatening. Such people have that edge of independence and that sense of personal space which makes Protestantism an attractive option, and moreover an option which will, however marginally, enlarge that personal space yet further.

El Petén, Guatemala

Research in El Petén, Guatemala, conducted by the anthropologists Norman Schwartz and Rubem Reina, gives some idea of the complex relation of Protestantism to local social structure.[4] The study begins by drawing on a point made over two decades ago by Emilio Willems that Protestants are found not only among migrants to the new rural frontiers or among those otherwise isolated in the city but also among people who own middle-sized plots of land.[5] These constitute a kind of frugal, land-working peasantry who farm for subsistence and are fairly independent of markets. What is important in such instances is a relative freedom from ecclesiastical and social authority combined with adequate means for sustaining an independent existence. Schwartz and Reina approached three communities in El Petén, northern Guatemala, equipped with an interest in such semi-independent middle groups. Does their susceptibility to conversion vary in some way in relation to their independence, their tendency to migrate, and their openness to change in general?

Schwartz and Reina comment on the weakness of the Roman Catholic Church in El Petén up to 1954. People still distinguish sharply between the religion of the clergy and the social identity of being Catholic. The three communities they studied are in an isolated frontier area which was spared any traumatic conquest and was never subject to patron-client relationships or to the hacienda system. Although the area theoretically ought to be ripe for conversion, in fact this potential is mediated and canalized by the precise nature of the different social systems. In the town of Flores, which is the main local center, there is a system of marked social stratification which prevents some potential converts from opting for innovation. Those who do become converted are middle-class, but less secure and less able to compete with the elite than are the "new" Catholics nurtured by the priests. The main area of conflict is between the old and the new Catholics, who respectively comprise the elite and the counterelite. In the community of San Andrés, by contrast, the system of stratification is less marked and people are more willing to work out their frustrations. "There is consequently more religious activity in San Andrés than in Flores and proportionately more people opt for innovation. There is, moreover, a base in the community culture for innovative agents."[6] This brief sketch shows how difficult it is to make statistical comparisons between Protestants and Catholics. Who is available for economic and/or religious innovation depends on the shape of the social structure.

Agencies of Change

The various agencies of change in such situations may be very complicated and feed one into the other. One has to imagine that with the movement of people and the extension of communication in every sense, the marginally better-off and the more dynamic, active, and intelligent start to adopt new styles and modes of behavior and have some increased sense of themselves as agents. It is at this juncture that they become conscious of the Protestant option and above all of what it can offer in terms of social relationships which allow them self-expression, self-control, and autonomous management. The question as to whether the Roman Catholic Church is aligned politically with right or left is at this point not so important as its long-term implication in all that has been. It covers the whole society and is the mainstay of its organic unities and hierarchies. It follows that a new religious group offers the one thing that dramatically signals change, which is a voluntary, active act of adhesion to a self-governing association outside the "system." It provides a free space in which people of several social sorts who are mostly above the lowest reach of misery and mostly well below the professional middle classes can be themselves and run their own show.

Basically, Protestantism in Latin America is a movement of withdrawal from all that was on the part of people who are on the move or who have been forced to move. That withdrawal includes the rejection of personal violence and of social violence. Those who become Protestants reject the machismo of the male personality and equally reject the path of political rebellion. Bitter experience has taught them that they have little to hope for from political action or from the political violence of the left or right. Rather they engage in a personal and peaceable reform which may yield them some tangible "betterment" in all the senses of the word betterment. The betterment is in the first place moral but it is also, in the second place medical and economic. One way or another they wish to get up off the dirt floor. They do not become converted *in order* to prosper but if their endeavors are prospered they are grateful for the kindly disposition of Providence.

For the moment, of course, the access of prosperity is for the most part very marginal, and may even be no more than some protection against total destitution. But with new generations and the persistence of a culture of striving in which cleanliness is next to godliness, they are well placed to take up whatever opportunities may present themselves and to assist one another in locating where these opportunities are most easily available.

Protestantism in Latin America is a fissile, highly adaptable phenomenon which is part of the breakup of organic wholes and of the antecedent religiopolitical system. It represents a mutation from religious monopoly to religious competition, from a territorial, automatic, and passive faith to the voluntary and mobile congregation. To that extent, it is at least congruent with competition and choice in the economic sphere. Add to that a discipline of person, of family, and of work, and there exists a psychology apt for capitalistic industry. It may be generations before this particular option of the poor produces captains of industry or corporate managers. Nonconformity even in industrial England took its time in producing the makers of chocolate, of corn flakes, soap, and biscuits, of flour and jam. In proper conformity with their origins, the British Nonconformists produced homely, useful objects. Something similar could be in train in the Latin America of today.

The Relationship of Religion to Development

The lesson to be drawn from studies of the relationship of religion to social and economic development is that the relationship is at one and the same time real and indirect. There is no way of telling whether it is those who are apt for change who opt for the new model of faith or whether those who opt for the new faith become as a result apt for change. What is required is an imaginative response to the way in which over a minimum of two generations, and possibly over several, a religion which encourages sobriety and personal discipline, and which is lay and participatory in style, which abolishes the hierarchy of mediations between man and God, and which is created by and helps create a competitive milieu, may also create useful and potent congruences with an entrepreneurial culture.

One final point concerns the wider ambit of the phenomenon just discussed. The cultural shifts coming about so dramatically in Latin

America and focused in Pentecostalism are observable much more widely. In sub-Saharan and southern Africa they are located in separatist and syncretic churches as well as in evangelical and Pentecostal Protestantism. In the Pacific Rim, India, and the Far East they are located in neo-Buddhist, neo-Islamic, and neo-Hindu movements, as well as in evangelical and Pentecostal Protestantism. There is, in short, a worldwide mobilization of familial and personal resources which is organized within and which corresponds to the exigencies of contemporary economic and social development.

Gillian Godsell

6

Entrepreneurs Embattled: Barriers to Entrepreneurship in South Africa

One of the Western stereotypes of the entrepreneur is that of the "Lone Ranger," succeeding in a hostile environment. S. G. Redding poses an alternative model—East Asian capitalism, which is successful but different,[1] with entire families—rather than individuals—entering the economic fray. This chapter will focus on the differing and complementary entrepreneurial roles of individuals and groups in South Africa. What light can African capitalism throw on these roles? Certainly the idea that capitalism can be non-Western and non-individualistic is compatible with African political rhetoric and tribal history. Indeed, Redding's exposition of Chinese capitalism received an enthusiastic response at a workshop in Johannesburg where many complaints were expressed about the inappropriateness of applying Western models to African economic practice.[2] Is this congruence between the African and Asian models reflected in economic reality?

More precisely, is there a unique African pattern of communal economic functioning, different from both Eastern and Western patterns? This chapter examines community support for the entrepreneur in three South African groups exhibiting more communalistic than individualistic inclinations, at face value at least: Indians, Afrikaners, and South African urban blacks. In addition to their communal orientation, these groups are economically significant in South Africa and provide interesting comparisons with one another. The Indians and blacks may be compared for their responses to the external prejudice and discriminatory legislation that have hampered their business enterprises; the Afrikaners and blacks may be compared for their response to an internal religious and social negation of business as a career. Although English-speaking whites were also interviewed in the study on which this chapter is based, findings from this group will not be discussed here.[3]

In addition to explaining a small part of the general entrepreneurial puzzle, the study can help South Africa itself. Most obviously, with a black unemployment rate of at least 20 percent,[4] and a per capita GNP of U.S. $2,290 per year,[5] entrepreneurs are desperately needed for the expansion of the economy. Even more important in societies in transition is the role Brigitte Berger ascribed to small-scale entrepreneurship: that of community- and institution-building.[6] We need to understand the way entrepreneurs function, not only as potential employers or even independent subsisters, but also as community-shapers and ultimately nation-builders.

The research for this study was carried out in the industrial and commercial heartland of South Africa, an area known as the PWV (Pretoria-Witwatersrand-Vereeniging) triangle, which centers on Johannesburg. Both group discussions and individual interviews were used to obtain data from forty Indians, thirty-seven blacks, and twenty Afrikaners who were either currently running a small business or had run a small business that subsequently expanded.

Indian Business: The Organic Network

The Indian business networks examined in this study are rich and varied. They cross generations and even oceans, and incorporate not only the obvious kin, but also more diffuse relationships such as "the small factory owner who was my dad's closest friend for forty years and whose son is to marry my niece."[7] The term "organic network" describes this type of relationship. An organic network is not consciously developed for a specific purpose, but is one of many reciprocal networks developing within a community and covering different functions. It is an ineradicable, and usually unconscious, part of an individual's life.

This type of network appears to be the primary tool of Indian business survival: family networks, religious networks, friendship networks, all play a role in the businesses studied. Every Indian interviewed had received business help from another Indian, whether this help amounted to thousands of rands in cash or credit, or simply the loan of a truck for transporting fresh produce from the market. Networks appeared to play a role in all aspects of the business, from the provision of initial credit and stock to help behind the counter to import/export contacts. This pattern is very similar to that of the Chinese families described by Redding who were the source of business socialization and provided both capital and apprenticeship opportunities.[8] The differences between Indians and the other groups are shown in Figure 6.1. Indians received start-up assistance in the form of cash, credit, supplies, and even shop fittings, from all sections of their community. Not only was the spread of their start-up resources wider, but more Indians also received help in each potential donor category. Some categories, such as ethnic group assistance, were significant only for the Indians: other Indians helped Indians, but other blacks did not help blacks and other Afrikaners did not help Afrikaners. Family provided no start-up assistance for Afrikaners and friends provided none for blacks. In common with other ethnic enclaves, Indian businesses do rely on consumers from outside the community,[9] supplemented by a strong ethnic loyalty, particularly relating to professional services.

Several factors have served to strengthen the Indian networks. The first Indian businessmen came to South Africa as "passenger Indians," that is, people who had paid for their own passage, as distinct from the indentured laborers who were brought there to work in the sugar plantations. The passenger Indians were mainly Moslems, and Moslems have since dominated Indian trading and commercial life. Only 20 percent of the Indians in South Africa are Moslem, but about 70 percent of Indian enterprises are run by Moslems.[10] The first ties that bound the passenger Indians were geographic; men from the same village traveled on the same ship and often shared accommodations to save costs. These early ties still bind the children and grandchildren with obligations and rewards—favors owed and trust offered.

In the early days, Indians were employed by other Indians, whether they were bookkeepers or sweepers. This was partly because of ethnic and religious loyalty, partly because of language difficulties, and partly because of prejudice on the part of other potential employers. Religion is an important component of ethnic loyalty, but not the whole of it. Preference will be given, or help offered, first to a family member, second to a coreligionist, third to another Indian. In some cases, such

Figure 6.1

Individual Sources of Start-Up Assistance for South African Entrepreneurs

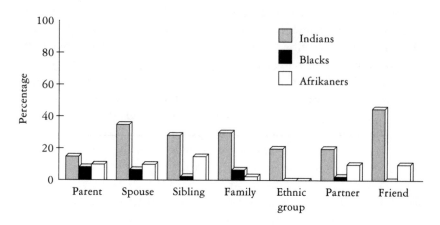

"Assistance" means financial and other help. The number of cases are: Indians = 40, Afrikaners = 20, Blacks = 37.
SOURCE: *Author*

as the preparation and sale of Halaal foods, employment only of coreligionists is essential.

Both religion and family play a role in the development of business skills and values. Family provides approval, as well as specific business teaching and socialization: "Mother was the keypin . . . she gave us our courage, pushed us, promoted us, showed us how to behave as business people and be enterprising."[11] Religion provides a general approval of business. There is no question of business in itself being an immoral occupation, or money being tainted: "God provided it that one should see to the increment of one's fortunes for the sake of the children. . . . Ultimately our belief is that if you have good intentions, if you're honest and straightforward and you do hard work, you must see success."[12] The sense of the speaker's being in control of his own destiny, the clear connection between individual action and results, is striking, and illustrates an important dimension of the Indian sense of communalism or community. This is not a community that expects or encourages individual passivity. It does not take care of the individual simply because he is a human being, or an Indian, or a Moslem; it assists him to take care of himself. It is not a hammocklike support into which the individual can gratefully collapse; rather, it is like a set of starting blocks from which the individual must begin the race.

In addition to generalized approval, religious beliefs incorporate specific business practices. The Koran is often quoted as the source of business advice: "We buy cheap and sell cheap—a ruling which has its foundations in the Islamic way of thinking—that is why we are successful."[13] This may well be a particular interpretation favored by entrepreneurially minded Moslems, as Walter Connor seems to suggest that in Eastern Europe the Moslems are more of an economic drawback than a resource.[14] Patronizing the businesses of coreligionists is also encouraged. One businessman said simply, "It is my duty to make another Moslem rich." Another described it in a more complex fashion, explaining that since Moslems are obliged to pay a religious tax of 2.5 percent of their income every year, he would prefer that the profits from the money he spent went to another Moslem, and eventually, through the religious tax, to the poor.

The proactive nature of this community can best be illustrated by the important role played by friends in the Indian businesses (Figure 6.1). Friends provided more start-up support to new businesses than did any other section of the Indian community. A family network may arrive ready-made, but a friendship network does not: it must be developed and nurtured. In our study, offering business help seemed to be an important sign of friendship, and several respondents said they preferred to obtain help from friends rather than from family because if family help you, you never hear the last of it. The virtue of the Indian network is not only that it exists as a resource, but also that by working in networks the Indian businessmen learn to use and develop networks and then apply this knowledge, first outside the family circle and second outside the Indian community altogether. The benefits of reciprocity are well understood. Time and again Indians explained that to increase your market you must extend credit to retailers and to hawkers. A sharp distinction was made between credit extended to sellers, which could develop a business, and credit to consumers, a practice that was frowned upon.

The Indians in South Africa were able to draw on their religious family, and ethnic resources to overcome the obstacles placed in their way by legislative and social discrimination. The earliest legislation, limiting Indian immigration and land ownership, probably had its origins in white envy of Indian business success and fear of business competition.[15] The worst blow to Indian businesses came from the Group Areas Act of 1950, which demarcated specific areas for occupation by members of particular racial groups and forced Indian businesses from the prosperous white areas into enclosed Indian areas. Nevertheless, the Indian businessmen not only survived but prospered, using white nominees and front companies, and attracting white customers to the areas where Indians could legally operate. Religious and community approval provided the spiritual capital: networks were the means, and survival and even prosperity the result.

Black Entrepreneurs: Individual Success and Strategic Networks

In every aspect of business, black businessmen and -women interviewed came across as sturdy individualists who relied mainly on themselves for help. Although the black township community is rich in helping networks—revolving credit associations, burial societies, women's church organizations—these did not appear oriented toward helping small businesses or generating capital for starting such businesses. Some family businesses were encountered, but these were not the rule, and they were also fairly carefully confined to immediate family.

In organic networks, linkages flow under, over, and through discrete sociological categories—from nuclear family to friends of neighbors and back to extended family. In an organic network it is logical to employ somebody because he is your ex-father-in-law's nephew. No such diffuse relationships were found in the black community. Whereas Figure 6.1 shows the interdependence of the Indian entrepreneur, Figure 6.2 shows starkly the independence of the black entrepreneur. Neither people (Figure 6.1) nor institutions (Figure 6.2) provide much assistance to the black entrepreneur. Savings and money generated from a previous business provided the major sources of start-up capital for more businesses in the black group than in any other group (Figure 6.2).

Where networks do operate in the black community, they are functional or strategic rather than organic. That is, they are single-element networks, consciously developed for a specific purpose. In this case they are usually consumption networks, and a black producer of goods or services calls on other blacks to choose his product in preference

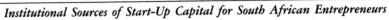

Figure 6.2

Institutional Sources of Start-Up Capital for South African Entrepreneurs

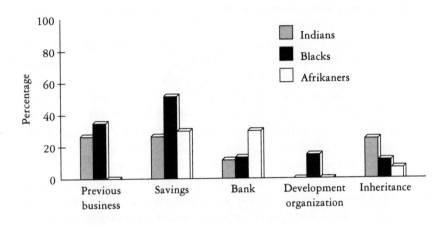

The number of cases are: Indians = 40, Afrikaners = 20, Blacks = 37.
SOURCE: *Author*

to a white-generated product, in the interests of black solidarity and black economic empowerment. The appeal is pitched at the political rather than the economic level. This usually occurs among more sophisticated users—in this study, a black computer consultant offering his services to the black professional community, and a black community organization producing school uniforms whose purchase was decided on by school principals rather than parents. The ordinary township consumer seems as likely to express suspicion as support of black-produced goods.[16]

Business in a black township does not enjoy high status within the community. There is no overt religious support or justification for it, as there is among the Indians. Indeed, some respondents expressed the view that as Christians, they should not be engaged in direct profit making. This view appears to have much in common with that ascribed by Walter Connor to the Russians, when he refers to the moral ambiguity of cooperatives in the public mind and the supposed moral inferiority of entrepreneurial skills.[17] Historically, because of the limitations on trading in black townships, people who did manage to get licenses were regarded as being, if not corrupt in an economic sense, then certainly politically corrupt and in cahoots with the white administrative bureaucracy of the township. In addition, these early traders were often people of little education, and therefore their choice of business as a profession contrasted poorly with the high-status professions such as teaching. Later, when the allocation of business sites was carried out by black town councilors, often themselves under attack for alleged collaboration with whites and supposed malad-ministration, the unsavory associations of business were strengthened.

Perhaps this lack of community status for business is one of the reasons black community networks and resources have not been made available for the development of small business. Another could be the lack of business socialization. Among the Indians, employing another Indian in your business is, apart from any other consideration, a safe bet from a business point of view. The interviews made clear the extent to which Indian children were involved in business from an early age. Not all South African Indians are involved in business, of course, but those from the business families may be sure that other family members have grown up with both a respect for and a competence in business, making them desirable business partners. They may be brought in as much for the good of the business as for the good of the family. In the black township, family members are brought into the business for the good of the family. In some instances this has worked, but there are many complaints of family workers being lazy, negligent, and impossible to fire. Such complaints are not unique to the black group: both the Afrikaners and the Indians express reservations, in principle, about the desirability of employing family, and in particular about their children coming into the business.

In practice, it seems to be only the township businessmen who are the targets of community and family contempt and hostility. Particularly worrying is the hostility expressed by the young people—a criminal hostility expressed in the form of pilfering and looting, and a political hostility expressed by coercion and even arson. When the businessman in the township is defined as part of a group, it is always to his disad-vantage. If he is defined as a businessman first, and black second, he is then also defined as wealthy and the legitimate target of theft, along with white entrepreneurs.[18] He is required to provide donations for funerals and other political events. If he is defined as black, it is not to make him the beneficiary of black solidarity, but rather to make him part of the black struggle and to demand support for a consumer boycott that might cost him his livelihood.

One of the businessmen interviewed had run into this sort of trouble during the Soweto rent boycott. He had supported the boycott by not paying rent on his house, but had paid rent and electricity bills for his shop because his business depended on large refrigerators to keep his products fresh and he did not want his electricity cut off. He was labeled a collaborator, and his house, shop, and car were firebombed. This was not an isolated instance. Hostile acts by children were cited as a problem by several respondents, and one elderly woman, when asked to list the disadvantages of being in small business, said simply, "when the children burns your shop."

Soweto is a poor, crime-ridden, violent city, and the researcher placing emphasis on isolated instances of violence may be overly naive. Ordinary citizens may become targets of coercion during boycotts. No instances are recorded of persons in corporate employment being attacked simply because of their job, but shopkeepers appear to fall into the same "legitimate target" category as policemen and community councilors. It may simply be that shopkeepers charging high prices for small quantities in convenient locations are targets of the rage of their poor customers the world over. Because of the legislation barring traders of other race groups in Soweto, this rage is directed by blacks toward blacks, whereas in other situations the Indian or Korean or Jewish or other outgroup traders are the targets of rage and frustration.

Because they are in a statistical minority, the Indian traders and manufacturers can strengthen their ethnic ties by offering discounts to other Indians without affecting the bulk of their profits, which derive from outside consumers. Blacks, being in a statistical majority, cannot employ this tactic. They must rely on black solidarity, offering political rather than economic benefits to develop a consumer network. Theoretically, black manufacturers, wholesalers, and retailers could rival their white counterparts without ever breaking into the white market, but this is hampered by the general attitude against the township trader.

The prototypical township entrepreneur, therefore, is an individualist, working without community good will and sometimes even in spite of community ill will. This was the case among the earliest recorded black entrepreneurs in South Africa, the commercial farmers who had to move off tribal land onto the mission stations "to avoid traditional sanctions against the accumulation of wealth."[19] A typical individualist emerged in the current study, an elderly coal dealer. Although he has an extensive family with whom he keeps in touch, none of them is involved in his business. He does have one friend who is also a coal dealer, but this friend uses donkeys instead of a truck to transport coal and is therefore unable to advise or help in any way. The dealer announces, half proudly, half fearfully, "If I am in trouble no one can help me, I can do it myself."

Both Indians and blacks responded at length to questions regarding help they have offered to other businessmen. The nature of this help, and in particular the reasons for offering help, differ for the two groups. For the black group, the need to help is based on the value of *ubuntu,* or humaneness: the need to extend dignity to another human being simply because he is a human being.[20] Often, the provision of employment for others was regarded as the main justification for running a business.

Although the charity tax is a clear indication of a philanthropic approach among the Moslems, in conversation the help was clearly reciprocal: "We know in our minds that you are helping a person, but while you're helping him you are building yourself."[21]

The Afrikaners: Individualists and Political Networks

Extensive business networks could be anticipated among Afrikaners because of the predominance of strong group or communal terminology. In the 1930s, when an Afrikaner economic consciousness was being developed, the rhetoric of togetherness was in full flight: the first Afrikaner bank was called *Volkskas* (people's chest), the first building society was *Saambou* (build together). With hindsight, these names appear to be as much an exhortation to Afrikaners to cooperate as a reflection of a cooperative reality. The slogan of these times, *'n volk red homself* (a nation/people saves itself), has enjoyed some popularity today among proponents of black economic empowerment, and indeed, much of the Afrikaner rhetoric of the 1930s found an echo in the black economic empowerment rhetoric of the 1980s. The Afrikaners expressed hopes of developing Christian national capitalism (labeled by O'Meara *Volkskapitalisme*—people's capitalism[22]) as a more acceptable form of capitalism than the oppressive Western variety. Some blacks have explored the idea of the development of a humane capitalism, incorporating *ubuntu.*

Like the blacks, however, the Afrikaners show no sign of anything equivalent to the Indian organic networks. Although not subject to the huge disadvantages of discriminatory legislation, in the 1920s the Afrikaners were in an economic position that may in some respects be compared to the position of South African blacks today. The most recent Carnegie Commission study on poverty carried out in South Africa referred exclusively to the plight of blacks.[23] In the 1930s the first Carnegie Commission focused on the plight of poor whites, the majority of whom were Afrikaners. Like the blacks today, the Afrikaners then associated capitalism with the foreign oppressor, and consequently rejected it.

The most marked similarity between the black and Afrikaner groups lies in the distaste for business as an occupation, and their interpretation of Christianity as regarding money to be tainted. For the penniless young Moslem immigrant, self-employment was the only possible means of survival. For the equally impoverished young Afrikaner in the Transvaal in the 1920s [24] and the young black in the township today,[25] self-employment was and is simply not perceived as an available option.

A difference in the black and the Afrikaner situations is the massive campaign launched in the 1930s to rehabilitate capitalism in the eyes of the Afrikaner, with the holding of two Economic *Volkskongresse* (people's congresses), and the formation of the *Reddingsdaadbond* (league for the act of salvation). The attempt to persuade ordinary Afrikaners, as consumers, to support Afrikaner manufacturers and retailers was not successful.[26] What did succeed was the rehabilitation of capitalism among the elite so that engaging in commerce and trade could be regarded as a service to the Afrikaner nation. It was the massive Afrikaner insurance companies, supported by government patronage, that were the first vehicles of Afrikaner economic success, not the small-scale traders. Although the attitude of the elite was changed, this filtered down only slowly to the man in the street. The financial support networks created for a political and national end find no obvious counterparts at the small-business level. The church, which played such an important role in the political mobilization of the Afrikaner, was not mentioned by any of the respondents as providing either tangible resources or approval, although some attributed their business success to the blessing of God.

The Afrikaner small businessmen and -women are largely individualists, neither benefiting from the community help of the kind provided by the Indians nor having to overcome the community hostility presented to black entrepreneurs.

Conclusion

The fact that business is carried on within a cohesive social group need have no bearing on the way that business is conducted. The community may actively assist the business, as is the case with the South African Indians, particularly the Moslems. It may tolerate but not help, as is the case with the Afrikaners. And it may disapprove, or actively hinder, individual activities, as appears to be the case with the blacks.

What factors shape these different relationships between community and business? The first is the status of business in the community. If it does not enjoy high status, community resources will not be mobilized for its support. This is not an immutable condition; if, for example, religious legitimation is absent, a conscious effort may be made to provide political legitimation. It is harder to affect everyday buying habits and consumer patterns by this type of legitimation, as the failure of campaigns to persuade ordinary people to buy black or buy Afrikaner indicates.

The black entrepreneurs in this study have not waited even for such tenuous legitimation; they have gone ahead with their businesses in the face of active social and political hostility. Contrary to the expectations with which the study was undertaken, the black entrepreneurs have turned out to be the most tenacious individualists of all. The Indian community, faced with external barriers, was able to draw on internal community resources, which the individual could use to help him overcome business adversity. The Afrikaner needed to overcome community resistance to the idea of individual trade as a respectable and useful occupation. He was forced to rely on his own resources, but at least had no external barriers to overcome. The successful black entrepreneur has had to overcome barriers both internal and external to his community, and the only resources available to him have been personal ones.

The structure or type of community may also play a role in entrepreneurship. The Indian community does not lift the responsibility from the individual; rather it rests on the carrying out of individual responsibilities. This individual-oriented community meshes in a felicitous fashion with the carrying out of entrepreneurial responsibilities. The Afrikaner community, on the other hand, is much more leader-oriented, and the fit with successful individual business functioning is more awkward, at least until the businessman reaches the stage of community leader, when he is honored by the community. The community resources might not be there for the support of the small businessman, but the recognition for the achievements of successful businessmen, in the form of honorary doctorates and other public awards, is tangible.

Successful businessmen, by contrast, barely feature among the leaders of the black townships. Both the small-scale networks and the large-scale recognition are absent. Although the combination of township difficulties and a history of communalism have produced a variety of helping networks, dealing with all sorts of modern consumption needs from school fees to electrification, somehow there is a gap between what is offered in a compassionate or practically helpful spirit and what is needed to launch a successful entrepreneurial career. In this case, the community structure does not mesh with the requirements of the successful individual in business.

This study does not support the existence of a different-but-successful model of African capitalism, certainly not at the small business level. The Indian family businesses seem to provide an interesting model of the meshing of individual entrepreneurial responsibility with the provision of community support and resources. The exclusiveness of this interaction carries the penalty of envy and hostility from other groups, and the threat of ultimate political exclusion as has happened elsewhere in Africa.

A form of exclusion may also be the price paid by the successful individualistic entrepreneur in the township. Until now, group solidarity has been a major political weapon in South Africa. In the economic field, as elsewhere in public life in South Africa, it remains to be seen whether the role of the individual will be enlarged or reduced. Will increasing numbers of successful black entrepreneurs develop, in themselves and the broader community, a heightened respect for the role and the resources of the individual? Or will pressures toward group conformity and absolute egalitarianism narrow the individual's space and limit entrepreneurial growth and influence?

Ashis Gupta

7

Indian Entrepreneurial Culture: Bengal and Eastern India

This study represents the first phase of an inquiry into Indian entrepreneurial culture, consisting of thirty-one interviews involving more than ninety prominent business owners, owner-managers, and managers. Some were first-generation entrepreneurs; others represented a second or third generation. Some had had little or no formal training; others had been trained in the top business and engineering schools in India, Great Britain, and the United States. Interviews were carried out in Calcutta, New Delhi, Bombay, and Poona—four cities among the half dozen or so major industrial regions of India. Two other centers in southern India—Madras and Bangalore—are soon to be studied.

We set out to explore the spirit that animates entrepreneurs to invest their time and money in Indian business, which is generally perceived as riddled with corruption, bureaucratic red tape, chronic shortages of power, poor communications, and localized labor militancy. We wanted to explore the origins of entrepreneurship, the conditions conducive to its growth and maturation, and the expectations and visions of entrepreneurs—their hardships and their frustrations.

Our investigations revealed a pattern of eclectic entrepreneurship forged out of the interaction between two distinct sets of forces. One set is represented on the plane of entrepreneurial autonomy by qualities of individualism, social conditioning, and the propensity to exploit structural opportunities. The second set of forces is made up of structural determinants such as religion, culture, and sociopolitical conditions. Figure 7.1 represents this model.

Figure 7.1

Eclectic Entrepreneurship: Individual Autonomy and Societal Structure

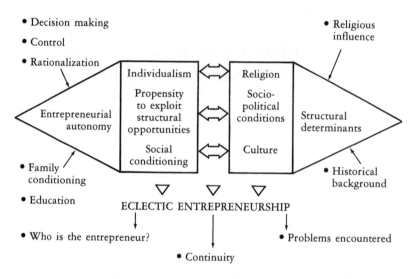

SOURCE: *Author*

Our study was designed to obtain information that might lend validity to the model. As such, we begin with the historical background, move on to family and other influences, examine the nature of entrepreneurial decision making, control, and rationalizations, and conclude with a discussion of religious influences. Our efforts to probe into the complex interpenetration of these forces and the unpredictable pattern of their outcomes meant a departure from conventional studies of successful business families or highly entrepreneurial communities, of which there are several.[1] We decided to focus on four distinct industrial regions of India located around major centers in the east, west, north, and south of the country. Cultural traditions, historical opportunities, and regional affiliations seem to have played significant roles in the economic and industrial development of all four regions, but the outcomes have been remarkably varied.

It seems inevitable that a complex society with a colorful and deep-rooted history tends to produce unique strains of entrepreneurship.

Therefore, rather than impose preconceived definitions to determine who is and who is not an entrepreneur, we allowed our respondents themselves to define their own roles. The definitions touch upon one or more of the traditional concepts, such as risk, innovation, startup, ownership, or growth orientation. What was most important to us was that our respondents had no doubt in their minds that they were indeed entrepreneurs.

The History of Entrepreneurial Culture in Bengal and Eastern India

Entrepreneurs from Bengal as well as from other parts of India maintain significant bases of operation in this region, but there is a more important reason for beginning our study here. The region presents a fascinating cycle of growth and decay, with the forces of imperialism, religion, nationalism, and regionalism playing different roles at different times. Through it all, the individual entrepreneur has actually functioned within the traditional sense of the word as a "go-between."

Many of us have a stereotype of Calcutta not far removed from the fictional image of the "Black Hole." Today, few can picture Calcutta as it was presented in *Hartley House, Calcutta,* a memoir published in 1789 by an unknown author:

> For the British Calcutta was, above all, a place for making and spending money. Lawyers' fees were enormous: "if you ask a single question on any affair, you pay down your gold mohur, Arabella, (two pounds)! and if he writes a letter of only three lines, twenty-eight rupees (four pounds)!". . . but the truth of the matter was that gold mohurs were "dealt about at Calcutta, as half crowns in England." A Calcutta memsahib would sometimes spend Rs. 30,000 or 40,000 in one morning at one of the shops specializing in European goods, for personal decoration alone, "on which account many husbands are observed to turn pale as ashes, on the bare mention of their wives being seen to enter them: but control is not an article of matrimonial rule in Calcutta; and the men are obliged to make the best of their conjugal mortifications."[2]

Other records tend to confirm the commercial pre-eminence of Calcutta even in the nineteenth century. East Indian trade was popular in the United States in the early 1800s. Dozens of boats filled with Indian goods docked in the ports of Boston and Salem, Massachusetts, each year. A descendant of Rajkissen Mitter, one of Calcutta's leading exporters, was recently quoted as saying, "I don't know the exact volume of business back then. But to give you an idea, in one year ninety-seven vessels anchored in the port of Boston from Calcutta. And [it] was all from just four families in Calcutta."[3]

In the halls of the East India Marine Society of Salem, one can still be startled by the life-size clay figures of Durgha Prasanna Ghose, Rajender Dutt, Raj Kissen Mitter, and Nusserwanjee Wadia. The first three were prominent Bengali merchants who lived in Calcutta in the eighteenth and early nineteenth centuries. Nusserwanjee was a Parsi, the son and grandson of shipbuilders for the British in Bombay. The following account of New England interactions with Calcutta is worth noting:

> In Calcutta, the firm of Rajender and Kalidas Dutt, Hindu *banians* (merchants) was a favorite of New England traders. In 1849 T. A. Neal, a merchant of Boston, gave the museum a life-size clay portrait statue of Rajender Dutt. Dutt himself, in 1850, gave the museum alabaster figures of the goddess Lakshmi and attendants. Charles Eliot Norton, later known for his influence on nineteenth-century arts and letters, began his career in the India trade as a super-cargo for his brother-in-law's firm, Bullard and Lee of Boston. Norton found Dutt "one of the most agreeable and intelligent Hindus that I have met here" (*Letters of Charles Eliot Norton*). Norton, who was privileged to visit the Dutt home on several occasions, wrote in his *Letters* that the Dutts were a family of two hundred members, who "lived together with all their property in common and with no division for seven generations." Norton . . . found Hindu practices easy to judge: "Is it not a strange thing that such ceremonies [the sacrifice of goats to the goddess Durga, observed at the Dutt home] should be continued in a family some of whose members are intelligent men, acquainted with the literature and science, and, more than all, the religion of the West?"[4]

Indeed, it was in and around Calcutta that the beginnings of the industrial age in India were seen. There is also now a sense of dismay at the depths to which Calcutta and Eastern India have fallen, compared to the growth and prosperity that have touched other regions of India

Table 7.1

Statewise Industrial Licenses (IL) and
Letters of Intent (LI) Issued

State	1981		1982		1983	
	LI	IL	LI	IL	LI	IL
Andhra Pradesh	69	39	66	26	79	63
Assam	7	4	5	1	3	22
Gujarat	131	79	121	69	116	115
Haryana	59	21	66	21	68	59
Maharashtra	144	114	148	95	155	171
Uttar Pradesh	77	24	111	22	130	99
West Bengal	43	34	37	27	45	71

SOURCE: Business Information Bureau, *March 27, 1984, no. 5.*

since independence in 1947. Table 7.1 suggests the commercial ascendancy of other regions of India compared to West Bengal and Assam.

The economy of Bengal and the rest of India has been in transition since the imposition of British rule over the subcontinent in the latter half of the eighteenth century. Earlier, the Dutch had come to Pipli in the province of Orissa in 1627; by 1655, they were trading both at Hughli and Balasore in Bengal. The French came to India in 1688, when they founded the trading post of Chandernagore, Bengal, in pursuit of Colbert's decision to establish French trading posts on the mainland of India. French trade with India reached impressive heights with the appointment of Dupleix as governor of Chandernagore in 1732. Chandernagore, which did not have a single ship in 1732, is reported to have "possessed fifteen or twenty vessels in daily use by the Company's employees when he [Dupleix] left in 1742."[5]

The British, however, outstripped the French and the Dutch.[6] A series of treaties between the British East India Company and the successive Nawabs of Bengal gradually transferred political powers and functions into the hands of the Company. The India Act of 1784 commanded the East India Company "to enquire into the alleged grievances of the landlords and if founded in truth to afford them redress and to establish *permanent rules for the settlement and collection of the revenue* and for administration of justice, founded in the ancient laws and local usages of the country."

Lord Cornwallis and the British government introduced the permanent settlement of land between 1789 and 1790. The idea was to raise the value of landed property and encourage capital investment in land:

> To the government it was immaterial what individual possessed the land provided he cultivated it, protected the ryots [farmers] and paid the public revenue. One third of the Company's territory was a jungle. . . . Cornwallis visualized Calcutta banians with their business-like habits displacing the happy-go-lucky old type landlords. These new landlords would clear waste lands and increase the value of landed property.[7]

Unfortunately, the permanent settlement destroyed many complex social relationships. Urbanites adjusted themselves to the "easygoing, indolent, and not altogether self-satisfied life" that prevailed in zamindari society.[8] Even more disastrous were the effects on the domestic handicrafts of Bengal, which, more than agriculture, were responsible for Bengal's prosperity. "The disappearance of domestic handicrafts followed closely on the wake of the Permanent Settlement. The weaver-cum-agriculturalist had now to depend entirely on agriculture . . . ."[9]

Early in the twentieth century came the stirrings of a movement whose "motive was to break the system of foreign monopoly capitalism and to enable the educated Bengalis to break out of the narrow confines of service and professions into the wider fields of commercial and industrial enterprise." The year 1905 saw the beginnings of the "swadeshi" movement—ostensibly a protest against Lord Curzon's decision to partition Bengal—whose principal objective was to boycott the use of British goods and develop reliance on indigenous products. Bengalis wanted to escape the narrow sector of the economy to which they had been confined:

> Living on an inelastic income derived partly from landed property and partly from clerical service in government and mercantile offices, the majority of the educated Bengalis found their economic horizon extremely limited. They were eager to enter the world of business

and industry, but lack of capital stood in their way. The big landlords and the successful lawyers and doctors who were in a position to supply the capital were reluctant to put money into the hands of young and untrained persons, and even a man with some training found it difficult to raise sufficient capital, partly because of the poverty of the people and partly because of the fear of powerful foreign competition. The fear was real and was bred from experience. Rabindranath's brother, Jyotirindranath Tagore, started an Inland River Steam Navigation Service in 1884 to break the exclusive European monopoly of river navigation. His swadeshi venture, however, collapsed from the unequal and unfair competition which he faced from the Flotilla Company managed by the Hoare Miller group. This pathetic yet magnificent gesture by the grandson of Dwarkanath Tagore taught educated Bengalis the lesson that swadeshi ventures were extremely likely to end in debt and financial ruin.[10]

The efforts of Bengali entrepreneurs came to naught, but the 1914 war provided something of a watershed in the realignment of economic power on the Indian subcontinent. In the business world of Calcutta, one saw a remarkable breakthrough for Indian capital, as illustrated in Table 7.2.

Table 7.2

Increase of Capital Investment in India, 1914–1922 (percentage)

	Calcutta	Bombay	Other India	All India
European	140.30	193.87	135.02	152.53
Mixed	234.22	420.03	43.61	251.56
Indian	1609.04	434.35	194.16	507.18
Total	197.40	333.06	111.35	240.30

SOURCE: Investor's India Year Books, *1914, 1922.*

In Calcutta, the investments of Indians rose by 1,609.04 percent between 1914 and 1922. Historians such as R. K. Ray have discovered "a remarkable correlation between the extent of European domination and the rate of growth in the different parts of India—the rate of growth being an inverse ratio to the strength of European capital."[11] The phenomenon has been explained as follows:

> Unlike the mill-owners in Bombay, who invested almost the entire profits of the war in new enterprises like the Scindia Steam Navigation Company, which at long last brought to an end the European monopoly of India's overseas shipping, the European managing agencies in Calcutta did not reinvest the whole amount of the considerable profits they made during the war, but transferred a large portion of these profits to England. . . . In Bombay the Indian capitalists now controlled 60 percent of the total capital investments, but in Calcutta the European houses were still in exclusive control of 65 percent of the rupee capital invested in the city, apart from the vast amount of sterling capital in Asia for which also Calcutta was the focus of concentration.[12]

European businessmen felt intimidated by the disappearance of the favorable prewar political climate and by the increasing transfer of power to Indians through constitutional reform. They quickly abandoned their long-term policies of reinvesting profits earned in India and began to transfer them to England as quickly as possible. A net import of British capital privately invested in India had existed until 1914, but the returns on former investments being withdrawn from the country now often exceeded the declining amounts of new private investments from Britain.

The effects of these trends were quite dramatic in Calcutta, where Indian businessmen, especially Marwaris, had amassed enormous profits during the war. The large fortunes in Marwari hands quickly turned a subservient merchant community from collaborators into fierce competitors. From the middle of the nineteenth century, migrating Oswal, Agarwal, and Maheshwari traders from Rajasthan in Western India had begun to settle in Calcutta and displaced the Bengalis as the principal collaborators of the expanding British companies. These businessmen kept to their traditional trading activities during the war. After the war, flush with capital, they aggressively began to finance new ventures. Unlike the swadeshi period of a decade earlier, shares in companies were fully subscribed in a very short time. Even Bengali businessmen began to make some headway, especially in such areas as tannery and leather works, chemicals and pharmaceuticals, pottery, cement, and coal mines. The Marwaris had already established a firm grip over the economy of Eastern India, however. Not content to move into the enclaves held by European businesses, some of the most powerful Marwari entrepreneurs of Calcutta—G. D. Birla, Kesoram Poddar, and Sukhlal Karnani—began to extend solid financial support to the nationalist movement under Gandhi.

Family and Other Influences

The successful entrepreneurs and top executives we interviewed for this study were either born into families with business interests or were drawn into business either by choice or, as they themselves liked to describe it, by some quirk of fate. Some were already successful in their chosen professions and were then seized with a desire to create an environment for themselves incorporating their deepest needs and aspirations—and this seemed possible only through the creation of their own organizations. Some of the enterprises they worked in before starting their own often filled them with a sense of frustration. We spoke to chartered accountants who found accounting intensely boring, advertising executives who chafed under the constraints of agencies controlled by others, and architects whose employers sent them out to see if water-taps were working and if the basins were clean.

Included in our group were Marwari businessmen, as well as entrepreneurs from West Bengal, Uttar Pradesh, Northern India, and Assam. The common element was that the center of their entrepreneurial activities lay in Eastern India generally, though not exclusively. The Marwaris we interviewed made no secret of their burning desire, from childhood, to be in business. It was not simply a desire to participate in business activities, but to outshine all others. This was radically different from the orientation of most Bengali entrepreneurs whose driving ambition, as they were growing into manhood, seemed to be to compete and excel in examinations, to be brilliant if possible. "We Bengalis believe and indoctrinate our children into believing," said one, "that business is *bad,* that the guy running around in a Mercedes-Benz is unquestionably evil." We also met Bengali businessmen who said, "Business is in my blood," or words to that effect. Other saw their fathers in business and admitted that the thought of going to work for someone else had never occurred to them.

Those who took up entrepreneurial activities as a matter of choice cited the need to be free, from a psychological if not an economic point of view. Entrepreneurship provided an avenue for proving to oneself that one could, after all, accomplish certain specific goals.

Clearly, the family environment proved to be the most critical in developing entrepreneurial instincts. "I lived in a business, so to say," reflected one entrepreneur who found himself reading the *Economic Times* when he was only fifteen. The family environment provided support as individuals went about acquiring engineering, accounting, or other professional degrees because they also believed in the necessity of becoming formally qualified. In some cases, the search for credible qualifications took the respondents to U.S. colleges such as Harvard and to M.B.A. degrees.

At least one current managing director made a conscious effort to stay away from the family business after graduation from high school. Through the help and prompting of his public school headmaster he joined a company in 1950 as a tea-taster. Today, he controls that company. The headmaster, in this case, was less than a mentor, but no less influential in helping individuals make vital career choices.

Career choices led, in a few instances, to identification with someone else's business. A single woman among our respondents considered herself as having been "thrown" into the role of manager. An alumna of the Harvard Business School's Advanced Management Program, she believes she could quite easily have been a contented Bengali housewife. She shared with other Bengalis a powerful drive for educational attainment. Another Bengali entrepreneur went behind his father's back (an unheard-of lapse in obedience) to enroll himself in an engineering program. The father wanted him to go into pure research in the sciences, after a customary stint at Cambridge or Oxford. He slipped into management, as it were, from engineering assignments at the start of his career.

Just as Bengal idealized the intellectual life, other parts of India held up other career ideals. One of our northern Indian respondents said, "Most of my family members are either in military or government service. My father discouraged me from government service. Instead, my aunt, a doctor, persuaded me to join medical college. I left after only ten days of classes."

Others had dreams to realize. An engineering graduate from a prestigious Indian Institute of Technology said, "I had dreams of a decent life, a car, a house. After a year working for a major managing industry house in Calcutta, I had a new car, a bungalow, a club membership, but a boring job." A trip to Japan was all he needed to make up his mind about starting his own business.

Our respondents identified a wide variety of influences that have shaped their lives. The Bengali owner-manager of an electronics company acknowledged the influence of swamis (Hindu missionaries) at the Ramakrishna Mission School where he studied, as well as the influence of American businessman Ross Perot. "My father didn't influence my career in any way," confided one respondent. "I spent many years in a boarding school as a boy. If anyone has influenced me, it is the religious singer, Dilip Kumar Roy of Sri Aurobindo Ashram. He brought me close to God through his singing." Another businessman acknowledged the powerful influence of Mother Theresa in helping him understand the meaning of compassion and human suffering.

The changing nature of industry and industrial relations often brings about unique opportunities for managers who might otherwise be quite content to work for others. The jute industry offers a typical example. A blue-chip industry of the pre-independence era, it was offering returns of 10 to 12 percent when the rest of the market provided from 3.5 to 5 percent. The industry required barely any working capital. Goods were sold on a prepaid basis, and expenses were deferred—payment for raw jute by one to three months; wages for labor, fifteen days; and salaries, one month. Veterans in the business maintain that nobody but a Scotsman could have created such an industry!

After India's independence, the industry was saddled with lack of flexibility. Labor unions and labor agreements limited management options in what was a labor-intensive industry. Competition from synthetics further eroded the industry's strength. "After twenty-five years in the industry as a manager," said one of our respondents,

I found the industry "sick" just when I thought I ought to be comfortably settled. Major stakeholders had lost interest in the industry. I was in a jute mill with 15,000 employees in a region where there were no alternate avenues of employment. Our mill was closed for two years. Now, I saw there was trouble ahead because workers were beginning to pawn their roofing tiles. With the monsoon setting in, that was the last straw. The situation was dismal. I called in the labor leaders with a plan to revive the factory. I trimmed the labor force to 10,000 and introduced labor participation in venture capital. Each worker was to contribute Rs 5,000 (U.S. $300) to build up an equity fund of nearly $3 million. Then I approached the West Bengal state government to chip in $2.4 million by way of equity, rather than take over the entire factory.

The factory's 1988 production was the highest during the previous six years.

A break from tradition, then, coupled with support and encouragement from some family member, often led to entrepreneurial beginnings. A base of family wealth that one could tap into, and counsel from in-laws, just as often proved to be the all-important catalyst.

Educating and Helping the Would-Be Entrepreneur

Among those we interviewed, the general consensus was that, compared with the rest of the country, there was less and less entrepreneurship as one moved eastward. "There's a lot of family education in Marwari and Gujarati families," said one. "They train their children for business, instill discipline, whereas Bengalis and Assamese don't." Some felt that many Eastern Indians had confused ownership with management, leading to the decline of entrepreneurial families. Because it was a family business, these entrepreneurs often felt they had the right to manage with little or no thought to competition. "As a result," said one Assamese tea-garden owner, "every single garden owned by Assamese families is being sold—to Marwaris."

A highly successful and visible entrepreneur from Northern India admitted that, within his community, it is taken for granted that business is a worthwhile and rewarding occupation; but the reliance is not merely on the process of socialization. "Good education has been responsible for my becoming a good entrepreneur," said the same person. "My father was very particular about imparting good education. He would say that money can come and go, but a good education is forever." The gentleman's own son has a recent M.B.A. from the Harvard Business School. Still, we found a firm belief among many of our respondents that the effectiveness of an individual ultimately depends on the individual alone, not on whether he or she has had a formal education. "Formal education merely gives one greater confidence, reduces inferiority complex," suggested someone.

Learning was a different matter. Learning was rated very highly by all the entrepreneurs we spoke to in Eastern India. "You learn as you grow," said a Marwari businessman. "I've learnt from bosses, colleagues, and clients. I have groups of people, in my own company and among my friends, to whom I go for specific assistance." Even clubs such as Rotary International provide a source for help and advice. Almost everyone believes that the ideal is to integrate the experiences of others as well as one's own to formulate effective action.

"I'd attend morning classes at college from 6:00 to 10:00 A.M., then I'd go to my father's office to sit and observe what was going on," said a young Marwari entrepreneur. "That's how I learnt business." Later, this experience was augmented by a Bachelor of Business Administration degree earned in New York City.

For Marwaris, the origins of entrepreneurial activity lie in initial apprenticeship in a business where one learns certain things and later becomes a competitor with help from a financier. For example, the Bangur brothers were ordinary share brokers until World War I when, with jute mills making huge profits and jute shares rising in value, they became millionaires by jute speculation. The firm of Surajmull Nagarmull started as raw-jute hoarders and later diversified successfully by buying a jute press, a hessian mill, and a sugar mill. Kesoram Poddar was another speculator who rose from ordinary conditions to become a millionaire during the war. He started his career in a Goenka firm, then went into the sugar business by selling sugar to Ralli Brothers. Later, he became an agent for a Japanese firm.

A special concept of capital seems to be fundamental to the success of Marwari businesses. "You are bound to fail in business," said a Marwari entrepreneur, "if you start with 25 percent capital and expect 75 percent from financial institutions. The money never comes on time. The clerks could go on strike, and the bank manager could become ill." Most Marwari businessmen grow up with a conservative attitude, not necessarily risk-aversive, toward capital.

Contrary to popular belief, Marwaris don't help others because they are Marwaris. The truth is they'd rather lend to a Marwari with a solid business idea than to a bank for a lower rate of interest. Typically, the Marwari businessman lends at interest rates of 18 percent or higher. Risk is so much a part of their psychological orientation that Marwaris rarely deposit money in banks. Even established Marwari companies continually borrow from private lenders.

Opportunities for lending and borrowing abound in this informal segment of financial institutions. As far back as 1978–1979, figures suggested that the size of the informal economy in India represented 48.78 percent of the official Indian gross national product.[13] It is a durable sector of the economy, vast and successful. Not only business, but also politicians and political parties look to this informal sector for help while promising policy concessions in return.

Unfortunately, not many Bengalis have access to this kind of informal financial facility. Bengalis are also loath to ask their parents or spouses for money, usually out of reasons more sentimental than practical or entrepreneurial. Most are fearful of losing money borrowed from family members.

Our respondents tended to agree that life was easy in Bengal once upon a time. "Making a living, providing for two meals for one's family, were comparatively easier in Bengal than in the rest of the country, especially arid spaces like Rajasthan and Gujarat," said one Bengali businessman. Although everyone agrees that the advent of the British East India Company gave an economic boost to this part of the country, there is also a perception that the desirable lifestyle in Bengal continues to be the life of the *zamindar* (landlord) or, by extension, that of the *bhadralok*[14] or *babu* (white-collar worker), modeled after the *zamindar's* lifestyle without the analogous base of landed property. This is hardly compatible with entrepreneurship. Besides, the recent history of failed Bengali entrepreneurs constantly casts a shadow on the aspirations of many Bengalis who would otherwise have wished to emulate them.

The British way of life and business has exerted a powerful influence on economic life well beyond India's independence in 1947. Said one respondent, "When I joined the company in Calcutta, I was taught by the senior Indian executive how to survive in a company dominated by Europeans." There were two classes of people in British-dominated companies and most Indians felt compelled to adhere to British social and recreational preferences. Golf and the club scene were big in Calcutta and other metropolitan cities.

The "club culture" of Calcutta is a tremendous help in entrepreneurial and other business activities. It is clearly linked to interfirm relationships that entrepreneurs find so critical to their survival and growth. These relationships provide unexpected sources of help and rare camaraderie. When a tea-brokerage firm was faced with a sudden, if temporary, shortage of cash, the chairman was overheard reflecting philosophically at a bar about his urgent need for about $150,000. A friend heard him and immediately came to his assistance. No papers were signed, no documents exchanged, but the money was in his hands the following day.

Role models are often provided by other Indian businessmen. Take J.R.D. Tata, for instance. "Because he takes care of everyone," explained one respondent, "employers, suppliers, customers, even the country. A young girl's father will readily marry his daughter off to a boy working for Tata's."

Our woman executive, the first to have been hired by a major cigarette manufacturer, claimed her father was the greatest influence in her life. "He had that rare ability," she said, "to laugh at things in spite of adversities of every kind." An Assamese tea-plantation owner considered his mother a significant force, someone who brought him a sense of direction in life. "She was widowed at forty," he said. "She didn't know any English, but had enough determination to send me to the Harvard Business School."

Another Assamese plantation owner found his father, in spite of the family tea business, actively embroiled in the Indian freedom movement. "In 1942," he said, "father saw a steel-rolling mill advertised for auction. He didn't know anything about rolling mills, but had to buy it on his own account when his partners backed out. There was so much to do in the business, even mother took to running the tea gardens."

As if to further highlight the maverick spirit that often lies behind entrepreneurial enterprises, a Bengali business owner told us of his grandfather, a school headmaster, and his father, who joined a cargo ship as a sailor. The father went to Japan and Singapore and secured an introduction to some Sikhs in Vancouver, Canada, who eventually smuggled him into Washington State as an illegal immigrant. He traveled south, enrolled in the University of California, Berkeley, and became a Marxist active in the revolutionary Ghaddar Movement, a society of Indians abroad. He returned to India in 1914, was immediately arrested as a communist and a subversive, and jailed for six years in Rewa. Later, the father started the business in Bengal. He is clearly a larger-than-life role model for his son.

Again, the jute mill owner who entered into equity participation with his workers owed many of his ideas to his father who was a leader in the cooperative movement. "My father used to tell me stories of people helping people to preserve and nourish businesses," he said, "and I was always full of admiration for what he had done."

One respondent remembered his father imparting wisdom before he went to work for another industrialist. "You must command, not demand, respect," said the father. "If you join a trade union you may be protected in your job, but you won't be protected from your family. I'll turn you out of the house."

European business executives also had a positive influence on some. "I thought managing directors worked only in air-conditioned offices and enjoyed the high life," said one Bengali entrepreneur, "until I saw this Englishman standing at the factory gate and helping people tuck their shirts inside their trousers. He also hired cobblers so the workers could wear clean and decent shoes. Finally, he taught the workers to sit on chairs in the factory canteen." Play hard and work hard was another principle picked up by one of our respondents, who recalled his British boss telling him, "I'll drink with you till any hour of the night, but you must be in the office at 9:00 A.M."

There are no quick ways to become an entrepreneur. The consensus of our respondents was that one needed to know about every aspect of the business to succeed—from purchasing to accounting to providing funds. Formal training was considered useful. It helps develop confidence. It is important for keeping abreast of the environment. Formal training, without the informal component, was generally considered to be somewhat deficient. It was felt, however, that informal training, without a formal component, might not be such a handicap after all.

The best place to get informal training is obviously on the job. Opportunities, however, are not easily or readily available to all. "I picked up the business from the company itself," said one respondent. "Tea tasting is a profession, but each one of my colleagues made it a point to teach me."

First-generation entrepreneurs face many limitations. "Our foolhardiness has carried us into many problems," admitted one Bengali entrepreneur from the electronics industry. It is not always difficult to find help, however, believed most of our respondents. Friends can often be very helpful, just as business competitors may often prove to be singularly perverse.

"I received a lot of help from my customers," said a North Indian entrepreneur. "For instance, in 1954, Sindri Fertilizers was importing cooling towers from the United States. During one shipment, the timber components caught fire on the ship. At the company's request, I produced the replacement components and forgot all about it. Five years later, Sindri asked me to build a complete cooling tower. They gave me the names of six international manufacturers from whom to obtain know-how and components. Two companies responded to our enquiries, and we eventually entered into a collaboration with Marley in the United States."

Other industrialists admitted to leaning heavily on their trade associations and on Chambers of Commerce for wage negotiations and other actions demanding concerted effort. "For industry-specific problems, we look for answers in our own resources or turn to our foreign collaborators," said one entrepreneur. "For other problems, we turn to specialists."

"I received no help from anyone," said a Bengali entrepreneur, "until I turned the company around." The woman among our respondents said, "I tend to keep my problems to myself. I share them with my husband, but I don't turn to him for solutions."

At least one Bengali entrepreneur in computer services, software, and video production identified the source of his venture capital as a Marwari industrialist. "He gave us money at 20 percent interest, but it was an unsecured loan. The financial institutions gave us no support at the startup stages, even though we now have banks chasing us with money." On the other hand, the Bengali owner-manager of a small tool-manufacturing company admitted his consistent dependency on financial institutions, "Without them," he said, "I'd be completely lost. When we started in the fifties, I believe our recently 'nationalized' banks gave us a lot more support than before."

Decision Making: Entrepreneurial and Other

"Some decisions I leave to the experts. Others I make myself." This seemed to be the general pattern of decision making acknowledged by most of the respondents. The head of a firm of consulting architects— often entering design competitions—employs a novel decision-making process: "Even an architect who has passed out yesterday can come up with brilliant, creative projects. So we have internal competitions. Recently, one of our architects with only two years experience submitted an entry for the Indira Gandhi Science Complex, and he won."

The chairman and owner of a state-of-the-art rubber consumer and industrial products facility said to our surprise, "Most of our decisions are taken at the lowest level. Our operating decisions, in particular, are discussed in great detail right down to the shop-floor level. It is sometimes quite chaotic. But with good moderators, we find it a very effective process."

Generally speaking, decision making is a participative process in companies controlled by our respondents. The chairman of an investment company said, "Twenty-five top executives get together once a month. Some plans emerge and we follow them. Even the managing director doesn't have a veto. Some facts and figures are documented, but there are no notes or systematic analysis."

Others, like the managing director of a diversified group of engineering and other companies, rely heavily "on various tools and statistical data which can support our decisions." "Often," he added,

> we end up in a greater mess than without it. Like the case of the filament factory. With rural electrification and power plants coming on stream, we projected a high demand for filaments. Unfortunately, the statistical data never came true. The hoped-for infrastructure never came to pass. So we ended up making a huge investment without there being adequate demand. Our hunch then told us to diversify into certain areas where we could get support. This wasn't the result of structured study. Even before we could start the new project, we received orders for Rupees twenty crores (U.S. $12 million).

A Marwari manufacturer of electrical consumer products said, "We collect views of others and eventually base our judgment on this information. Our major decisions are *not* based on feasibility reports or market research. Give me three options and I can tell you without a calculator which I believe to be the right one."

The Marwari managing director of a telecommunications equipment company described their decision-making process as follows: "By habit, we would definitely like to have data collected and available. Afterward, in the case of major decisions, we discuss the data among top executives and board directors. But we may well come to a decision which goes against what is suggested by the data."

Even where decision making is not formalized or documented, it is still thought out in as much detail as possible. Many respondents laid strong emphasis on what some called a "sixth sense," or the application of one's total knowledge, background, and experience. Sometimes, within the same organization we find some major decisions made informally, and others through a rigorous, formal process. Often, operating decisions are left to the various operating divisions. They tend to be more structured than some other nonoperational strategic decisions. For instance, the acquisition of plant and machinery might require meticulous justification, whereas incursions into new business areas may not demand or permit similar levels of documentation.

It was suggested that managers tend to be more formal and less entrepreneurial when they are controlled by powers located thousands of miles away, as is the case with many multinationals. In such instances, the degree of accountability to local and overseas shareholders is so high that managers necessarily become more circumspect and formal. Size can often be another determining factor. "When we were small," suggested the owner of an electronics-component manufacturing firm, "we used to work together much more informally. Today we have a more formal structure."

"Our family members (the owners) still make the key decisions," remarked a North Indian respondent, "but we do consult top executives. More and more authority is being delegated as the company grows. One family cannot possibly look after the entire enterprise. But we do have trouble finding good managers in India."

The Great Divide: Control

"I've never believed that being a member of the controlling family in a company entitles you to anything more than a fair return on your investment. The organization must claim precedence over the family. If the organization prospers, the family prospers. If you want anything more, you must prove your competence." Indeed, none of our respondents shied away from imposing appropriate standards of evaluation on their family members within the company. An Assamese entrepreneur told his son, "During working hours you're not my son. After 5:00 P.M., yes."

Whenever an Indian family business has experienced rapid and high levels of growth, it has become necessary to bring in professional managers; otherwise there is danger of the company's breaking apart. For instance, the vast industrial empire of the Modis is on the verge of splitting up today. The Modis have a large number of third-generation family members, all very qualified, who want a piece of the action. With remarkable foresight, the great G. D. Birla split up his empire a long time ago.

Today, several major Marwari industrial enterprises have a fairly cosmopolitan group of senior managers, in marked contrast to several other entrepreneurial communities. For example, one has to be a Tata to be head of the Tata group, a South Indian to be head of a South Indian group, and a Punjabi to head a group of Punjabi companies. Highlighted here is the danger of assuming stereotypically close and consolidated family relationships throughout the Indian subcontinent.

Family members control the shares of several of the companies involving our respondents. Generally speaking, working members of the family depend on each other for advice, regardless of whether there is a crisis. "Those family members who'd actually like to run the business should develop appropriate skills. Family members should be professionally qualified, but they must also prove themselves. In any case, 'fringe' members of the family shouldn't be admitted."

Everyone considered family loyalty to be important. For the sake of efficiency, however, the need for professionalism was also considered imperative. "It is best to leave family businesses to professional managers," suggested one entrepreneur, "so that jealousies do not crop up and affect the day-to-day workings."

A Marwari entrepreneur said, "Psychologically, a man wants that whatever he earns be passed on to children and grandchildren. That's why people don't like to buy apartments on leasehold land. I want the same for my sons. But I also want the sons to be *more* competent than me. If they're incompetent, I'd rather entrust the company to the hands of someone who'll keep it safe." A tea-plantation owner said, "I can't risk the jobs and lives of eight thousand people. If necessary, the son must stay on the sidelines and be a mere shareholder."

Marwari entrepreneurs seemed to assume, in spite of occasional reservations, that their sons, if not daughters, would naturally drift into business. One father described how, as soon as his son completed high school, he was placed in the factory. He attended college from 6:00 A.M. to 10:00 A.M., then spent the rest of the day until 6:00 P.M. in the factory. "When I see him working hard and to the best of his ability, I know he needs a pat on his back. And he gets it."

One of our respondents, not an owner, observed, "Children of a business family are often a different kettle of fish from nephews and cousins. Often, sons will come into the business whether they're any good or not. This thought crosses the minds of prospective employees as well as employers. I've heard owners say: 'My son is two years old and you're forty-two: what's your problem?' The close relationship between father and son is unique to the Indian psyche." In most family-owned companies, one observes four or five favorites for whom much is done. These people know that, eventually, power will pass from father and son. A little less is done in such companies for those lower down.

Larger business houses must necessarily depend on professional managers. In a group consisting of twenty-six companies—not untypical of the larger Marwari enterprises—finding twenty-six presidents becomes very difficult. "The reason seems to be that the best of our intelligentsia have gone abroad," suggested one Bengali entrepreneur recently inducted as a board member of a large group of companies. "They may not have been the best engineers, but they are capable of taking risks. They would've been good managers. What's left behind in the thirty- to forty-year-old age group is not of very high quality. Unfortunately, we can't pay the equivalent of U.S. salaries. That would wreck the rest of the company."

Bengali and Assamese entrepreneurs were somewhat more circumspect about steering their children into careers in business. "What right do I have," asked one "to force my son into the business? He may wish to be an artist or a singer!"

There was also a certain amount of ambivalence about the role of family relationships. It was pointed out that earning a livelihood from the business was generally not such an immediate concern for others as it might be for a founder. The key seemed to lie in a consistent set of family values that everyone believed in and that established, in turn, certain relationships and expectations between the company and individual family members. A Bengali entrepreneur noted with a sense of loss, "The values we followed are not considered relevant by youngsters today." A North Indian respondent pointed out that the next generation is probably more ambitious. "They're looking for greater material gains than we could've hoped for. But they probably work just as hard, if not harder, than us."

Often, family members are investors in the family business. They constitute a dependable core of people who are always motivated. "They're committed and intrinsically honest and loyal," said one. "Family members, especially women, can also play an indirect role in increasing harmony within the organization by planning and participating in social and religious events."

The impact of family relationships appears to surface in a family-owned company every fifteen to twenty years. The emergent differences can often imperil the continuity of operations. The basic problem generally lies in a generation gap. Many from an earlier generation still believe in a father-son type of relationship between management and workers. Younger entrepreneurs, on the other hand, believe more in financial results than in sentiment. This situation is often very disconcerting to workers who don't know how to respond to the changing environment. "The trick is to be able to segregate personal values from those more practical and relevant to the organization," suggested one respondent—clearly of the modern breed.

There were, however, some dissenting voices regarding the wisdom of hiring M.B.A.'s merely on the strength of their degrees. The owner of a major appliance-manufacturing firm said he was somewhat amused after attending a training course for entrepreneurs at one of the prestigious Indian Institutes of Management. "If I learnt whatever they taught me," he said, "I would've closed down my business." On the subject of M.B.A.'s, he said, "M.B.A.'s think they're ready to take on the managing director's job right away. They don't try to learn from their juniors and peers. These are the people who are always deceived by their subordinates. If you always tell others to do things, you can be certain they'll act on your errors first."

Entrepreneurial Rationalizations

Fairness rated very high with the interviewed entrepreneurs. "Employees are always happy with a tough but fair boss," explained one. "If my father allows me to purchase drugs, I might love him for his generosity today, but I'll curse him when I'm older for not punishing me when he could have."

The legitimacy of one's authority derives from one's character, according to most of our respondents. "The authority figure must be an exemplary person, a man of integrity, honesty, commitment, and dedication." Others expressed similar views: "The top man must set an example. He must work the hardest. Corruption starts from the top. If the head is corrupt, corruption will trickle down and cover every part of the body."

"I am still the first to come in and the last to leave," said one managing director. Another recalled a piece of advice from a British boss which he has turned into a guiding principle: "Don't hide under an umbrella when your men are out working in the rain."

Eastern Indian entrepreneurs tend to be gregarious. They are involved in a lot of social work through organizations such as the Chambers of Commerce, the Rotary and Lions Clubs, and others. "I'm sure there are better managers and engineers in my company," remarked the managing director of a power-generating firm, "but I have a singular advantage in that I get along well with people."

"Managers must guard against ego. Ego and a businessman don't go together." Today, many observers feel that one can trace the rise and fall of some Bengali industrialists to an ego problem. Ego, and a certain amount of the zamindari mentality that creates an affinity to things like a garden house and inevitable neglect of the business. "Bengalis are highly sentimental people, and that's their downfall," reflected one Bengali respondent. "When I am in a situation where I can't pay the bank, I go to the bank and ask for time. Most Bengalis can't bring themselves to ask."

A fairly pragmatic sense of the meaning of authority was found. Many respondents agreed that one's designation in an organization doesn't necessarily entitle one to any special privileges. Authority was seen as implying endless responsibility. One is responsible to one's seniors and accountable to one's subordinates—always *more* responsible than persons lower down in the hierarchy.

A Bengali managing director justified his authority by saying, "I am more interested in the welfare of my workers than union leaders are, because I don't have to be voted to power at the end of the year." A North Indian business owner found justification for his authority in the happiness and satisfaction of those working in his organization.

The highly respected chairman of a group of tea plantations, a Muslim by religion, observed, "My entire attitude to my staff and the business would change if I came to *own* the business. My entire character would change. This may be a naive observation, perhaps reflecting a weakness in my character. But that's why I never thought of changing from a professional manager to an owner."

Our respondents felt it was easy to lose one's effective authority—by making decisions that put the organization at risk, by failing to admit mistakes, by making the wrong compromises, by being unfair and, most importantly, by being corrupt and dishonest. Several of our respondents believed that workers invariably look to their bosses as being better than themselves. There's trouble when this perception breaks down: "When a man has invested money, even if he makes a wrong decision and loses money, nobody questions him. But a dishonest man is never respected."

It would seem that the key to an entrepreneur's authority is his competence. "An owner who is not 'professional' will not remain an owner," said one. The owner's justification for his authority lies in a general acknowledgment by others that he has contributed to the mutually accepted goals of the organization. It seems that there would definitely be a loss of influence if the principal entrepreneur failed to fulfill his commitments. This could happen as soon as he lost concern for customers, employees, or shareholders, failed to adapt to environmental changes, or lost touch with political allies. The close parallels between such thinking and prevailing ideas on the subject in North America are not surprising. North American business principles have made considerable inroads in certain sectors of the Indian economy. This is not to say that there isn't a deep-rooted mistrust of North American business practices in many other sectors, however.

A certain environmental concern appeared to dominate the thinking on life-styles. "You look vulgar in a small town in Assam driving a Mercedes or a BMW. It doesn't seem so if you're in Hamburg or staying at the Savoy. Still, if I haven't cheated anybody, I don't feel guilty if I have champagne and caviar and a Mercedes-Benz." The attitude of this Assamese entrepreneur appeared to cover the three aspects of day-to-day living most entrepreneurs wished to talk about: desired lifestyle, feelings of guilt, and a contextual propriety.

"Lifestyle is very important for a professional," said a North Indian respondent. "In the past, we had people who worked to *maintain* a life-style. Nowadays, we have difficulty attracting people, especially people with good family backgrounds. In the north and west of the country, most such people want to go into their own business."

In the Eastern region, it was felt that people generally wanted authority without responsibility; hence, the tremendous attraction of government jobs. Employees often leave higher-paying company jobs for lower-paid government positions. Clearly, the priority is security, the kind found in government jobs and, to some extent, in professions such as medicine or law. Social status is secondary. For persons in business, these two are rarely the top priorities. "Such cautious attitudes stand in the way of entrepreneurship. For a businessman, security is number two on the list of priorities. You stake your security on yourself."

The Bengali chairman of a large rubber consumer-products company believed that Bengalis were slowly trying to change. "The bright boys still opt for security. Others find opportunities limited in the Eastern region because of lack of growth. However, Westernization weakens their roots, and these boys move to other areas. Interestingly, they are not going out of the state for jobs as clerks."

The culture of ostentation appears to be different in different cities of India. As one respondent described it, "In Bombay they pick up material objects, in Delhi they throw money in your office, in Calcutta there are lavish private cocktail parties." Ostentation is generally considered a waste of time, but is not considered the same as "spoiling" company staff with benefits so they may be self-sufficient when they one day leave the company.

The entrepreneurs agreed that ostentatious consumption is becoming more and more evident in India. Some very successful people are flaunting flamboyant lifestyles. "There shouldn't be a vulgar display of wealth in a nation where millions go hungry," said the North Indian president of a chemical company. "Lakshmi (the goddess of wealth and prosperity) comes to those who respect Lakshmi."

There is a recognition that the ostentatious rich build up social pressures against themselves. "We may be creating new wealth, but it is certainly not being equitably distributed."

Ultimately, respondents said, one's lifestyle tends to be based entirely on the values one chooses as guides. "I'll live the life I choose to live, the way I feel comfortable," proclaimed an Assamese entrepreneur. A Bengali respondent said, "In my scale of operations, I wouldn't like to have a Mercedes-Benz. However, in absolute terms, yes, I'd love a Mercedes, even a private plane." He rationalized by pointing out that a level of high consumption, if cultivated at an early stage of growth, reduces the capacity for taking risks.

Others rationalized differently, but no less pragmatically. Sometimes, business needs dictate the level of expenses. For instance, if one needed to host a visiting foreign collaborator, it might be necessary to put him up in a five-star hotel, to drive him around in an imported, air-conditioned car, and to usher him into an elegant office. These gestures might build up his confidence in the Indian environment.

On the other hand, there was the recognition that "a flamboyant office may be counterproductive in that the collaborator might think you're ripping him off."

The second-generation owner of a multinational firm, a Harvard M.B.A., admitted, "This is a terrible conflict we face, especially when we are doing international business. This is a backward country, and it is very difficult to operate in the midst of widespread poverty. International business can probably go anywhere else in the world. Such business is largely based on perceptions."

A Marwari entrepreneur recalled how, when faced with difficult times, he once elected to save money by traveling between Calcutta and Delhi by train rather than plane. A fellow passenger on the train, following introductions, recognized him as the owner of a major Calcutta-based engineering company, and said, "If a person like you travels by chair-car in a train, what are we ordinary mortals to do? Shall we hang outside by the doors?" This entrepreneur, regardless of his own personal orientation toward a certain degree of asceticism, agreed with his North Indian counterpart that "to satisfy the expectations of the modern consumer, his perception of quality, one often has to spend unnecessarily."

The same entrepreneur recalled visiting the federal government offices in New Delhi just when two executives from a competing firm pulled up alongside in a flashy Japanese car. His own car was the ubiquitous Indian Ambassador, and his chauffeur ruefully asked him later (quite aware, no doubt, of his net worth) when he would trade up to an imported car. "I told the driver one must be *able* to afford a Mercedes. And what about the escalating costs? The quality of my pen, my shoes, my briefcase, my driver's clothes, these must all match my Mercedes-Benz. It's easy to increase expenses, very difficult to bring them down. Eventually, you'll kill the business." He regretted the country's proliferation of people who *deceive* others by vulgar show, just as they deceive by giving larger dividends than the company can afford.

By and large, thrift is still considered important for generating wealth. "Some individuals can be ascetic, others may be pleasure seekers," said a Bengali entrepreneur, "but as long as one gives adequate time to the business, as long as salary levels and benefits are legitimate, it's fine."

The Shadow of Religion

In any study of the entrepreneurial culture of India it is difficult to unburden oneself of Max Weber's thesis suggesting a passive and permissive role for Hindu beliefs in industrialization, as opposed to the positive, dynamic role of the kind presumably played by the Protestant ethic in the development of European industrial capitalism. More recently, one finds a major shift in the emphasis of Weber's thesis whereby what is stressed is the *"rational adaptability* rather than the *irrational resistance* of Hinduism to change."[15] Others have shifted the discussion of obstacles to modernization from emphasis on religious belief and ritual and traditional social structure to the more immediate problems of shortages in capital, skills, and management expertise. In the former case, we may be in danger of ascribing very little freedom of choice to individual actors; in the latter, there is a danger of exaggerating one set of variables at the cost of another.

Religion did not affect our respondents in any uniform, predictable way. The Bengali owner of a major newspaper chain made a telling statement concerning religion which confirmed earlier findings by Milton Singer:

> In my study of the Madras industrialists, as well as from my observation of other Hindus, I found that Hinduism also generates in its believers a "salvation anxiety" about how to escape from the effects of one's own past actions and the endless cycles of rebirths. The anxiety is not an intolerable one, however, that leads to an overwhelming pessimism and defeatism or to a despairing burden of sin and guilt. That one becomes good by good deeds and bad by bad deeds is taken as an inexorable law of fate (karma) but not necessarily as a denial of freedom of choice and action in the present or as a reason for not exercising effort, intelligence, foresight, and resourcefulness in taking advantage of opportunities to improve one's condition in this life and the next.[16]

What our respondent said was: "I'm happiest in situations where there are no contradictions. In my corporate life, I try not to introduce values from the *Bhagwad Gita* or the *Upanishads."* These values, highlighted in Figure 7.2, are so fundamental that they tend to leave no facet of Hindu life untouched.

Figure 7.2

Key to the Culture of Hinduism:
Master and Dominant Symbols/Concepts

KARMA
(Service)

| BHAKTI | | | JNANA |
| (Devotion) | | | (Wisdom) |

DHARMA	ARTHA	KAMA	MOKSHA
(Right action)	(Wealth)	(Artistic/ cultural life)	(Spiritual freedom)

BRAHMACHARYA	GRAHASTHA	VANAPRASTHYA	SAMNYASA
(Period of training)	(Period as householder)	(Period of retreat for loosening bonds)	(Period of renunciation)

SOURCE: *S. Radhakrishnan*, The Hindu View of Life

A somewhat different feeling came from several North Indian respondents. "Religion has played a great part in my life," said one. "Faith in God has given me strength. My religion has helped me tide over numerous crises." Another said, "I have a little temple in my office. I have Lord Krishna in my office, and he has played a big part in my life." He reminded us that his was a major British company. A third person said, "Religion is a great corrective. I don't go to temples, but I have a temple in my own house. I spend some time in it every morning. Religion pulls you back when you're on the verge of doing something wrong."

Most entrepreneurs kept religion out of their business on a day-to-day level, but there were some exceptions. In some companies, a priest visits every day to offer prayers and flowers to Lakshmi, or Ganesh, or Krishna. The practice is much more widespread around special festivals when new images of the gods are installed in many organizations. A Marwari entrepreneur remarked, "Religion motivates you to remain honest. After all, I have to go to God. How do I answer him? A man wouldn't want to adulterate if he's conscious of his religion. I can't adulterate medicines that might kill a person. Ultimately, God is there to take the final account."

The other Indian religion that plays a major role, especially in the lives of many businessmen, is Jainism. All businessmen from the western Indian state of Gujarat, and most of the Marwari traders, are either Jains or Vaishnavas, a sect of Hinduism founded in the early sixteenth century. The basic vows of the adult Jaina householder, according to the *Tattvarthadhigama Sutra,* are as follows:

1. Must not destroy life.

2. Must not tell a lie.

3. Must not make unpermitted use of another's property.

4. Must be chaste.

5. Must limit possessions.

6. Must make a perpetual and daily vow to go only in certain directions and certain distances.

7. Must avoid useless talk and action.

8. Must avoid thought of sinful things.

9. Must limit the articles of diet and enjoyment for the day.

10. Must worship at fixed times, morning, noon, and evening.

11. Must fast on certain days.

12. Must give charity by way of knowledge, money, etc., every day.

Weber has written: "The compulsory saving of asceticism familiar from the economic history of Puritanism worked also among them [the Jains] toward the use of accumulated possessions, as investment capital rather than as a fund for consumption or rent."[17] Although the Jain's quasi-Puritan ethic pointed to successful entrepreneurial activity, in the case of the Vaishnavas this ethic was compensated for by social networks and customs such as discipleship and consequent travel, which were conducive to trading activities.

One of our younger Marwari respondents, commenting on the subject of religion, said, "Personally, I couldn't care less. The elders of the family are more traditional. So we never start anything new, never hire anyone, on a Friday. I see no logic in it."

Religion often determines what businesses one stays out of. The mighty Birlas chose to stay out of the hotel business because of the necessity to consider serving nonvegetarian food. "My family are all vegetarians," said one Marwari entrepreneur. "They didn't want me to make potato chips with artificial chicken flavor. They felt if the public had the slightest suspicion that the same oil is used to fry vegetarian and nonvegetarian products (even if artificially 'flavored'), they wouldn't buy the chips." Another Marwari said, "My wife wouldn't want to earn a single penny from the death of a single bird."

One of the Bengali respondents said, "I'm not antireligion. It's just that I don't practice any religion. I'm a Hindu. I got married by Hindu tradition. My sons will probably get married in the Hindu tradition." Another Bengali entrepreneur revealed through his response a conscious separation between personal and business values. "At a personal level," he said, "I don't believe in God. In business, we are marginally involved with the concept because we grant religious holidays and generally acknowledge that religion does touch many lives. New buildings are consecrated religiously. Workers organize the periodic worship of Vishwakarma (patron god of craftsmen and artisans). It gives them satisfaction, so why not?"

Several of our Eastern Indian respondents were categorical in denying that religion played any part in their business. They admitted, however, that most successful Indian businessmen are probably quite religious, even if religion had no part in their success. "He sticks to his religion," suggested one entrepreneur by way of explanation, "because he is afraid to upset the mental equanimity, the balance, which he derived from religion and which was a *part of him* when he became successful. He will not part with religion, then, for fear it will upset the overall configuration that he knew as present when he found success."

"I've seen businessmen, otherwise very astute," noted one respondent, "who have changed the direction their desks are facing at any point in time, because they imagine a particular direction to be shuv (auspicious) for the next three months."

Other entrepreneurs made no secret of their skepticism over the avowed religiosity of many of their contemporaries. "Notwithstanding the 'tika' (a sandalwood or vermilion mark) on the forehead and the images of Ganesh and Lakshmi in the office, what generally overrides religious principles is the desire to make a profit either for oneself or one's company," said one. Some companies encourage religion as they would encourage sports and fitness.

At least one voice of dissent asked why business was not secular in India. Our respondent felt that religious symbolism should not intrude into the workplace, and regretted that most religious groups were seemingly moving toward fundamentalism.

Finally, a first-generation Bengali entrepreneur pointed out a common paradox. He said, "In earlier times, I was an atheist who didn't believe in God. Today, I am not an atheist, but I don't believe in myself any more." The paradox apparently has not affected his performance as a dynamic entrepreneur, nor has it arrested the impressive growth of his computer services and software company.

It is perhaps impossible to demonstrate the effect of religion on entrepreneurship in any empirical manner. We found, however, individual entrepreneurs who attest to the significant impact of religion in their lives, both private and business. We also have statements from those who claim absolutely no role for religion in their lives. The rational adaptability of Hinduism may be an acceptable concept on a global scale, but the rational adaptability of the Hindu would seem to be more pertinent to our study.

Who Becomes an Entrepreneur?

Almost everyone seemed contemptuous of upstart entrepreneurs who flaunt their money and power. An entrepreneur earns respect, they felt, only when he behaves in a way acceptable to society. "You'll act responsibly," said one, "only when you get accustomed to handling wealth."

As in any other country, many entrepreneurs in India are honest, but many also feel driven to make a quick buck. "The political climate," remarked one respondent, "doesn't permit one to have a very clean image of business. One has constantly to get around the rules before one can become a Birla or an Ambani (two of India's leading industrialists)." This need does not seem to present any moral conflicts.

Many respectable and qualified people are turning to entrepreneurial activities. This shift reflects changing attitudes toward business, even though most people seem to believe that businessmen, by and large, are all blackmarketeers. Families still prefer to marry their daughters to government servants or to those holding clerical jobs rather than to businessmen. Bengali mothers discourage sons from joining businesses. It is not uncommon for generations of Bengalis to find in their family circles lawyers, doctors, and teachers, but no businessmen.

A Bengali entrepreneur therefore had often to be something of a maverick. "My grandfather was entrepreneurial and started a mica mine," said one, "but I never saw him." "And so it is," commented the same individual, "that my son may get a job with the World Bank and forget all about entrepreneurship."

On the other hand, we also talked to Bengali businessmen who said, "My two daughters are with me in business, and they'll continue to be in it until they're ready to start their own businesses. I'd expect other relatives of mine to get into business because it is so rewarding and satisfying."

Entrepreneurship is full of hazards, of course. The raw entrepreneur runs the risk of being taken for a ride by bureaucrats, politicians, as well as less-than-scrupulous competitors and suppliers. It would seem that an exposure to business practices and activities before starting a business is just as critical as an ongoing support system after starting operations.

Problems Entrepreneurs Face

The contemporary Indian experience with entrepreneurship seems to suggest that it is inseparable from a spirit of nationalism. In the 1990s, nationalism is more than likely to translate into regionalism. Government controls and bureaucratic interference in the free market represent two of the biggest sources of dissatisfaction for the entrepreneurs we interviewed. Some complained bitterly about the government's planning mechanism which has discriminated blatantly against Eastern Indian interests. "During the British Raj," one Bengali businessman complained, "we stood up against a ruthless, alien government. But now we seem to have lost the will to confront a less ruthless government of our own people." He pointed out that India's First Five-Year Plan committed as much federal government investment to the city of Bombay as to the entire province of West Bengal. Other provinces such as Maharashtra, Gujarat, and Tamilnadu have all benefited from considerably higher federal government investments compared to Eastern India, in spite of the severe problems (like five million refugees and more) that have plagued provinces in Eastern India.

Those we spoke to acknowledged certain generic problems for the region, especially the nonavailability of power. They noted, however, an abundance of certain raw materials and a profusion of skilled labor. "In communications technology, especially software development, Bengal has a tremendous comparative advantage, a great cerebral capacity. What prevents its exploitation is lack of money," noted one entrepreneur. Large numbers of entrepreneurs are prepared to sell jute and tea, but few are interested in high-profit, high-risk ventures. This reluctance may betray the absence of sophisticated understanding of venture capital.

Bengali entrepreneurs, in particular, feel that regional advantages must be exploited. "If you believe in capitalism," suggested one of them, "you have to believe in regional advantages." Through non-adherence to the theory of comparative advantage, "it is not Bengal that's sliding back relative to the rest of India, it is India that is sliding back relative to the rest of the world."

Many of our respondents shared the view that the present political structure of a strong federal government works against individual regions. Those in manufacturing industries were almost unanimous in calling for a de-equalization of factor prices (of coal and steel, for example), and for greater revenue-raising authority for the regions. The Bengali owner of a computer-services firm said, "The government really doesn't have a good grasp of how to encourage business and its growth. The eastern region is not a suitable market for entrepreneurs. In West Bengal you survive because you're a survivor, not because anyone else helps you survive. Incentives for startups are *not* communicated by the government. It's cheaper to set up a project in Orissa (a neighboring state) than near Calcutta."

One of the recurring sources of dissatisfaction lies in the lack of commitment among bureaucrats. A prevailing premise in India is that no government official is supposed to make mistakes. As a result, they all tend to be overcautious rather than overzealous. Evaluation of major projects takes from two to three years, and the delays permit huge cost escalations. As if to slow down the process even further, the government's personnel-transfer policy prevents senior bureaucrats from gaining extended experience on the job. Additionally, senior bureaucrats tend to make themselves virtually inaccessible. "The same rule is applied differently to different people by the government," complained one entrepreneur. "That's my greatest source of dissatisfaction."

Some of the entrepreneurs we spoke to shrugged off the barriers of government regulations and controls as inescapable challenges of doing business on your own, but others were less philosophical. Even a simple product such as a new brand of potato chips involved one of our respondents in endless running around to obtain licenses. He didn't think there were deliberate hurdles placed in his path. "It's the system," he said. "The system is like that." Another respondent added, "We are a most unwanted lot. Every second person thinks he can stop you, if you don't grease his palm."

Thanks to a basic overregulation of industry, entrepreneurs often feel at the mercy of petty officials. Excise inspectors refuse to approve the manufacturer's classification, and foreign-exchange enforcers are deeply suspicious. In fact, vested interests are so entrenched that it is often impossible to break through them.

The lack of a congenial work culture is also a significant problem. "We look after our workers very well, but the work culture has been deteriorating in West Bengal," a Bengali businessman remarked. "People are not prepared to work any more than they have to. I've offered workers up to 30 percent more in wages for extra work, but they've refused on the plea that it will shrink job-creation opportunities." Said another, "I find union leaders of opposing camps having greater influence over my workers than I do. I find myself inadequate to combat this. This causes me great anguish. Opposing unions vie with each other for the workers' support. They foment dissatisfaction among workers who don't seem that dissatisfied. Political forces muddy the situation." Several other respondents echoed such sentiments.

The nature of the Indian market also bothered some. "The buyer is not at all quality-conscious," regretted one respondent. "He is price-conscious, and that works as a disincentive for higher quality. Otherwise, we're quite capable of products of international quality. There are instances where our foreign collaborators have confirmed our products as superior to their own. In spite of this, we had to sell at the price of our competitors. Since the manufacturer doesn't get a premium for higher quality, he is quite prepared to produce anything that will sell." Several respondents insisted that India has to overcome this dilemma before they could remove the bias—'Why buy from India?'—and seriously enter international markets."

Why Remain an Entrepreneur?

The creative aspects of entrepreneurial work provided the single greatest source of satisfaction to our respondents in Eastern India. The chairman of a multinational company manufacturing cooling towers literally glowed as he said, "Initially, we would import 70 percent of our components; today, we're exporting these same components."

Other entrepreneurs saw themselves as part of a process in which they were helping to build something that transcends individuals and, certainly, individual efforts. Some described it as a position where one is influencing events, rather than being part of something over which one did not have much control. "One of the greatest satisfactions," said a Bengali entrepreneur, "is when you can conceive a plan, start a business, and find that it meets your projections and expectations. Here's something new that you, and you alone, have thought out."

Opportunities in Eastern India for introducing new blood into dying, neglected businesses have also been a source of intense satisfaction for many. Some dramatic turnarounds have taken place. "I took over a company which was closed for sixteen years. Everyone had written it off. I turned it around."

Relationships with unions can also provide a source of satisfaction. The part-owner and managing director of a jute mill started off with fourteen different trade unions exercising sway over his workers. He succeeded in persuading all fourteen to work together, even to the extent of not staging political meetings in front of the mill gates. When one of our respondents started a new electronics plant near Calcutta, he was faced with a demand that all workers involved in the plant's construction be provided with alternate employment. Instead, he offered them jobs as trainees with the promise of permanent employment if certain criteria were met. Fifty workers opted for training, at wages considerably lower than what they were earning during the construction phase.

In the late 1960s and through the 1970s, labor militancy reached frightening proportions in West Bengal. Several of our respondents made adjustments to coexist peacefully with the labor unions. "We fight often," said one respondent, "but never on small matters, only on matters of principle." With financial instability a chronic problem destabilizing many Eastern Indian companies, management has often had to agree to reduce its own salary levels to persuade labor unions to forgo wage increments and save a company from ruin.

For many of our respondents, growth and the successful adaptation of technology are sources of great pride. Many are quickly becoming multinational from the very nature of their operations. One owner pointed out, "We're manufacturers of tea-processing machinery. We started by setting up a plant in a backward area. Now we're into project exports. We've set up complete tea factories in Uganda and Vietnam."

Entrepreneurial energy often transcends ideological barriers. West Bengal offers a good setting for such breakthroughs. One of our respondents, a Marwari managing director of a telecommunications equipment manufacturing firm, described his company as an example: "An organization which is a joint venture between a multinational and a communist state government, and whose success depends largely on cooperation between a communist state government and a non-communist central government in New Delhi. We're on a fast track, and our product has met the stringent standards of various agencies. We've successfully bid against the government's own public-sector companies and secured telecommunications-equipment contracts." That's no mean source of satisfaction.

Indian entrepreneurs attach a high value to their ability to touch the lives of others. Employees often expect this of their bosses. Regardless of occasional eruptions of labor unrest, India continues to be a largely paternalistic society. The CEO is often a father-figure. The employees see him as a protector, the one man who has the strength to ensure a healthy, sound corporation.

The numbers of lives affected by entrepreneurial actions can reach into hundreds of thousands. The tea industry alone, confined largely to Eastern India, looks after one million people directly. Assuming each employee supports a family of five, the industry actually helps sustain five million people. A Bengali-owned finance and investment company controlled by one respondent services twenty million certificate holders through 100,000 active agents. The chairman believes each of his agents earns enough to comfortably feed a family of five.

The manufacturer of a highly successful brand of potato chips would be happy if, twenty years from now, he could look back and say, "I educated my countrymen about snack foods." He took care to point out that India produces the world's third largest crop of potatoes, but that 40 percent goes to waste for lack of storage facilities.

An Assamese plantation owner wants to be remembered for building an organization capable of running on its own. A Marwari entrepreneur would like to be remembered as a "fair" person. However, a Bengali respondent pointed out that, "in reality, you are never perceived as being fair to all."

One Bengali respondent would like to be remembered "as a person who has produced a truly high quality product." A somewhat more philosophical managing director of one of the largest managing agency houses said, "I'm quite positive they won't remember me. But I'll be happy if they remember me for someone who always tried his best."

Conclusion

The Indian entrepreneurs we studied presented a complex view of life and entrepreneurial activity. Some had role models and others did not; some received help from predictable or unexpected quarters, others did not. Clearly, powerful family influences worked into the lives of most of them. The religious influence took on an added dimension when individual entrepreneurs came in contact with religious figures, sometimes from religions other than one's own, as in the case of Mother Theresa.

In spite of waves of historical influences and unfettered interaction with other major religions, entrepreneurs from Eastern India remain acutely conscious of their culture. Some are increasingly impassioned about their regional identity. Unlike certain ethnic groups of entrepreneurs who often feel under pressure to modify their behavior, even their cultural antecedents, to fall in line with aspects of the dominant culture, Indian entrepreneurs find themselves utterly free of such anxieties, regardless of which part of the country they are from and which region of the country they are located in. "Excel, not integrate," seemed to be watchwords animating most of our respondents.

It is far from certain that cultural and religious influences give rise to an aspect of entrepreneurial behavior that may be considered remotely "otherworldly." If anything, Indian entrepreneurs appear to have established a remarkable balance between the known demands of this world and the less-than-certain demands of the next.

If it is humanly possible to cut through this intriguing web of goals, aspirations, beliefs, and values, is it possible to be left with a few common strands, certain cultural commonalities? Perhaps the single emerging perception we can be certain of is the diversity of backgrounds, motives, and strategies that runs through the nature of entrepreneurship, even in a single region of one country. This diversity seems to be a reflection of the diversity that is tolerated, even courted, by Hinduism.

If our findings point to a mutually accommodating diversity, it may be possible to trace it back to the curious way in which Hinduism links this life to anything that may lie beyond—as much through action as outside of it. This may explain many of the curious attitudes through which Indian entrepreneurs justify their actions as well as their inactions. This can only partially and momentarily reflect the truth. For truth has many faces, and the culture of India is in the throes of monumental changes. Hinduism may emerge from this period essentially unscathed, but the individual Hindu may not.

S. G. Redding

8

Culture and Entrepreneurial Behavior among the Overseas Chinese

This chapter reports findings from an empirical study of overseas Chinese entrepreneurs, and more specifically the beliefs and values they bring to bear on the processes of organizing their especially successful economic activities. Two issues will be addressed before using the empirical findings to illustrate the larger theoretical questions. The first broad issue concerns the significance for theory of the East Asian alternative model for development—alternative, that is, to Western industrial capitalism or to the Soviet bloc industrial system. (This latter has become, of course, a substantially less convincing alternative than it was until quite recently, as its disintegration proceeds. It does, however, still retain a form of coherence in China and North Korea as well as in the USSR itself and may thus continue to stand, if only on crutches.)

Two points are clear from an observation of East Asian economies. First, economic success equal to that of the West has been achieved. East Asian enterprises are successfully competitive in world markets, and in many fields they are dominant. Japanese GNP per capita now exceeds that of the United States, and Hong Kong and Singapore are richer in per capita terms than several European countries. Second, East Asian economic success has been achieved with an economic system that displays substantial variations from its Western equivalent. Organizations take on different shapes, relations between government and business are differently structured and maintained, and workforce attitudes to employing organizations—and to work itself—are different. Besides the macro East-West difference there also exists significant variety inside the East Asian sphere itself, to a point where only the most general homogeneity can be identified. There is, for instance, very limited typological overlap between a Chinese family business and a large Japanese corporation. There is nonetheless, and significantly, some similarity.

Thus the East Asian case is both successful and different from the Western. In crude terms the same destination has been reached, but using a different vehicle and going a different route. The ramifications for sociological and development theory are large, especially for theories of modernization, which rest heavily on the assumption that the distinctive individualism generated in the West has had a reciprocal relationship with modernity. The implication is succinctly stated by Peter Berger:

> It can be plausibly argued that East Asia, even in its most modernized sectors, continues to adhere to values of collective solidarity and discipline that strike the Western observer as very different indeed from his accustomed values and patterns of conduct. . . . Could it be that East Asia has successfully generated a non-individualistic version of capitalist modernity? If so, the linkage between modernity, capitalism, and individualism has not been inevitable or intrinsic; rather it would have to be reinterpreted as the outcome of contingent historical circumstances.[1]

This warning about the limited applicability of much of the sociological theory dealing with modernization is likely to be valid in parallel or subsidiary fields such as organization theory, where the proponents of universalism (such as Lex Donaldson[2] and Henry Mintzberg[3]) are being faced with empirical counterexamples that undermine the basic premise of a universal organizing principle valid across cultures.[4]

An attempt to come to terms with this variety, and to examine the East Asian cases on their own terms, is visible in the work of the Beyond Bureaucracy project outlined by R. D. Whitley and S. G. Redding.[5] The theme of this research is that distinct patterns or "recipes" for economic activity appear to stabilize in different societies, and can be explained in terms of the institutional contexts in which they develop. Such explanation necessarily incorporates historical, geographical, and political features to inform what is essentially a sociology of firm behavior. This attempt to explain variety, while searching at the same time for patterns, is seen as a means of moving debates to the middle ground between the culturalists and the institutionalists—where perhaps the most fertile understanding lies.[6] Some indication of the range of hypotheses within this complex project may be gained from the summaries, given in the appendix, of the characteristics of dominant economic actors and their related contexts. An example of such an approach is Richard Whitley's analysis in this volume of patterns of entrepreneurship in Europe.

The second broad issue is the need for a paradigm shift in theories of entrepreneurship, an issue first illuminated by S. M. Greenfield and A. Strickon in a review of the way the topic has been addressed in the half-century since Joseph Schumpeter's formulation of a theory of economic development.[7] Their characterization of the changes in approach and the epistemological problems faced begins with the original interest of economists in the institutional mechanics of equilibrium. This interest tended to deflect attention from questions about how growth was achieved, since equilibrium theories were by definition not addressing growth and change. Moreover, as Schumpeter suggested, the expansion of economic activity rests upon noneconomic factors, and specifically on the actions of individuals in the market.

The problem for economics then was that much of the inquiry necessarily moved outside economics and began to focus on the historical, sociological, and psychological determinants of entrepreneurship.[8] From this form of inquiry came, for instance, the psychological work of David McClelland on the need for achievement and the historical/sociological work of Everett Hagen in explaining the stimuli present among disadvantaged minorities.[9] As described by Greenfield and Strickon, the two postwar decades were periods in which "attention gradually shifted from the functions of entrepreneurship in economic growth to the psychological traits of persons designated as entrepreneurs and to the social conditions that produced them."[10]

At the same time a concern with nourishing underdeveloped economies encouraged certain assumptions that were both unchallenged and greatly influential:

- The preindustrialized, nonmarket economies were seen as being in a state to be left behind as quickly as possible. The agenda was to have them emulate the developed West. These economies were therefore generally not studied on their own terms.

- In the study of entrepreneurship, it was seen as adequate to describe and analyze the society, economy, and behavior of human populations that are either developed or underdeveloped, but in either case are assumed to be in a steady state. This approach is one of "comparative statics" and does not provide a model of how to move from one state to the other.[11]

- The traditions of nineteenth-century evolutionism are visible in the implicit notion of "stages" of development, a paradigm perhaps now due for revision.

To avoid the distortions implied in these three assumptions, Greenfield and Strickon propose an unmasking and rejection of "the essentialist/organic metaphor that has informed Western social thought for some two millenia."[12] They contend that it is misleading to conceive of societies as being composed of entities that are essentially organisms capable of growth. Instead, they say, it is more revealing to concentrate on the individual organisms within a population, observing the way they deal with survival, thus being less concerned to theorize at the level of the type or species.

The "Darwinian population ecology" approach to the study of entrepreneurship is claimed to benefit understanding by integrating the behavior of key agents into an explanation of the social process. Entrepreneurs make choices, and larger patterns of change reflect aggregations of these choices. An important component of this view is that it allows for different evolutionary processes and combinations to be conceived of as optional routes toward the current condition. It removes the essentialist view of modernization, and thus the notion of convergence. What were previously seen as anomalies thus take on the role of viable alternatives.

The argument concludes by example:

Even the introduction of the same new behavior or resources such as industrial technology into a range of populations would not be expected to produce similar statistical patterns of behavior. Instead, each community, in terms of its views of the universe, human relations, and values, would be expected to develop its own patterns. Given the new resources, individuals in pursuit of goals that are meaningful to them would make choices and decisions with respect to their behavior. The outcome of the selective process then would give us the new patterns for the group. Japanese factory owners or managers, dealing with a population of workers whose expectations of relations with authorities differed from those of their English or American counterparts, would be expected to make decisions and choices that differ from those of the English and Americans in the same situation. Consequently, patterns of industrial relations to emerge in the several societies would be expected to be different. The choices made in each case would reflect both the "objective demands" of the technology and the culturally given goals and values shared with their respective workers. The outcomes of the evolutionary process then would differ in each case, even though each is industrializing.[13]

In any move to focus explanation on the individual decision maker there is a danger that the account may be so reductionist as to prevent comparison or useful middle-range theorizing. To protect against this danger, it is necessary to make a clear distinction between what C. C. Ragin calls "observational units," which in the entrepreneurship literature would normally be entrepreneurs or their firms, and "explanatory units," which are the categories used to account for the pattern of results.[14]

Given this caveat, the practitioner of comparative social science may then begin to address some of the key questions that lie in the potentially fertile middle ground between the culturalists and the institutionalists. Examples of such questions for the field of entrepreneurship are:

- What do entrepreneurs do (as opposed to what personality traits do they have)?

- Why do they act as they do?

- When an entrepreneur creates a new combination, what is the process by which it is copied by others, and how is it selected to replace a previously dominant mode of behavior typifying a larger group?

- What is the importance of the entrepreneurial factor among the totality of determinants of the shape and efficiency of an economy?

- Do such explanations themselves vary by society?

The Overseas Chinese Entrepreneur

This research illuminates the first three questions above and provides empirical information that may contribute to attempts to answer the last two. The research is based upon a study of seventy-two overseas Chinese owner-managers in Hong Kong, Taiwan, Singapore, and Indonesia, aimed at reconstructing their belief systems and values and relating those patterns to what was already known about managerial behavior in the Chinese family business.

Although the discussion here will concentrate on the connection between managerial beliefs and managerial functioning, it is located within a larger field of inquiry. In simple terms, the managerial functioning is what these entrepreneurs do, the beliefs are why they do it, and the wider framework explains why such behavior becomes dominant in this economic culture.

This research was conducted by extended tape-recorded interviews, usually with two entrepreneurs together over dinner.[15] A semistructured process of questioning was used to explore ten main topics chosen to illuminate the espoused views of the self, relationships and kin, management and organization, and society. The statements were transcribed, analyzed, and categorized to create a picture of the mind-set of the group of people. Explanation took account of the social history of Chinese culture, and also of patterns of present-day economic behavior.

The Spirit of Chinese Capitalism

By definition, Chinese capitalism refers to economic behavior in areas outside China itself, and the research reported here represents the overseas Chinese in Hong Kong, Taiwan, Singapore, Indonesia, Malaysia, and Thailand. Figure 8.1 attempts to capture the spirit of their entrepreneurial behavior; it represents their way of explaining why they behave as they do, based on the analysis of their statements. Because levels of analysis need to be separated in the interest of having valid explanations, the subject matter is treated at four levels: perceptions of the self, relationships and kin, the organization, and society at large. Connections exist between the levels, but their conceptual frameworks are respectively psychological, social-psychological, organizational, and sociological.

Three main legacies of Chinese social history seem to act as primary determinants of present-day behavior. *Paternalism* derives from the predominantly Confucian ethics that lie behind the structure of Chinese society and provide the legitimation of hierarchy based on an exchange of deference upward and a responsible but humane strictness downward. *Personalism* is a powerful force that deals with the problem of establishing trust relations in the absence of institutions and societal structures, such as law, that would otherwise support the reliable conduct of exchanges. *Insecurity* is traditionally endemic for the mass of Chinese people. The majority of social experience is of subsistence agriculture, unpredictable government intervention with no countervailing defense, and a lack of understanding and identification between the people and the ruling elite. The traditional pattern of elite dominance through the retention of monopoly on the interpretation of official state dogma (either Confucian or, more recently, communist) has left the average Chinese with low expectations of benevolent welfare and a deep reliance on family-based resources.[16]

At the level of the self, these forces are played out as if there were a state of tension between, on the one hand, a high level of self-confidence emerging from the knowledge that a Confucian role is being fully complied with and, on the other hand, a defensiveness and wariness deriving from underlying societal insecurity. This tension is released by a powerful urge to control by ownership. Possession of the capacity to control a source of wealth makes use of the inner strength a person derives from complete role compliance in a culture where roles are very clear and widely understood.[17] It also depends on societal threats, principally poverty, and the low status associated with it. This status sensitivity is especially keen in societies where alternative status avenues are closed off, as is commonly the case in the colonial context or where the ethnic group exists within a culture dominated by a different ethnic host group. These features occur or have occurred for long formative periods of recent history in all the areas in East and Southeast Asia where the overseas Chinese now flourish.

The urge to control is clearly important to entrepreneurship: It provides the motivation to initiate risk-taking and to search for the new combinations of elements that will release wealth. It is fundamental to entrepreneurial behavior and possibly a universal prerequisite. Although the urge to control is a psychological force, it emerges from the web of social forces that surround the individual

Figure 8.1

The Spirit of Chinese Capitalism

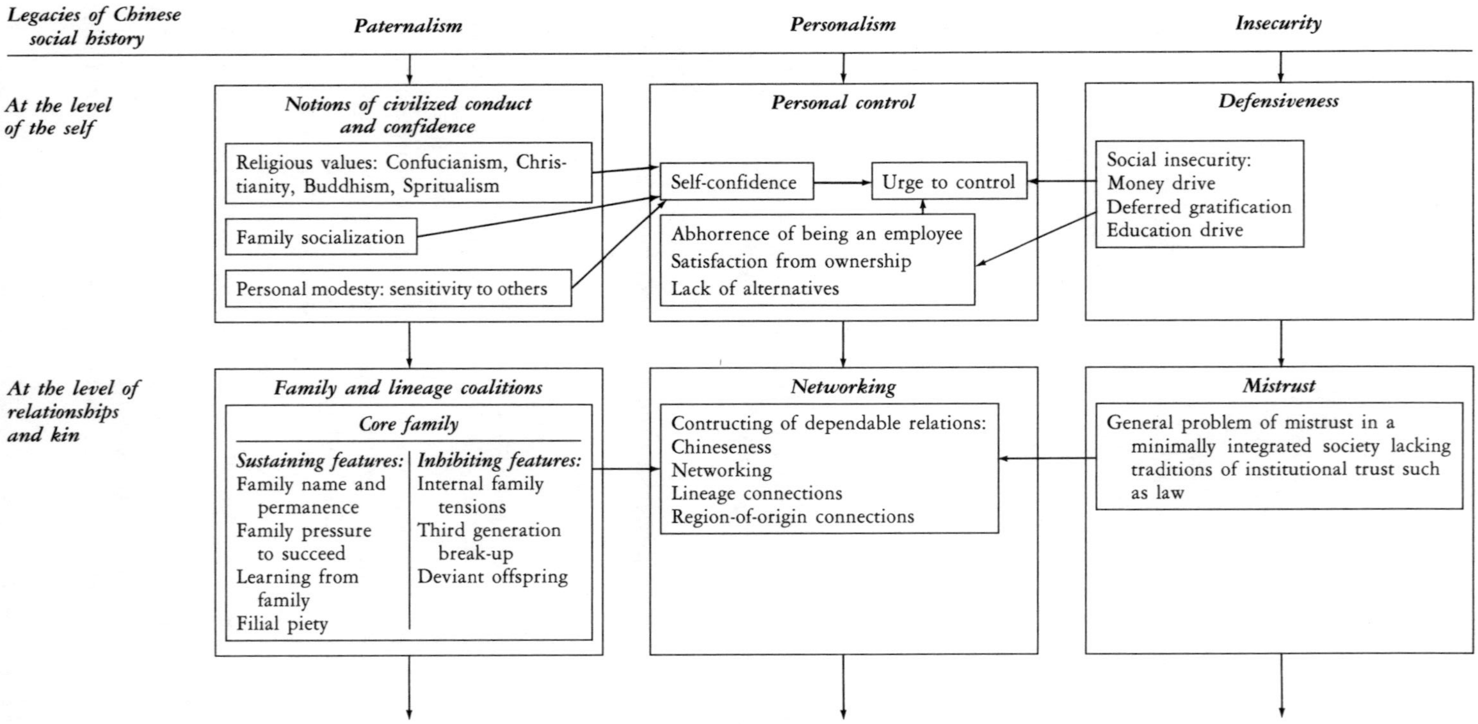

Legacies of Chinese social history	Paternalism	Personalism	Insecurity

At the level of the self

Notions of civilized conduct and confidence

Religious values: Confucianism, Christianity, Buddhism, Spritualism

Family socialization

Personal modesty: sensitivity to others

Personal control

Self-confidence → Urge to control

Abhorrence of being an employee
Satisfaction from ownership
Lack of alternatives

Defensiveness

Social insecurity:
Money drive
Deferred gratification
Education drive

At the level of relationships and kin

Family and lineage coalitions

Core family

Sustaining features:
Family name and permanence
Family pressure to succeed
Learning from family
Filial piety

Inhibiting features:
Internal family tensions
Third generation break-up
Deviant offspring

Networking

Contructing of dependable relations:
Chineseness
Networking
Lineage connections
Region-of-origin connections

Mistrust

General problem of mistrust in a minimally integrated society lacking traditions of institutional trust such as law

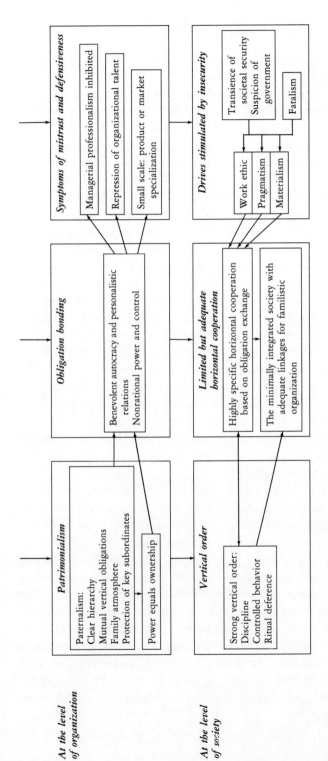

At the level of organization	*Patrimonialism*	*Obligation bonding*	*Symptoms of mistrust and defensiveness*

At the level of organization

Patrimonialism

Paternalism:
Clear hierarchy
Mutual vertical obligations
Family atmosphere
Protection of key subordinates

Power equals ownership

Obligation bonding

Benevolent autocracy and personalistic relations
Nonrational power and control

Symptoms of mistrust and defensiveness

Managerial professionalism inhibited

Repression of organizational talent

Small scale: product or market specialization

At the level of society

Vertical order

Strong vertical order:
Discipline
Controlled behavior
Ritual deference

Limited but adequate horizontal cooperation

Highly specific horizontal cooperation based on obligation exchange

The minimally integrated society with adequate linkages for familistic organization

Drives stimulated by insecurity

Transience of societal security
Suspicion of government

Fatalism

Work ethic
Pragmatism
Materialism

SOURCE: *Author*

and account for the strength of the drive. In this area, the key feature would appear to be societal mistrust.

At the level of relationships and kin, it is possible to discern the playing-out of the same tension seen earlier, but this time at the social-psychological level. There is a general problem of mistrust in Chinese society, which has no tradition of institutionalizing cooperation, and which consequently remains "minimally integrated" and reliant upon "utilitarianistic familism" for its stability.[18] The crucial unit of identity and reliance is the core family; cooperation across society relies upon social networking for the construction of dependable relations. This reliance is a natural development of the personalistic tendencies inherited and reproduced in the culture over a long period.

This form of networking, as Janet Landa has pointed out, is an institutional alternative to contract law.[19] It is also capable of producing high levels of business efficiency by the reduction of transaction costs[20] and by the fostering of organizational flexibility and strategic adaptiveness.[21] It is important to note that the perpetuation of such efficiency in the system, for example, the Chinese-dominated textiles and apparel industry of the Philippines[22] or the banking industry of Thailand[23] requires that organizations remain under the control of key individuals. If such a personalistic trust system is to work, then the individuals who make up its crucial nodes must have the authority to control economic action. This constraint is apparently understood and built into the Chinese capitalist economies as an unspoken design principle.

This point is reflected at the next level of analysis, that of the organization. Here the patrimonial traditions of the Confucian order serve to legitimate power where it coincides with ownership and leadership behavior expressing paternalistic benevolent autocracy.[24] In such a context the binding-in of people to a cooperative relationship with the organization proceeds through the obligation-bonding of paternalism, a system that allows for the perpetuation of personalism and creates a nonbureaucratic organization. In such an arena, it is difficult to incorporate managerial professionalism on a large scale, and the inevitable limits to delegation also act to restrain the scale of organization possible. It should be noted, however, that such organizational scale limitations can be at least partly transcended through the linking of organizations in the highly networked wider social context. "Molecular" organizations can thus be created from the atomistic entrepreneurial units.[25]

In this kind of environment, the entrepreneurial role is then sustained and encouraged. The system works if key individuals retain control of the units of economic action. Large numbers of controlling owners thus serve as examples to others seeking control of some economic domain. New entrepreneurs are commonly encouraged and aided by established ones as the building of networks and the creation of bonds of obligation proceeds.[26]

At the level of the society as a whole, stability rests on the strong vertical order and the disciplined role compliance that families inculcate, maintain, and perpetuate. The various drives stimulated by insecurity, such as pragmatism, materialism, and the work ethic, are directed into the creation of carefully bounded, limited, but adequate forms of horizontal cooperation. This cooperation is based on the exchange of obligations and a process of what in a negative sense might be seen as mutual exploitation. In a more positive sense, a strong moral order persists and acts to reinforce, in a Weberian sense, this form of non-Protestant capitalism.

To formulate the Weberian thesis in the sharpest way—including an acknowledgment that Protestantism was *one* of the causes of certain aspects of capitalism, and thus necessary but not sufficient—is to say: "No capitalist development without an entrepreneurial class; no entrepreneurial class without a moral charter; no moral charter without religious premises."[27]

The moral charter of the overseas Chinese is based on Confucianism and consists primarily of the construction of a "moral community," described in a recent study of the overseas Chinese of Penang as follows:

> The raison d'être of the clan and territorial associations was to promote the welfare and unity, not only of members, but also of all potential members. This ideological aim was often explicitly stated in the printed rules of the associations in formulations such as: "give mutual assistance," "promote cordial relations between clansmen," or "strengthen the unity of all Hui Aun fellow countrymen and plan for their welfare." Such formulations also occurred constantly in speeches made by the leaders, which always were reported in the newspapers. Any constellation of people affected by such a morality I will call a moral community.[28]

Entrepreneurial Behavior: Patterns, Predeterminants, Persistence

Earlier in this chapter, questions were posed that represent gaps in the entrepreneurship literature: What do entrepreneurs do? Why do they do it? How is entrepreneurship replicated? It may now be possible in the overseas Chinese case to answer such questions, using the accounts of the overseas Chinese as a basis.

What do they do?

If we use the organizational level of analysis from the previous model, the seventy-two entrepreneurs in our study provide a picture of the perception of the organizing process. This picture does not directly represent their behavior as organizers, but a series of parallel studies of overseas Chinese organizations allows this behavior to be brought into focus.[29] From these sources it is possible to propose models of organizational processes and structures that convey an impression of what such entrepreneurs do, at least at the level of managing and organizing. Although this is not the full gamut of an entrepreneur's behavior, it nevertheless illuminates an area so far only dimly lit.

Figures 8.2 and 8.3 propose patterns of determinacy that link the Chinese entrepreneurial organization to its ideological matrix and its host culture and traditions. The detail will not be given here, but an observation is appropriate: Although at a superficial glance it is possible to recognize universal characteristics of small business, it is difficult to explain them from universal determinants. This is a Chinese set of influences, and the challenge of generalizing from them to some universal "law" of entrepreneurship is daunting.

Why do they do it? How is the system perpetuated?

In summary, Chinese entrepreneurs act as they do for the following reasons:

- Societal insecurity heightens the need to accumulate wealth against an uncertain future.

- Responsibility for wider family welfare is strongly felt.

- Responsibility for wider family status and respect is strongly felt.

- Ownership is a source of status (and employment by someone else is disparaged).

Figure 8.2

The Chinese Family Business: Ideological Determinants of Organizational Structure

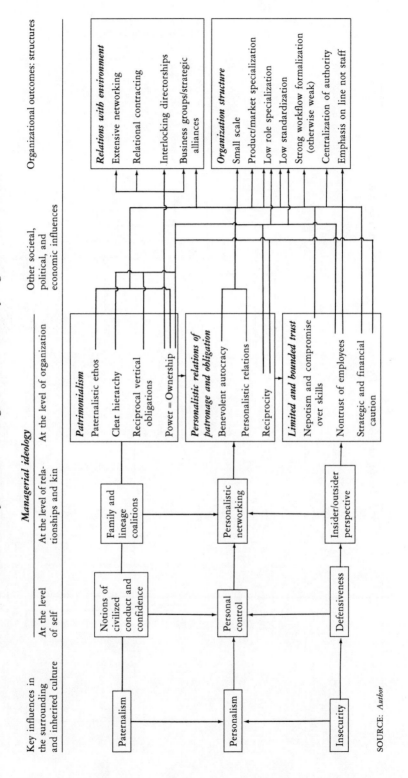

Key influences in the surrounding and inherited culture	Managerial ideology			Other societal, political, and economic influences	Organizational outcomes: structures
	At the level of self	At the level of relationships and kin	At the level of organization		

Patrimonialism
- Paternalistic ethos
- Clear hierarchy
- Reciprocal vertical obligations
- Power = Ownership

Personalistic relations of patronage and obligation
- Benevolent autocracy
- Personalistic relations
- Reciprocity

Limited and bounded trust
- Nepotism and compromise over skills
- Nontrust of employees
- Strategic and financial caution

Relations with environment
- Extensive networking
- Relational contracting
- Interlocking directorships
- Business groups/strategic alliances

Organization structure
- Small scale
- Product/market specialization
- Low role specialization
- Low standardization
- Strong workflow formalization (otherwise weak)
- Centralization of authority
- Emphasis on line not staff

Paternalism

Notions of civilized conduct and confidence

Family and lineage coalitions

Personalism

Personal control

Personalistic networking

Insecurity

Defensiveness

Insider/outsider perspective

SOURCE: *Author*

Figure 8.3

The Chinese Family Business: Ideological Determinants of Managerial Functioning

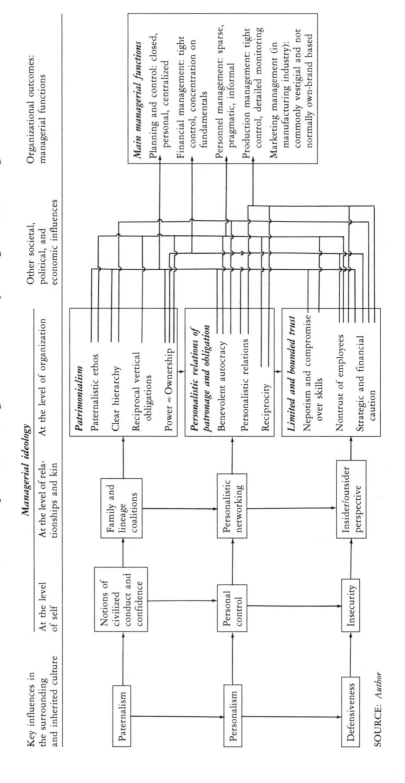

SOURCE: *Author*

- The society's moral ideal of caring for others can be most prominently exercised by those with wealth, thus providing an avenue for gaining respect.

- Inner self-confidence derived from Confucian role compliance is strongly felt.

All these features may be seen as reasons for risk taking and creative behavior by the individual entrepreneur. At the same time, certain features of the context might be seen as reinforcing the tendency for personal control of economic action. They partially answer the question, Why do entrepreneurs act as they do? The answers also overlap to some degree with the answers to the question about how the system perpetuates itself. The key components here are:

- The lack of trust. By placing clear restrictions on relations of exchange, and limiting them to specific social networks of direct relationship or clan or regional connection, the Chinese make the entire system reliant on specific individuals. The system is totally dependent on their personal characteristics and personal obligation bonds. Western-style transcendence to an impersonal ownership model destroys the coordination of the system.

- These key individuals need to command their field of action unequivocally, otherwise, in crude terms, they are not worth bonding to.

- The moral precepts of the society reinforce the specifically delineated networks of cooperation, while at the same time introducing notions of sharing, or welfare, and of civilized, nonaggressive competition.

These surrounding features, together with methods of practical encouragement such as socialization in the family context, assistance with capital raising, and apprenticeship techniques for entrepreneurial development, help to amplify the society's ability to produce entrepreneurs and refine their quality.

In light of this analysis, any theory derived to explain the entrepreneurship of the overseas Chinese must begin with the social conditions that so heighten the importance of ownership and the urge to control. There are clearly common denominators tying the overseas Chinese to other culturally defined and notably entrepreneurial groups, and a search for those common societal features is likely to be productive. Similarly, there are also likely to be common reinforcements to entrepreneurial ownership that explain its encouragement and perpetuation, and that can be defined as universals. In the middle, as it were, lie the personal characteristics of the entrepreneurs themselves, already seen as inadequate for explanation and now, in a wider context, visible as relatively small components of the total picture.

Conclusion

This chapter began with the proposition that the East Asian development model was as successful as that of the West, but followed a different route, a route more appropriately seen as a set of separate paths going in roughly the same direction and visible in at least three clearly separate instances—the Japanese, Korean, and overseas Chinese.

The movement toward modernity has not been accompanied in these cases by a noticeable rise in individualism. These societies are fundamentally paternalistic,[30] and operate to secure trust and cooperation by bonds of obligation rather than by legal contractual relations. A universal model of development is thus apparently not tenable. The entrepreneurial organizations are, as elsewhere, embedded in their societal contexts and cannot be comprehended without reference to those contexts.[31] The construction of a universal typology of organization is thus frustrated, and a more fruitful line of inquiry is how different recipes can be put together from different ingredients in varying contexts to produce effective structures for economic exchange and growth. By using the example of the family businesses so typical of the overseas Chinese, we gain some understanding of how the "embedding" occurs. Economic efficiency suggests how this particular organizational type flourishes and becomes representative of its society.

One universal conclusion remains tenable, the most fundamental of Weber's assumptions: A moral base in religious values is a necessary precondition for the legitimizing and encouraging of entrepreneurship, itself a necessary precondition for economic growth. For the overseas Chinese the moral base lies in a secular Confucianism and the resulting ethics that surround familism and communalism.

The example of overseas Chinese entrepreneurship suggests that a paradigm shift in entrepreneurship theory is needed, one that seeks to explain what entrepreneurs do, why they do it, and how a particular recipe for entrepreneurship becomes dominant. This middle ground is likely to be a more fruitful area of inquiry for those concerned with development than the psychological realm of individual characteristics, or the institutional realm of macro structures and policies.

Appendix

Societal Contexts

1. Dominant authority principles and structures
   Patrimonial rather than legal-rational administration
   Reigning without ruling
   Integrated vertical loyalties
   Obedience to role or person

2. Trust mechanisms between strangers
   Formal institutions of trust production
   Reciprocity of obligations
   Compliance mechanisms

3. Collective loyalties
   Primacy of kinship and other particular links over universalist principles
   Rational or emotional commitment to collectivity and leader
   Extent of individualism
   Primacy of horizontal or vertical loyalties

4. Skill organization and markets
   Formal certification of skills
   Individual ownership of general skills
   Labor-market control of skills by practitioners
   Integration of formal education system and practical skill training
   Standardization of payments systems across employers
   Significance of occupational identities

5. Developmental state
   Integration of economic and political elites
   State responsibility for and coordination of development
   Prestige of economic ministries
   Prestige of business careers
   Basis foundation of legitimacy of ruling elites
   Autonomy of ruling elites

6. State management
    Discretionary management of sectors and firms
    Control of credit and imports
    Control of labor organizations and wages

7. Financial integration
    Dependence of financial systems on domestic enterprises
    Organization and role of capital markets
    Connections between banks and firms

Structures for Coordination

1. Functional specialization and homogeneity
    Low self-sufficiency
    Low diversification of activities and markets
    Common training and experiences
    Market share goals
    Reduced coordination costs
    Permeability of legal/financial boundaries

2. Industry commitment to subcontractors, suppliers, and customers
    Long-term mutual dependence relations with
        subcontractors
    Risk sharing within sector
    Information and innovation sharing with subcontractors

3. Intermarket networks
    Long-term mutual support groups across sectors
    Preferential access to capital, materials, and customers
    Risk sharing across sectors
    Information sharing
    Joint ventures

4. Intersector coordination and planning
    Central coordination of activities and policies
    Preferential access to credit and suppliers
    Parameter manipulation
    Field augmentation
    Risk reduction

5. Authority principles and structures
    Personal or legal-rational
    Ownership and control relationships

       Centralization of decision making
       Dyadic, diffuse authority relations
       Formalization of rules and procedures

6. Employer-employee commitment
       Long-term membership of organization
       Seniority-based promotion
       Extensive firm-based training
       Enterprise unions
       Enterprise loyalty and identity
       Limited differences in rewards between strata
       Rigidity of employment boundaries

7. Roles and responsibilities
       Specificity and separation of individual posts
       Internal mobility and flexibility
       Collective performance standards and reward system
       Facilitative managerial role

Types of Enterprise Structure

Characteristic	Japanese Clan	Korean Patrimonial Bureaucracy	Chinese Family Business	U.S. Diversified Corporation
Specialization	High	Medium	High	Low
Industry commitment	High	Medium	Medium	Low
Intermarket networks	High	Low	High	Low
Intersector coordination	Medium	High	Low	Low
Personal authority	Low	High	High	Low
Employment commitment and enterprise solidarity	High	Medium	Medium	Low
Division of labor and responsibility between individuals	Low	Low	Low	High

Differences in Societal Contexts

Characteristic	Japan	Korea	Taiwan	Hong Kong	United States
Personal authority	Low	High	High	High	Low
Formal trust	Medium	Low	Low	Low	High
Nonkinship collective loyalty	High	Low	Low	Low	Medium
Certified skills and market-based wages	Low	Low	Low	Medium	High
Developmental state	High	High	High	Low	Low
State management	Medium	High	Medium	Low	Low
Financial integration	High	High	Medium	Medium	Low

Richard Whitley

9

The Revival of Small Business
in Europe

The analysis of relations between cultural and economic phenomena has relied on many different concepts and frameworks, which are rarely integrated, especially in the literature on cross-cultural management.[1] Sometimes "culture" seems to be invoked as a *deus ex machina* that accounts for large-scale economic transformations, as in some accounts of the newly industrialized East Asian countries, and sometimes it is reduced to aggregated responses to attitudinal questionnaires, as in many international surveys.[2] In accounting for variations in entrepreneurship, culture is often construed in terms of dominant values and beliefs that either encourage or inhibit risk-taking behavior. The emphasis here is on personal and collective values that legitimate and direct energies toward individual material goals or, contrarily, toward other activities.[3] This focus on individual and family priorities often ignores broader social structural incentives and barriers to new firm formation and economic development, such as those by C. Johnson[4] and others in discussing East Asian industrialization.[5]

Common values and beliefs, however, need to be integrated with other social institutions if we are to account adequately for economic change and variation, since personal preferences are organized through institutional frameworks in particular ways. Variations in these frameworks generate different results from the same predispositions, as the contrast of the overseas Chinese with those in China shows.[6] Consideration of the relations between culture and entrepreneurship in Europe, then, requires analysis of the institutional frameworks through which economic motivations and values are expressed and realized.

In addition to "culture" being understood in a wide variety of ways, the literature on entrepreneurship also reveals a considerable range of concepts and wages. In particular, the extent to which entrepreneurs are regarded as innovators varies greatly, with the followers of Schumpeter emphasizing the radical and discontinuous nature of entrepreneurial activities and others focusing more on their risky nature and the exploitation of uncertainty.[7] Most empirical analyses, however, equate entrepreneurial activity with new-firm formation, even though it is obvious that existing firms pursuing high-growth policies undertake considerable risk and often introduce major changes to markets. Certainly it is these fast-growing firms that seem to provide the bulk of new jobs in the small- and medium-sized enterprise sector.[8]

Because most of the research on entrepreneurship in Europe over the past fifteen or so years has concentrated on small-firm development and management, I shall focus here on variations and changes in the significance of small businesses in different European countries and regions without specifying their particular entrepreneurial qualities. Similarly, since explanations for these variations cover a wide variety of factors, and since institutional environments are clearly important, I shall interpret "culture" broadly and not restrict the discussion to personal values and beliefs. Thus, it is the relations between new firm formation, small business management and the wider societal context across Europe which are the central focus of this paper.

The analysis of the small-firm sector in Western European economies is bedeviled with a variety of definitions and indicators across nation states, time periods, and individual researchers. Additionally, the significance of recent changes in the size of the small-firm sector in many European countries is controversial. Some view the growth of small firms and self-employment in the 1980s as a short-term response to large-scale unemployment and large-firm restructuring;[9] others regard it as the product of a longer-term shift in economic structure that will have positive benefits.[10] However, there does seem to be broad agreement that, first, the decline in small-firm employment in manufacturing, which has been a marked feature of most European countries since the 1940s, has been reversed since the mid-1970s, and, second, that there are major regional differences in the rate of new-firm formation and in the types of new small businesses that have been established.[11] These regional variations have led to a number of studies of the particular characteristics of different regions that are correlated with varying levels of new-firm formation, to attempt to formulate aggregative indexes of regional entrepreneurship and analyses of the attractiveness of different regions for small businesses.[12]

The policy orientation of many studies, however, has led them to concentrate on the sorts of factors that could be influenced by government actions, so that the social processes by which such factors affect small-business growth are not always systematically analyzed. General correlations of rates of new-firm formation with rather *ad hoc* lists of socioeconomic variables need to be supplemented by more systematic accounts of the factors responsible for particular patterns of growth of particular kinds of small firms in particular socioeconomic contexts. Accordingly, after summarizing the statistical evidence about small-business revival in Europe and some general economic explanations of it, I shall discuss the reasons that have been put forward to explain regional and national variations, and consider some of the different types of small-firm growth that have been identified and the contextual features that seem to have been influential. These types can be compared in terms of their market scope, dependence, novelty, and level of industry expertise required—dimensions that help to highlight their differences and the particular processes that generated them.

The Statistical Evidence of Small-Business Growth in Europe

Statistical analysis of changes in small-business significance within countries, and of variations between countries, is fraught with problems, especially in the case of very small firms and the self-employed. As well as changing legal definitions and registration requirements, the nature of the small firm varies between industrial sectors and is defined in different ways by different nation states.[13] Additionally, in some countries, small "craft" businesses employing under fifteen people are separately classified and so omitted from some statistics. Because of these difficulties and the greater availability of statistics for the manufacturing sector, where size is usually measured by number of employees, most international comparisons focus on the importance of small- and medium-sized enterprises (SMEs) in this sector, although manufacturing typically covers only 10 percent of all small businesses in a country. For four European countries, though, the OECD has summarized the changes in the proportion of total employment found in firms of under twenty employees and those having over five hundred employees in selected years from 1972 to 1983.[14] As Table 9.1 shows, the figures suggest that the significance of small businesses has grown in Belgium and France, remained static in the Netherlands, and declined in Sweden.[15] Overall, small firms are more important in Belgium and the Netherlands than in France and Sweden.

In the manufacturing sector, figures for nine European countries show an increase in small-firm employment in Austria, Denmark, and France; Belgium, Finland, the Netherlands, and Sweden show relatively little change; and Luxembourg shows a slight decline. If we consider firms with up to one hundred employees in manufacturing industries to be "small," then most European Community (EC) countries, except for the Netherlands, Belgium, Portugal, and Greece, have increased the proportion of employment in this category. But, again, the percentage increases are not very large, except for the United Kingdom, which changed the basis of calculation in 1979 (Table 9.2).[16] In certain industries, however, the proportion of employment in small firms did increase substantially. In Sweden between 1969 and 1979, for instance,

Table 9.1

Percentage of Total Employment in Small and Large European Enterprises, 1972–1983

Country	Firm size	1972	1973	1975	1980	1981	1983
Belgium	1–19		20.6	21.9	23.8	24.3	25.0
	500 +		34.9	34.1	33.2	32.8	32.6
France	1–19	15.2		17.8	18.5	19.7	
	500 +	53.5		41.3	40.4	39.2	
Netherlands	1–19				25.5	24.6	
	500 +						
Sweden[a]	1–19		17.4	17.6	15.5	15.9	15.6
	500 +		53.2	54.6	59.6	59.1	58.6

a. *Includes public-sector enterprises.*
SOURCE: *Author*

Table 9.2

Percentage of Manufacturing Employment in European Community Enterprises with Fewer than 100 Employees, 1970-1984

Country	1970	1971	1973	1977	1978	1980	1981	1983	1984
Belgium						28.1	28.2	28.6	28.9
Denmark			31.3	34.3	34.0	33.0	34.3	35.1	
France		23.6		24.7	25.8	26.7	27.7		
West Germany[a]	12.5			15.9		15.4		16.0	
Greece	47.8				39.3				
Ireland			36.6			38.1			
Italy		53.1					59.0		
Luxembourg			18.0	17.9	18.5	19.2			
Netherlands					34.9	34.8	34.7		
Portugal	46.0						42.6		43.8
Spain							56.4	57.6	57.8
United Kingdom		15.5	15.3	17.1	17.3	18.8	20.3	22.0	

a. Excluding those employing fewer than 20 people.
SOURCE: Author

share of the labor force employed in small firms rose from 27.6 to 33.5 percent in mining and from 61.6 to 68.3 percent in textiles, largely because large firms reduced their labor force at a faster rate in recession than did smaller ones.[17]

This dominant role of large-firm labor shedding in the growing share of SME employment is a more general phenomenon (Table 9.3).[18] In most EC countries the SMEs in manufacturing did not actually increase the number of people they employed in the 1970s and early 1980s. Rather, the rate at which they reduced their labor force was lower than that of large firms. This was especially true of the United Kingdom and West Germany, where large firms reduced their employment by 36 and 23 percent, respectively. Much of the recent proportionate growth in employment in the small-business sector in manufacturing in Europe, then, is due to large firms responding to economic recession by reducing their labor force at a faster rate than SMEs.

Nonetheless, when compared with the steady decline of the small-business sector in European countries since 1950, this increasing significance of SME employment since the early 1970s is noteworthy, particularly when combined with the increase in new business registrations in some countries. In Britain, the number of businesses registered for Value Added Tax (VAT) has risen consistently since 1974, with new registrations growing particularly in the 1980s. The largest increases in the number of businesses occurred in the "other services" category—mostly in business services—which grew by 79 percent between 1980 and 1988, and in property, financial, and professional services (62.3 percent).[19] The construction, production, wholesaling, and transport industries also grew in the number of VAT-registered businesses. Of course, not all these registrations refer to new firms since some are subsidiaries or associated companies of existing firms and some simply reflect turnover growth that has pushed them over the VAT-registration threshold.[20]

A similar rate of growth in new business registrations in the 1980s in West Germany is discussed by C. Hull in his review of a number of studies of job generation by SMEs.[21] Between 1979 and 1984 the number of new registrations there rose from 156,000 to 298,000, although the exit, or "death," rate also rose from 138,000 to 254,000 over the same period, so the total rose by only 16.7 percent. However, since all changes of ownership have to be registered in Germany,

Table 9.3

Changes in Manufacturing Employment by Firm Size in European Community Countries

Country	Period	Firm size	Base year employment (000)	Final year employment (000)	Absolute change (000)	Percentage change
Belgium	1978–1983	SME[a]	267.9	228.7	–39.2	–14.6
		Large	548.1	446.9	–81.2	–14.8
Denmark	1970–1982	SME	156.9	142.7	–14.2	–9.1
		Large	261.7	215.8	–45.9	–17.5
France	1980–1984	SME	2,978.3	2,787.8	–199.5	–6.7
		Large	3,781.2	3,171.4	–609.8	–16.1
West Germany	1971–1985	20–99	1,049.6	1,073.5	+23.9	+2.3
		Large	7,346.9	5,635.6	–1,711.3	–23.3
Ireland	1973–1980	SME	79.6	92.3	+12.7	+16.0
		Large	138.0	150.2	+12.2	+8.8
Italy	1971–1981	SME	2,713.0	3,379.6	+666.6	+24.6
		Large	2,422.4	2,368.5	–53.9	–2.2
Netherlands	1960–1980	SME	524.0	389.0	–125.0	–24.2
		Large	751.0	641.0	–110.0	–14.6
United Kingdom	1971–1982	SME	1,159.0	1,078.0	–80.9	–7.0
		Large	6,299.8	4,040.9	–2,258.0	–35.9

a. SME refers to firms employing fewer than 100 people.
SOURCE: Author

many of these "births" are simply the result of takeovers. On the basis of other studies, Hull considers these to form about a quarter of the new registrations, although in the hotel and restaurant sector the share rises to over half. Overall, he suggests that recent changes in the proportion of small-firm employment in West Germany may be more a result of cyclical processes than of major changes in economic structures. Similar rates of growth in new-firm formation were found by Egbert Wever in the Netherlands between 1970 and 1980,[22] and also occurred in other European countries in the late 1970s and early 1980s, although there were strong regional variations within countries (which I will discuss later).

In summary, then, the past fifteen or so years have seen an increase in the rate of new-firm formation in many European countries, although this has been more marked in some than in others and has not been a steady growth in all sectors. Although small businesses have not grown as significantly as is claimed by some enthusiasts—and there is considerable variation in this between countries and regions—the postwar decline of SMEs appears to have been reversed and more new businesses have been registered in the past ten years than in previous decades. This increase in the rate of new-firm formation has not, though, led to a major shift in employment away from large enterprises toward small firms because most of the new businesses are in the service sector and employ fewer people than do manufacturing firms; their failure rate is higher than that of large firms so that the overall number of firms has increased at a lower rate than that of new firms; and some new firms displace existing ones, especially in declining industries and regions, so that the net effect on employment is neutral or negative.[23]

Economic Change and Small-Business Growth in Europe

As explanations for the reversal of the decline of the small-business sector in many Western European countries and the growth of new firms, a number of macroeconomic factors have been suggested, together with the changes in the structure and policies of large firms induced by these factors. Although authors differ in the importance they attribute to these, and there are few, if any, statistics that could be used for quantitative resolution of these debates, five major changes are commonly cited for the increasing importance of small businesses:

First, the decline of manufacturing employment and the growth of the service sector, second, the rise in unemployment since the early 1970s, third, income growth in the 1960s and 1970s leading to changing market structures for consumer goods, fourth, technological changes reducing the minimum efficient size of plants, and fifth, a move by many large firms to "disintegrate" their activities and rely on subcontractors to a greater extent.

Growth of the Service Sector

One of the most striking features of industrial societies in the postwar period has been the growth of service-sector employment relative to manufacturing, although part of this movement reflects the separation and "disintegration" of some service functions from manufacturing firms.[24] In particular, the increase in white-collar service occupations has been especially marked over the past three decades, both in the public and private sectors.[25] Since the service sector is more dominated by small firms than is manufacturing, this shift should have led to the growth of employment in small firms. For example, enterprises employing fewer than twenty people in the service sector in France accounted for 41.8 percent of all employees in that sector in 1986, whereas they accounted for only 18.8 percent in the manufacturing sector in 1980. Similar figures for the Netherlands were 35.9 and 10.7 percent in 1980, and for Belgium 33.8 and 12.1 percent.[26]

Although this shift has had some impact on overall firm size, it has not been as marked as might be expected and, in particular, has not led to a steady increase in the employment significance of small businesses since 1950.[27] This may be partly due to the emergence of large service firms in retailing, financial services, and the like in some countries, and therefore presumably some economies of scale in some parts of the service sector. Furthermore, the growth of the service sector obviously does not explain the growing significance of SMEs in the manufacturing sector in many countries.

Unemployment

The rise of unemployment in many EEC countries over the past ten to fifteen years has been seen as an important cause of the growth of small businesses in two ways.[28] First, it functions as a displacement factor, pushing people into considering self-employment for the first time, both by making them redundant and by reducing promotion prospects and the overall attractiveness of employment relative to setting up in business for oneself.[29] The significance of this can be seen in the study by Weitzel (cited by Hull[30]) in West Germany, which suggests that the proportion of businesses started by people who were unemployed or judged their previous employment to be insecure rose from 41 percent in 1981 to 61 percent in 1983 during a period of considerable increase in unemployment. Second, recession can increase business opportunities by increasing the supply of cheap second-hand equipment and making available market niches for new flexible, specialized firms with lower overhead costs than large enterprises. However, it should be noted that while unemployment may increase the potential supply of entrepreneurs it need not always increase the small-business share of employment, since new firms may simply displace existing ones by undercutting them, especially where markets are relatively limited and local.

The evidence for "recession-push" explanations of growth in small businesses is rather mixed. Whereas the high rate of increase in self-employment in the United Kingdom between 1979 and 1983 does seem attributable to the massive increase in unemployment during that period, and some studies of firms' founders have discovered close links between increases in unemployment and firm foundation rate in some regions,[31] others have found either little direct relation between these rates or a negative relationship.[32] These differences highlight the need to distinguish between different types of new-firm formation and the different contexts in which they appear, as well as the importance of considering perceptions of future employment prospects in addition to actual unemployment. Decisions to start a window-cleaning or car-repair business in a declining region are clearly different from those to set up a technologically innovative manufacturing firm in an economically booming region, and responses to unemployment differ considerably between different regions in the same country.[33] Thus, severe recession is a significant factor in the growth of new-firm formation, especially self-employment, in some of the industrialized regions of northern Europe, but it is by no means the only one.

Income Growth and Market Change

The third macroeconomic factor adduced as an explanation for the rise of small businesses involves changes in markets rather than the supply of entrepreneurs. The overall growth in disposable income in the industrialized world in the 1960s and 1970s, it is suggested,[34] has led to a shift in demand patterns away from mass-produced, standardized goods toward more varied and customized commodities that can be efficiently produced by small-scale producers. Flexible, specialized small firms can outcompete large enterprises in these growing markets and so their significance has increased. This growth in demand for specialized goods and services—although not necessarily a mechanical outcome of income growth—has certainly assisted the growth of the "industrial districts" model of firm organization in north-central Italy,[35] and probably also the increase in personal and other services firms. High-quality "craft" outputs are clearly encouraged by an increase in the demand for special goods and services and these are often supplied by small firms, particularly where an appropriate form of business organization can be established. The degree to which this change in market demand is responsible for the increase in new-firm formation in many European countries is difficult to establish, however, and the precise causal processes are not at all obvious.[36]

Technical Change

The microelectronic revolution and other developments in production technologies over the past few decades have both reduced barriers to entry in some manufacturing industries, by enabling smaller plants to be as efficient as large ones, and increased the flexibility of machinery. Coupled with the growth of market demand for specialized products, and hence the importance of flexible responses to changes in customer needs, these technical changes facilitated the growth of small firms by improving their adaptive abilities. Both in sectors where technological innovation is a significant competitive advantage, and in more traditional ones where new technologies can enhance flexibility, the small firm can capitalize on its inherent advantages of quick response to market change and ability to produce high-quality, nonstandard outputs to compete effectively with large firms relying on economies of scale to reduce costs.[37]

The development of relatively cheap electronic control systems has certainly reduced the minimum efficient size of plant in many industries and so facilitated small-firm entry to them. As M. J. Piore and C. F. Sabel point out, however, some large firms in the steel and chemical industries have also taken advantage of these developments to increase their flexibility.[38] Increased flexibility is not an exclusive property of SMEs and technical change per se cannot be guaranteed to increase the economic significance of small firms. To be effective in enhancing their competitiveness, it has to be integrated with changes in markets and in organizational forms such as the "industrial district" model.[39] Additionally, many of these technological developments occurred after the reversal of large-firm growth in the 1970s.[40]

Large-Firm Fragmentation

Finally, the resurgence of small firms has been attributed to the changing strategies of large enterprises, especially in the United Kingdom.[41] In addition to labor shedding on a large scale in the late 1970s and early 1980s, many large firms responded to the increasing uncertainties of market demand, technical innovation, and labor markets by disintegrating their operations and subcontracting, licensing, or franchising many activities.[42] Although this trend has encouraged the growth of small firms in complementary but distinct activities,[43] J. Shutt and R. Whittington suggest that these should more properly be regarded as dependent subcontractors rather than genuinely independent enterprises, in the same way that the growing strength of the unions in Italy encouraged Fiat to set up nonunionized, quasi-independent component companies in the 1970s.[44]

The extent to which large-firm fragmentation has been responsible for the increase in new-firm formation in the 1980s in the United Kingdom is a matter of some debate. Although there seems little doubt that many large manufacturing firms have increased their reliance on subcontractors and that the overall level of concentration in this sector has declined since the mid-1970s, the degree of disintegration does not appear large enough to account for the rise in firm births since 1979. Furthermore, the degree of dependence on a single large customer varies considerably between small businesses. For instance, only 17 percent of new East Anglian manufacturing firms in 1983 reported a high level of such dependence.[45] The majority of new-firm founders, in addition, tend to come from SMEs rather than from large firms, and most regional studies conclude that districts with a large number of SMEs are more likely to generate new businesses than those dominated by a single large employer.[46] Although the changing policies of large firms have increased the number of small firms, and many of these are undoubtedly closely linked to large-firm customers, it seems improbable that fragmentation strategies alone could account for a large proportion of new-business starts.

This brief survey of the major economic changes that have been adduced as possible explanations for the growth of small firms in Europe emphasizes two points. First, many factors are interrelated and cannot be considered in isolation. Second, there are substantial variations between regions and countries in the kinds of new firms established and in the processes that led to their establishment. With regard to the interdependence of economic factors, both market change and technical change are important in increasing the need for, and providing the means of, flexibility in manufacturing and so providing small firms with significant advantages. Similarly, economic recession coupled with the growth of service occupations and the growth of the demand for specialized non-standard services where capital requirements for new businesses are low can be seen as encouraging specialist employees to set up their own firms. Equally, recession and labor-market inflexibility combine to encourage fragmentation strategies in some countries; these, in turn, increase new-firm formation. Clearly, identifying discrete economic causes for variation in the growth of SMEs is a difficult, if not mistaken, task given the interconnections of many contributing influences and the lack of detailed explanations suggesting exactly how underlying processes account for specific changes.

Considering the second point, it is intuitively obvious that the socioeconomic processes leading to the establishment of small, new technology-based firms near Boston, Massachusetts, are different from those leading to the growth of self-employment in depressed industrial areas in northwestern Europe, and simple statistical correlations or regression equations describing general relationships are unlikely to reveal a great deal about such variations. However, a substantial amount of research into spatial variations in the rate of new-firm formation, and the significance of SMEs, has been undertaken in different European countries and this has led to some consideration of how varied institutional contexts do affect the sorts of new businesses that become established, as well as changes in their growth rates.[47] Some of the major conclusions of this work will now be discussed, before considering more general ways of analyzing types of new-firm formation and their relationships with contextual features in different situations.

National and Regional Variations in Small-Business Growth in Europe

The data presented in Table 9.2 suggest considerable national variation in the employment significance of SMEs in manufacturing between European countries. As mentioned earlier, though, cross-national comparisons are fraught with difficulty because of variations in the unit of analysis and coverage of businesses. The figures for West Germany, for instance, only include firms employing more than twenty people and so clearly underestimate the importance of SMEs there. Similar problems arise in comparing rates of new-firm formation since the British figures refer to VAT registrations but the German and Dutch ones refer to all new business registrations, including changes of owner-ship and name. Thus any detailed explanations of variation in the importance of small firms and in entrepreneurship, or in the rate of new-firm formation across countries, relying entirely on national statistics, may be limited in their validity and applicability.

Nonetheless, there seems to be general agreement that the signifi-cance of the small-firm sector in Britain is considerably less than that in most other European countries, and that large firms dominate the manufacturing sector to a greater extent in Britain and West Germany than elsewhere.[48] Small firms appear to be especially significant in Italy, Spain, Portugal, and Greece, and also seem to provide over a third of manufacturing employment in Denmark and the Netherlands.[49]

These national differences suggest that one major factor in the continued importance of small-business employment in the manufac-turing sector is the significance of agricultural employment and pat-tern of late industrialization. W. Korte suggests that the less-developed rural and peripheral regions of the European Community are in general characterized by overproportional shares of SMEs in labor-intensive industries because they cannot support larger enterprises.[50] There are, however, important regional differences within these countries, especially Italy, which highlight the need to distinguish between different kinds of small businesses and their relations to their socioeconomic environment.[51] Additionally, the ways in which agriculture and other primary industries are organized are important factors in explaining variations in the significance of small businesses. Independent peasant proprietors and share-croppers are more likely than agricultural laborers to generate a thriving small-business sector.[52] Sven Illeris, for instance, suggests that the importance of small firms in rural Denmark is related to the continued significance of the "self-employment life mode" among farmers, artisans, and fishermen there.[53] Economic independence in these areas is a dominant cultural ideal that is exemplified by many members of the community. These small-business owners function as role models and can provide information and skills informally for those starting new businesses.

At the other end of the distribution, the relative insignificance of the small firm in the British manufacturing industry is mirrored by the dominant position of the largest firms, who produced over 40 percent of net output in the 1970s.[54] Although the decline of SMEs in Britain continued into the 1970s, most of it occurred in the 1950s when concentration in manufacturing grew sharply. According to S. J. Prais, this growth of large manufacturing firms in the United Kingdom was assisted by the contemporaneous growth of financial intermediaries, such as pension funds and insurance companies, and their shifting of investment to industrial debentures and equities.[55] This change led to a massive shift of ownership of shares from individuals to financial institutions, which encouraged the formation of large industrial enterprises because of these institutions' preference for large firms' shares to maintain liquidity and reduce their likelihood of being locked in to ownership of a particular firm's shares. Risk-reduction goals thus channeled funds to the largest firms.

As Prais points out, this separation of financial institutions from individual industrial firms in the United Kingdom has not been evident in continental European countries and the financial pressures to amalgamate have been weaker there.[56] By 1972 the importance of firms employing over 40,000 people in the manufacturing sector relative to total manufacturing employment in the United Kingdom was twice as great as that in most other European countries and, in the case of Italy, three times as great.[57] An important component, then, of the decline in employment significance of SMEs in Britain in the postwar period relative to that elsewhere in Europe is the growth of the largest manufacturing firms, encouraged by the growth of financial intermediaries and their preferences for portfolio management rather than industrial involvement.[58]

The decline of the small firm in Britain has, however, been continuing for much of the present century, with the 93,000 establishments employing ten or fewer people in 1930 reduced to 35,000 in 1968,[59] and appears to have been more marked than that in other European countries, allowing for differences in large-firm growth.[60] This condition may partly be due to the persistence of part-time rural industries in France and other countries with substantial agricultural employment, but it may also result from broader characteristics of British society such as those discussed by John Child and his colleagues, by G. Ingham, and by others.[61] These concern the relatively low social status of work in a manufacturing industry relative to that in the higher civil service, the financial services sector, and the established professions; the preference for "pure" science and the traditional humanities over more practically oriented subjects and skills in the universities; and the low status of the "self-made man" in English culture since the late nineteenth century.

Although these features cannot be directly connected to new-firm foundation rates or other indicators of entrepreneurship, they are likely to encourage a preference for professional types of service employment in which prestigious, nontechnical, and diffuse competences guarantee access to specialist "staff" roles rather than direct management of one's own business. The recent decline of promotion opportunities and conditions of employment in the public-service sector and many large private managerial bureaucracies in Britain may have reversed this preference to some extent and, perhaps, led to an increase in the rate of new-firm foundation in the more prosperous regions.[62]

Turning to consider regional variations in SME significance and rates of new-firm formation, substantial differences exist in the importance and growth of small firms, and in the types of new businesses that are established, in different locations. Four major kinds of European regions have been identified by economic geographers and others as sites of distinctive patterns of small-business activity.[63] First, there are the old industrial regions dominated by large firms in the same or related industries such as iron and steel or shipbuilding. Examples include much of northern England and Scotland, northeastern France, and southern Belgium. In these regions small firms are not very important sources of employment and the rate of new-firm formation is relatively low. High rates of labor shedding have not led to the formation of many new businesses because of the combination of depressed market conditions, traditional dependence on a small number of large employers, and relatively low levels of education and managerial expertise among the population.[64] Where new firms have been started, they are often in different sectors where existing skills and knowledge are of little use because of large minimum-efficient plant sizes in traditional industries and, if successful, they often displace existing ones.

In contrast, diversified growing metropolitan regions, especially the suburbs and semiurban areas on the outskirts of dominant cities, manifest high rates of new-firm foundation in both manufacturing and service sectors.[65] Here the growth of market opportunities, coupled with high proportions of managerial and technical personnel, high levels of education, easy access to startup capital through home ownership, and the existence of a diverse range of industries and firm sizes, encourage new businesses,[66] especially when employment prospects in large firms appear less attractive than they once did. Many of these are in the new service sectors where close links to clients are especially important. As Pom Ganguly shows, the southeast of England generated about half of all new VAT-registered firms in financial, professional, and other services between 1980 and 1983, although containing only 30 percent of the country's population.[67]

Two types of rural regions have been distinguished by R. Aydalot, P. Keeble and T. Kelly, and others.[68] The first are largely agricultural areas in attractive parts of the country with at least one major city with some manufacturing activities, where public and private service facilities are of a high standard, and communications with the rest of the country are good. In these regions manufacturing activities in the urban area are relatively diverse and decentralized among medium-sized firms rather than in a few large plants. Such "sun-belt" regions have attracted relatively well-educated and managerially experienced immigrants from the metropolis and elsewhere who often set up new businesses in new sectors, sometimes in association with staff at the local universities. However, specialized, craft-based firms linked to high-quality technical education facilities are also important and provide "incubators" for new firms.

The second type of rural region, the peripheral rural region with no large urban focus, few substantial service facilities, and poor transport connections, is characterized by considerable unemployment and underemployment, few manufacturing firms, high rates of emigration by many of the skilled and young people, and a largely artisanal small-business sector serving local markets.[69] Limited growth, relatively low educational levels and facilities, and the lack of managerial experience and expertise limit new-firm formation in these regions, unless they become the focus of state-inspired investment activities that encourage subcontracting on a significant scale. This seems to have happened in southern Italy in the early 1970s, although it is not clear how well this small-firm growth will be sustained.[70]

Some of the factors affecting these different rates of new-firm formation and small-business vitality have been combined by D. J. Storey into an index of regional entrepreneurship in Britain, but as R. Whittington has pointed out, many of these interact and the precise causal relations are not always clear.[71] In his regression analysis of these factors relating to the rate of new VAT registrations in different U.K. regions, Whittington found that the best predictors were recent changes in unemployment, the incidence of home ownership and, negatively, the proportion of the labor force in manual occupations. It is clear, however, that these connections do not hold in the same way in other countries, and that they may change as circumstances alter. New-firm formation in manufacturing industries in different French regions, for example, was quite strongly negatively correlated with average firm size in 1974 but this relationship had weakened by 1983 because the nature of the regions exhibiting high rates of firm creation in the earlier period had altered.[72]

Three Configurations of New-Firm Formation

This sort of correlation analysis may be helpful in suggesting contributory influences on new-firm formation rates in different areas, and in rejecting alternative factors, but it clearly cannot provide detailed explanations of variations in these rates, nor can it identify the processes by which broad background characteristics impinge upon them. This requires more sustained analysis of particular cases or models that would reveal the particular combination of underlying processes responsible for them and the more general factors that appear to be significant in different situations. These models constitute distinctive configurations of new-firm formation generated by certain interdependent features of their contexts. Three distinct models have recently been identified by Storey and Johnson: the Italian industrial district; Birmingham, England; and Boston, Massachusetts.[73] The first has attracted the most academic attention and required the development of novel forms of combined economic and sociological explanations[74] in a comparable

manner to the institutional cross-cultural accounts of the successful
Chinese family business discussed by S. G. Redding in this volume.

Italian industrial districts specialize in the production of high-quality
consumer and engineering goods for competitive national and international markets. The districts are composed of large numbers of small
firms, often with fewer than ten employees, who form extensive
networks of interdependence and reciprocal trust. Production is frag-
mented between these specialized small businesses, which continually
negotiate new contracts with a wide variety of buyers and suppliers
and so encourage high rates of flexibility and generate constant pressure
to reduce costs and improve quality.[75] Links with consumer markets
are provided by merchants in provincial cities who buy the finished
goods and suggest new designs and products. Economies of scale are
achieved by those businesses that create specialist niches in particular
production processes and have a considerable number of customers
for their specific output.

As A. Amin emphasizes, an essential element of exchange relations
in these industrial districts is their personal and direct nature.[76] They
are not impersonal market exchanges between anonymous partners
dealing with standardized, fixed commodities, but rather negotiations
between personally known parties that cover design, materials,
technologies, prices, and delivery. Sharing of new ideas and business
information through the principle of reciprocal benefits ensures
rapid diffusion of best practices and market needs. The close geographical proximity of, and intensive family involvement in, these
small businesses facilitate information flow in a manner comparable
to that of Hong Kong.[77]

Between 1971 and 1987 nearly all the growth in the number of
plants in northeastern and central Italy came from those with fewer
than ten employees (81 percent), as did a third of the total growth
in employment.[78] The dominant role of small firms in this part of
Italy reflects the success of the industrial-district model in both the
traditional consumer-goods market and in newer engineering ones.
Increasingly, firms making advanced machinery for the ceramic, textile,
and farm-machinery industries, including industrial robots, have
become an integral part of these industrial districts, thus making them
more technologically self-sufficient.[79] The increasing and successful
use of advanced technology in the smallest firms of this "third Italy"

demonstrates their ability to develop and innovate and the general viability of the industrial-district form of business organization.[80]

The success of Italian industrial districts, especially in the 1970s, has encouraged a number of studies of their origins and reasons for their continued vitality, as well as discussions of their generalizability as a model of flexible specialization in manufacturing.[81] Explanations of their development in this part of Italy focus on the particularly favorable combination of contextual features there. The first of these was the dominant pattern of agricultural organization in the late nineteenth and early twentieth centuries, which combined sharecropping with the involvement of large extended families in agricultural production and selling. Because landlords had a strong interest in ensuring that their land produced the maximum possible, they exerted considerable control over the size of the productive unit, the family, and tried to match this to the size and type of farm. This ensured that sharecroppers and, later, tenant farmers had to manage the family labor force and the whole agricultural enterprise producing cash crops in a way that the daily agricultural laborer did not. Large and complex family units thus dominate areas where this form of sharecropping was prevalent, whereas the nuclear family is more characteristic of southern Italy where waged agricultural labor dominated. These large families are important elements in small firms today, both as means of raising capital and as providers of flexible, committed labor.

The second important feature of northeastern and central Italy is the relative independence of the provincial cities and towns and their significance as local centers of trade, commerce, and finance. They served as the coordinating foci for agricultural trade, connecting the farms to the wider national markets, and often were the loci of extensive artisanal and later factory production. Many of the new industrial entrepreneurs of the 1960s and 1970s started as traders and the patterns of interdependence and trust between producers and merchants that developed over many centuries have been transferred to newer industrial activities. It is important to note in this context that industrialization in this part of Italy was a relatively slow process until the 1950s and 1960s, and it has not resulted in widespread geographical mobility. Thus, earlier patterns of social organization and control have survived and conditioned the development of new economic activities. This situation can be contrasted with the more rapid industrialization of northwestern Italy, where large firms and plants dominate and many workers have migrated from the south.

Large plants have been prominent in parts of the "third Italy" as well, but not dominant over a long period, and they often were branches of major firms centered elsewhere. These factories have been seen as a third important ingredient of the industrial districts because they provided some training in mechanical and other skills. In some cases their closure resulted in workers taking over plants and running them as cooperatives. The essential point here is that the institutional context of such closures encouraged skilled workers to establish their own businesses instead of searching for employment elsewhere, as has occurred in other European regions. Thus, the new skills were not lost to the area.

Finally, most writers emphasize the important role of local technical schools in producing skilled workers and technicians and developing new skills. These schools were established in the early twentieth century in most towns and have been important training institutions for the local communities. Allied to this feature is the positive and supportive role of local links and governments. Both financial and political institutions are committed to local economic growth through SMEs in these areas, and appear to be well-integrated into local networks.[82] Linda Weiss has also suggested that the national government has played a major role in stimulating small-business ownership in Italy, but this does not account for the particular prevalence of small firms in this part of the country.[83] In general, it is the widespread diffusion of managerial, technical, and commercial competences throughout these local communities—and not just among a narrow stratum—that seems to be a key feature of their success. As S. Brusco points out, about one in ten of the economically active population in Emilia-Romagna is self-employed or running a small business so that virtually everyone has direct experience of the associated problems and procedures for dealing with them.[84] This broad diffusion of knowledge and skills together with established networks of trust and reciprocity have created and reproduced a collective capacity for efficiency, flexibility, and innovation that is very competitive, in a manner comparable to business networks in Hong Kong.[85] It is this collective capacity of industrial districts as a system of organization that makes them effective, rather than particular features of individual businesses.

The second model of small-business growth suggested by Storey and Johnson is typified by the city of Birmingham in Britain. This type of model is also found in parts of Belgium, France, Italy, and Germany, but is most noticeable in the traditional manufacturing regions of the United Kingdom because of the sharp decline in large-firm employment there. Essentially, Storey and Johnson suggest that in such regions of economic decline small-firm growth is more an expression of industrial restructuring than of dynamic resurrection. The withdrawal of many large firms from unprofitable markets and the increasing reliance on subcontracting for many components and services—although this has not gone as far as some suggest[86]—have both created opportunities for new businesses and pushed some former employees into considering self-employment for the first time. Because this restructuring has affected managerial and technical employees to a greater extent than before, the potential supply of knowledgeable entrepreneurs is greater. The birthrate of new firms is therefore likely to be greater than in more depressed regions dominated by large branch plants where the proportion of highly educated managerial and technical staff is lower. The limited overall impact of this sort of small-firm growth is exemplified by the low rate of adoption of new technologies and the predominant dependence on local markets rather than national or international ones, in strong contrast to the Italian industrial districts. It is more a matter of reducing average wage costs and increasing labor flexibility than leading to an industrial renaissance.[87] Many of the new firms replace existing ones rather than forming the foundation for new economic activity.

The third type of small-firm growth is typified by that found in Boston. It is also found in parts of Europe, such as in the Munich area and around Cambridge and other parts of southeast England, but to a much more limited extent. It reflects the growth of new technology-based firms in the Boston area since the mid-1970s, which in turn boosted the growth of service businesses. These high-technology firms are closely linked to the concentration of higher-education institutions in particular areas and, in the case of the United States, high levels of state expenditure on military and space exploration products and services. D. Keeble and T. Kelly note the importance of universities, especially in Cambridge, Massachusetts, in explaining the spatial concentration of new firms in the computer electronics industry as well as the high rate of new-firm founders coming from very small businesses.[88] However, as G. P. Sweeney points out,[89] prominent science-based universities on their own are not sufficient to generate large numbers of new technology-based firms.[90] More significant are a technological orientation and close links between research universities and firms as well as considerable decision-making autonomy in the industries and infrastructure of a region. Direct state support of research-based small firms, or indirect support through subsidies to aerospace companies, and encouragement of technological innovation in small businesses also appear to be important factors in new technology-based, small-firm growth.

These three distinctive patterns of small-firm growth, and their dependence on different combinations of contextual features, emphasize the need to distinguish between types of new-firm formation and their contributory factors if we are to understand better the reasons for variations in small-firm growth over geography and time. This, in turn, requires the identification of the key dimensions that differentiate new firms so we can identify the distinctive processes involved in their formation and development in particular circumstances. These dimensions can be developed from the three distinctive configurations just described, together with other accounts of different types of SMEs such as those by S. Brusco, Roy Rothwell, and others.[91]

New-Firm Formation and Types of Small Business

In his brief discussion of small firms in Italy, S. Brusco distinguishes between the three main types—traditional artisan, subcontractor, and members of industrial districts—in terms of their relations to their markets.[92] In particular he emphasizes two dimensions: the degree to which they are dependent upon a single or small number of customers and are only indirectly linked to the final market, and the scope of the market—local, national, or international. While the traditional artisan has a variety of customers, he is limited to a local market. Subcontractors depend on a few large customers that tend to be locally based. The industrial-district firm, as we have seen, is not dependent on a single large customer and often produces goods for the international market.

These market-based distinctions can be usefully supplemented by two others. First, there is the degree of novelty and innovation involved in the product or service being provided or the processes by which they are produced. This is related to the degree of technical uncertainty about products and processes and the extent of standardization of outputs. It is also connected to the type of knowledge required for new-firm formation—in particular, to the reliance on systematic research into materials and processes as contrasted with more craft-based knowledge. Thus, Rothwell distinguishes between traditional firms in long-established areas, such as garments and metalworking, which make incremental quality and design improvements; niche-strategy SMEs in the scientific instrument and specialist machinery industries, which develop novel products and processes largely with existing formal knowledge and developing craft skills; and new technology-based firms (NTBF), which rely on new formal knowledge, often self-generated.[93]

Second, the degree to which specialized knowledge of the industry and involvement in its business networks are required varies considerably between types of small firms. Many personal and household service activities, for instance, can be undertaken by the self-employed on their own without extensive industry knowledge. On the other hand, firms offering specialist services to businesses or those manufacturing complex products need considerable knowledge of how their industry functions and of suppliers and customers. As a result, new firms in these areas are likely to spin off from existing ones rather than develop from outside the industry. Generally, the more industry and business specific knowledge and contacts are required, the more new-firm formation is dependent on current employers' structures and practices, and the likely prospects for that particular sector, rather than more general societal processes.

The importance of these two dimensions lies in their implications for risk/reward relations and entry barriers. Novelty and technical uncertainty increase the risks associated with new-firm formation but, equally, imply high rewards if technical and market difficulties can be overcome. They usually require considerable technical and business knowledge and so restrict entry. More standardized products and services are easier to provide and markets for them are more predictable but, by the same token, competition is usually greater and entry barriers are lower. Both risks and likely rewards, then, are lower.

The need for high levels of industry and business knowledge and contacts raises entry barriers and therefore limits the ability of outsiders to move into an industry. Competition from outside is thereby reduced but may still be high internally, as the example of the Italian industrial districts indicates. The more interdependent and specialized such firms are, however, the more likely is such competition to be tempered by cooperation and trust, as reciprocity and information sharing are essential to efficient operation. Individual-firm risk is thus attenuated, but industry risk remains considerable. On the other hand, the need for relatively low levels of sector knowledge and contacts facilitates entry and so competition from new entrants is high, especially when technical skills are low, as in much retailing and franchising.

Novelty and the need for considerable industry-specific knowledge can be combined with market dependence and market scope to generate sixteen possible kinds of small firm, although many of these combinations seem unlikely. A high level of dependence on a single large customer, for example, obviously restricts the scope of the market for a firm's outputs, at least in the short term. Similarly, highly complex and innovative goods and services are unlikely to be produced by independent small firms with few industry contacts or little industry expertise. Such firms are also not likely to sell goods or services to national and international markets because that usually involves networks of contacts and access to market knowledge. These exclusions result in eight major types of small business distinguished by these four dimensions, listed in Table 9.4.

The traditional artisanal and personal/household service firm provides relatively standardized outputs direct to the final consumer without relying on intermediaries or extensive networks. Market scope and dependence are low. Examples of this type are the small shopkeeper, machine repairer, and hairdresser. Entry barriers are low and new-firm formation is highly influenced by changes in macroeconomic conditions together with general social predispositions. Second, craft-based services that rely on networks and require extensive knowledge of the industry to produce the final product or service for a predominantly local market form a distinct type of small firm characteristic of the construction industry—the specialist craft business. New-firm formation here is dependent on the organization and control of skill production and certification as well as economic cycles and the contracting practices of large firms.

Third, where products and services are highly dependent on direct, personal contacts between their providers and consumers, so that markets are essentially local, but are relatively novel and innovative—

Table 9.4

Types of Small Business

Market scope: Low

Novelty and industry expertise/networks	Market dependence	
	Low	High
Low innovation and low industry expertise	Traditional artisan Personal and household services	Franchisees
Low innovation and high industry expertise	Construction Wholesaling	Subcontracting component manufacturers
High innovation and industry expertise	New business services	Subcontracting business services and new technology-based firms

Market scope: High
Market dependence: Low

Industry expertise and networks required	Novelty	
	Low	High
Low	Unlikely	Unlikely
High	Italian industrial district firms	New technology-based firms

SOURCE: *Author*

such as some business services—small-business growth is clearly dependent on the development of the requisite skills and on the inability of
large firms to meet the considerable demand for them. Often this
kind of firm is created by people who became frustrated as employees
of large firms or are unwilling to move geographically to further their
careers. Typically, they are not totally committed to small-business
ownership and are able to move back into employment if their firms
fail. Risks are therefore relatively low for this group, and new-firm

formation depends on their perception of the relative attractiveness of remaining with their current employer or establishing their own business. In Illeris's terms, they exemplify the career-life mode.[94]

Where dependence on particular large firms is high, three further types can be distinguished. The fourth type of small business consists of franchisees who often have relatively limited technical and business skills and provide a relatively standardized service for final consumers. Fifth, the dependent subcontractor is part of a network of specialist component manufacturers for final assembly plants. The growth of both of these types of small firms is obviously highly dependent on large firms' policies and practices, as the example of Japan demonstrates.[95] Because of the greater technical complexity of many subcontracting businesses and their membership in industry networks, barriers to entry are greater than that of most franchisees. In general, as J. Curran and J. Stanworth point out, franchising is a relatively low-risk means of starting one's own business and is particularly likely to be attractive to those lacking the confidence, information, and capital needed to found an entirely new enterprise.[96] It is less likely to attract people who value independence above all else since it is essentially a joint venture between franchisor and franchisee. The sixth type of small firm is typified by the innovative business that spins off from a large firm on the basis of guaranteed orders and assistance for a limited time. If it becomes successful it usually seeks broader markets.[97]

Small firms producing goods for national and international markets are likely to be quite specialized and to require considerable industry expertise and access to networks. Thus high market scope and low market dependence tend to be associated with high levels of industry knowledge and membership of trust networks. The major difference between many firms in the Italian industrial districts and new technology–based firms (NTBF) lies in the degree of innovation they are committed to and their reliance on highly educated staff. Both compete internationally and are not usually dependent on a single large customer, at least not after being successfully established for some time. It seems unlikely that large numbers of these businesses will appear in countries where strategic decision making is highly centralized within industrial sectors and within state and financial institutions, such as Britain. The high risks associated with NTBF are likely to inhibit new-firm formation unless the state or another large customer provides some slack in procurement policies to encourage small-business growth, or the state redirects substantial financial support toward small business as in postwar Japan[98] and Italy,[99] or the local economy is sufficiently buoyant to provide a variety of employment opportunities if the new ventures fail. Both of these types of small business require high levels of knowledge about whom to contact for advice, contracts, and supplies. They are therefore likely to be relatively specific to particular localities and greatly dependent on high levels of what P. Bourdieu calls social and cultural capital, that is, highly valued competences and social status that can be transformed into control over resources.[100]

This point highlights the importance of the social distribution of knowledge and access to networks of help, finance, advice, and customers/suppliers for many kinds of small business. In particular, those requiring high levels of education, knowledge of markets, products, and processes, and the capacity for mobilizing networks have high entry barriers and depend on perceptions of opportunities and costs among those with considerable social and cultural capital. These perceptions are, of course, considerably affected by the practices of large firms and state agencies as well as the dominant prestige hierachy of different kinds of employment and self-employment in a society.

Where market risks, at least in the short term, are reduced by large-firm contracts, new-firm formation is obviously facilitated, especially if founders have considerable industry experience. Thus, Mike Savage and his colleagues point to the rapid growth of small firms in pro-ducer and consumer services in Berkshire, England, during the 1980s, many of which are spin-offs from larger companies and have major contracts with them.[101] They suggest that this reflects the development of occupational and entrepreneurial careers among the highly technically skilled staff of large firms, instead of organizational careers. Where these skills are in high demand, and firms increasingly subcontract such services, separate labor markets develop around them and mobility between firms, and between employment and self-employment, grows. If successful, such spin-offs naturally try to broaden their customer base and become less dependent on a single client. In the case of southeast England in the 1980s this tendency has probably been encouraged by the growth of two-income households and the increas-ing disparity of house prices between the regions, which restrict geographical mobility and hence diminish the attractiveness of a corporate career that requires it.

In the case of specialized, interdependent businesses providing more traditional goods and services, the nature of the social and cultural capital required is more specific and local. The extensive reliance on networks of contractors in the Italian industrial districts, for example, clearly excludes those from outside these districts and places a premium on reputations for quality and efficiency among the members of the networks. Although the basic technical skills may be generally available from the technical schools, and are theoretically generalizable and transferable, they require additional knowledge of how to apply and develop them in the particular context of the industrial district if they are to be the basis for a successful business. This knowledge is, of course, typically acquired by working there or from family experiences. New-firm formation rates may, then, be high within these districts, but entry from outside will be highly restricted.

Businesses in traditional sectors that do not rely on extensive networks, or that depend on local contacts for local markets that can be acquired in the industry at relatively low levels, such as construction, have low entry barriers and constitute the most common type of new-firm formation. Traditional artisanal activities, small-scale retailing, and franchising with low capital requirements are examples of this kind of small business. High unemployment rates push those with little cultural and social capital into these forms of self-employment, especially where there are already many small businesses. Racial discrimination also pushes many ethnic minorities into self-employment, although the degree to which this happens and the sector entered vary considerably between them. These variations depend on the pattern of immigration in terms of levels of education, prevous work experiences, and urban concentration, as well as family structures and dominant values.[102]

Generally, we would expect the "push" factors encouraging small business growth to have the most effect on these kinds of firms because they require relatively little knowledge and are not highly dependent on the ability to mobilize networks of assistance and obligation. They are also attractive to groups seeking upward mobility in societies and communities where independent business ownership is valued highly, especially when compared with working as a skilled employee. Thus small-scale retailing and artisanal self-employment remain attractive to many French people[103] and to others adhering to the life mode of self-employment, especially in rural areas.[104] On the other hand,

where substantial knowledge, skills, and contacts are required, the rate
of new-firm formation is dependent on the social and geographical
distribution of such "capital," the relative attractiveness of employment and career structures in large firms, and the existence of institutional policies and practices for reducing technical and market uncertainties associated with small businesses. In particular, the accessibility
and commitment of local financial and political institutions, together
with trustworthy sources of market information, seem crucial.[105]

Conclusion

This discussion suggests that the increasing significance of small
businesses in many European countries since the mid-1970s is as much
a result of change in large firms' policies and practices as it is a consequence of an upsurge in entrepreneurship in Europe. Changes in the
economic, social, and technical environment have led to a considerable
reduction in large-firm employment and a growth in subcontracting
in many industries. These changes have been especially marked in
Britain where new-firm formation rates have increased considerably
over the past fifteen years. Other general factors encouraging small-
business growth have been the expansion of the business and personal
services sector, which usually has more small-business employment
than manufacturing; the growth of demand for high-quality, nonstan-
dardized consumer goods, which are often produced more efficiently
by small- and medium-sized firms; as well as the development of new
production technologies that have reduced the relative economies of
scale achieved by large plants.

Variations between European countries in the significance of small
firms have been attributed to a variety of influences, ranging from
the growth of large financial institutions in Britain to the political
importance of small businesses in France and Italy. Undoubtedly, a
major factor has been the much greater importance of agricultural work
in many southern European countries, especially its organization
around peasant proprietors. This trend has resulted in the development of rural and semirural industries with many small firms of the
traditional artisanal type, and has also ensured that family structures,
values, and attitudes associated with self-employment have been
reproduced, as in the case of many Mediterranean immigrants to the
United Kingdom.[106] Attractive rural regions containing at least one

major city with a number of different industries and not dominated by large plants have also been associated with considerable small-business growth, especially that generated by domestic immigrants. In general, regional studies have emphasized the importance of industrial diversity, low plant-concentration rates, high levels of formal education and training, and considerable managerial expertise with access to capital through home ownership in generating high rates of new-firm formation. Conversely, declining economic regions dominated by a few large branch plants with little local subcontracting and low levels of formal education and managerial expertise have displayed low rates of small-business growth, at least in northern Europe.

The success of the Italian industrial districts emphasizes the importance of considering overall patterns of economic and social organization in analyzing small-business growth. Correlational analysis alone is insufficient to explore the reasons for the expansion of this particular form. Instead, patterns of historical continuity and development, particularly with respect to family structures and trust relationships, have combined with urban autonomy, local technical educational institutions, and particular trading relationships to generate a highly flexible and effective system of small-firm networks, which appears to constitute a viable alternative both to the large, diversified firm in Anglo-Saxon societies and to the Japanese reliance on "relational contracting."[107]

The significance of this form of economic organization lies not only in its viability and distinctiveness (as Becattini[108] and Bellandi[109] both point out, Marshall discussed industrial districts many years ago), but also in its development in a particular socioeconomic context and the key role of interfirm networks. As a distinctive system of organizing small businesses—or "business recipe"[110]—the Italian industrial districts highlight the importance of considering how small firms are interconnected and the nature of the whole system, rather than simply focusing on the growth of individual businesses. They also emphasize the need to analyze the social processes through which such business recipes become established and successful in particular institutional environments. This analysis involves going beyond the simple listing of associated factors that appear to be correlated with them and formulating a model of the important generative mechanisms that shaped them in particular ways in particular contingent circumstances. This, in turn, requires a way of characterizing different kinds of small-business growth, and ways in which small firms are organized, that facilitates the identification of such mechanisms and of the contingencies affecting their operation. Distinctive patterns of new-firm formation and small-business organization need to be distinguished as a preliminary step toward such an analysis, using the kinds of market, output, and expertise dimensions that have been suggested here.

Walter D. Connor

10

The Rocky Road: Entrepreneurship in the Soviet Economy, 1986–1989

The USSR Mikhail Gorbachev inherited in late winter 1985 was a state-socialist economy par excellence. While the Soviet model had been modified, or incompletely implemented, in many of the East European states, leaving some room for limited individual/private enterprise for those who would choose to live and work outside the state sector, those who did so in the USSR operated, in virtually all cases, outside the law. Not for Moscow was the private farm sector of Poland or Poland's licensed small-scale shopkeepers, craftsmen, and the like. Not for Moscow were the complicated leasing arrangements and other legislation that had accommodated a whole range of entrepreneurial activity in Hungary since the introduction of the New Economic Mechanism in 1968.

Some Soviet economists had, over the years, suggested that concessions to individual moonlighting (for example, taxi drivers, repairmen) or small-scale collective enterprise (for example, leasing of state cafés and snack bars to families) would not damage socialism and could only improve the woefully deficient service sector. Until Gorbachev, however, these arguments had fallen on deaf ears. "Private enterprise" amounted to two things: the legal sale, by collective and state farmers, of produce grown on their auxiliary private plots at market prices and the large, illegal, but loosely policed second economy of moonlighting repairmen, builders, and so forth.

Gorbachev's perestroika, based on a grim diagnosis of the state and prospects of the Soviet economy if left unaltered, finally made some room, among its broad provisions, for what the economists had advocated. As early as late 1985–early 1986, however, generally positive discussions of the contribution some private enterprise might make to the economy became mixed with a focus on eradicating various forms of speculation and illegal activity that generated "unearned income"—somewhat echoing the "crackdown on corruption" policies of the short-lived Andropov period. A Politburo session on March 27, 1986, addressed the bugbear of "unearned income," and *Pravda*'s report of the meeting indicated that "plans call for the implementation of legal and other measures aimed at eradicating unearned income from illegal operations, theft, bribery, speculation, and unauthorized use of state-owned transport, machines, and equipment for personal profit."[1] This prose was not especially auspicious, it seemed, for those who hoped the proenterprise and anticorruption themes could be disentangled. Indeed, the first application came in a decree and resolution in May 1986 against "deriving unearned income," which led in the summer of 1986 to what one economist called a pogrom against private hothouses, gardeners, and feedlots[2]—enterprises in the farm sector that were generally legal. In retrospect, what looked like antienterprise moves from the top probably reflected something more complex—a combination of compromise on matters of real policy conflict and, for the reformers at least, a "clearing of the decks" for proenterprise moves to come. This *enabling legislation* comprised a draft law on cooperatives in October and a decree on individual labor activity in November.[3] Cooperatives were set in motion under the draft legislation. At the local level, where licensing took place, there was evidence aplenty of bureaucratic resistance and restriction, leaving the central authorities in the uncharacteristic posture of demanding legal support for the rights of entrepreneurs and reminding local authorities that the enabling rules meant that all business that was not specifically prohibited was to be permitted.[4]

Given the new internal political atmosphere, the provisional quality of the legislation, and their novelty, fitting the cooperatives and individual workers into the economy's provisions was, and remains, controversial. What sort of taxes would be paid by private sector enterprises and those who worked in them? Early guidelines, which applied more or less through 1987–1988, aimed at encouraging the cooperatives to go into business and to expand. "Corporate" tax rates were set at 2–5 percent of income for a start-up two years, then at about 10 percent for succeeding years.[5] Yet fears that cooperatives would not take this cue to reinvest, but instead would pay out large wages to their members and exacerbate social tensions, led to proposals to tax the individual earnings of cooperative members once they rose above 500 rubles per month (roughly a bit more than twice the average state sector wage), at a higher and more progressive rate than earnings of state sector employees. It was proposed that the personal income tax system, which had left many low earners off the rolls and had been progressive only up to a rate of 13 percent, tax private sector incomes of 1,500 rubles per month or more at a marginal rate of 90 percent![6] Rejected by the Supreme Soviet in May 1988, this eventually gave way to the draft law on income taxes of April 1989, which equalized rates for state, cooperative, and individual earners and peaked at a 50 percent marginal rate for those earning 1,500 rubles and over. To some degree, this reduction represented a balancing of corporate and individual tax concerns—in February 1989 new guidelines, which slightly raised taxes on cooperatives' income, at least partially satisfied the Finance Ministry's concerns about the "take" from the new forms of activity.[7]

The tax regulations supplemented and gave more concrete meaning to the final law on cooperatives, enacted in mid-1988, some twenty months after the draft.[8] That law legitimated a rather broad range of cooperative activity, from restaurants and small-scale trade to consulting businesses, production of consumer goods, and the like. It came, however, after a major expansion of cooperatives, which along with the high real incomes of the cooperatives and their members—a mark of the massive overhang of demand for goods and services—had made for controversy. A resolution of late December 1988 restricted cooperatives' room for maneuver in two ways. In the words of two researchers who follow the development of cooperatives closely, the first article

> established that cooperatives do not have the right to engage in certain activities. Some of these activities, such as making weapons, munitions and narcotics it seems sensible to prohibit. But the same article banned a large number of medical activities which had become important in the cooperative sector, such as obstetric services or treating patients with infectious diseases or drug addiction, and also prohibited the manufacture of wine and vodka and the right to publish. Hence, for the first time, the state defined what areas of the economy it wanted

to monopolize. The second article defined a number of areas in which cooperatives could legally operate only when they were under contract with state organizations. These include buying and processing secondary materials and providing certain kinds of medical services not otherwise banned.[9]

A more detailed examination of the December resolution indicates a mixture of "normal" government concerns simply made explicit and those, such as restrictions on publishing, that accord poorly with reform.[10] The resolution, as well as the public moods to be discussed later, underlines the continuing ambiguity of cooperatives and new patterns of entrepreneurship in the Soviet economic, political, and social context.

Growth

The rapid growth of the number of cooperatives, as well as the number of full- and part-time workers in cooperatives and the number of individual operators, gives some indication of demand in three senses: previously unmet consumer demand for the goods and services provided by the private sector, demand for entrepreneurs (the emergence, under the new enabling laws, of would-be entrepreneurs), and a "demand" for the legal protection the new laws provide, under which previously illegal operators can emerge and various holders of large amounts of hidden rubles, much of it ill-gotten, launder their money as cooperative income.

The rapidity of the growth is shown in Table 10.1, which presents a rough picture of the number of cooperative enterprises, the number of full-time members and employees, and the total number of workers in cooperatives, including part-timers and moonlighters.

Given the limits of statistics, it is unlikely that the picture presented is complete or entirely accurate, but the trends it reflects are real enough. Cooperatives grew very rapidly over a rather short but tumultuous period in recent Soviet history. Full-time employment in cooperatives effectively grew tenfold between the beginning and the end of 1988. Estimates of the value of cooperative output, 350 million rubles in 1987, rose to 6 billion rubles in 1988 and 12.9 billion for the first half of 1989.[11] The contribution of cooperatives to national income was 0.1 percent in 1987, 1.0 in 1988, and an estimated 2–3 percent

Table 10.1

Growth of Cooperatives in the Soviet Union, January 1987–July 1989

	Number of cooperatives	Full-time members and employees	Total members and employees
Jan. 1, 1987	—	15,000	—
Oct. 10, 1987	8,000	—	88,000
Jan. 1, 1988	14,000	155,800	—
Apr. 1, 1988	19,539	245,700	—
June 1, 1988	32,561	458,700	
Oct. 1, 1988	—	777,000	
Jan. 1, 1989	77,000	1,500,000	
Apr. 1, 1989	100,000	—	1,951,000
Jul. 1, 1989	133,000	1,660,000	2,900,000

SOURCE: *Carla Kruger, "Early Swallows of Transformation: Alternative Property Forms in the Soviet Union under Perestroika"* *(Department of Political Science, Massachusetts Institute of Technology, September 1989); Anthony Jones and William Moskoff,* *"New Cooperatives in the USSR,"* Problems of Communism *38, 6 Nov.–Dec., 1989 27–39.*

in 1989, with the nearly 3 million people involved representing only a small percentage of a labor force of around 130 million.[12] Part of the growth is real and part is attributable to rising prices charged by cooperatives; both are responses to a long-starved market and the pressures of taxation politics discussed below. Nevertheless, some of the growth must also be understood as a shift of enterprises, human resources, and capital to the private sector, or the investment of previously idle funds and unused time to take advantage of new opportunities. As one close student of the cooperatives explains,

> In 1988, cooperatives produced goods and services worth about six billion rubles, as compared with only 350 million in 1987. Nearly half of the total in 1988 was earned in the production of consumer goods (1.5 billion rubles) and through the rendering of everyday services (1.3 billion). Still, by the end of 1988, cooperatives contributed only about 1 percent of total Soviet national income and 0.4 percent of consumer goods output. Part of the reason that cooperatives' share of total Soviet output has grown as quickly as it has is because many

cooperatives are not really new enterprises but former state enterprises that have been taken over—either wholly or in part—on leasing or on other arrangements by a cooperative collective (often a group of employees of the former state enterprise). This practice became especially popular in the last quarter of 1988, and it was responsible for the creation of 37 percent of the total number of cooperatives that year—a share that accounted for a staggering 57 percent of total cooperative output for the entire year. This is in part explained by the fact that cooperatives that are attached to (*pri*) a state enterprise tend to be larger and have easier access to equipment and inputs through the "sponsoring" state enterprise or ministry, than do totally independent cooperatives.[13]

To these numbers can be added the smaller, but not inconsiderable number of *individual operators*—those who function in individual labor activity, largely in activities ranging from repair to photography and independent taxi service to the manufacture and sale of handicrafts.

Table 10.2

The Number of Individual Operators in the Soviet Union, May 1986–January 1989

May 1986	100,000[a]
May 1987	80,000[a]
Jan. 1, 1988	437,254
July 1, 1988	512,100
Oct. 1, 1988	627,603
Jan. 1, 1989	800,000[a]

a. Numbers are approximate.
SOURCE: *See Carla Kruger,* "Early Swallows of Transformation: Alternative Property Forms in the Soviet Union under Perestroika" *(Departement of Political Science, Massachusetts Institute of Technology, September 1989),* 45.

As Table 10.2 shows, their number grew about eightfold between mid-1986, when the new enabling legislation was passed, and the beginning of January 1989.

Vague constitutional provisions had offered backing for individual operators before 1986. Nevertheless, the generally antiprivate climate and the difficulties of detection and enforcement meant, and continues to mean, that at the level of individual enterprise much remains underground. Rather than pay taxes at special rates, individual operators typically pay a high fee for a *patent* (license) to operate—a compromise that reflects, probably accurately, the state's recognition of the impossibility of keeping track of actual earnings. This fee, however, plays a role in the decision of many operators to ply their trades in a nonregistered legal limbo.

Some Soviet sources estimate that as many as 18 million people are engaged in nonregistered activity of this sort, especially in the repair of items ranging from shoes to appliances and cars to apartments.[14] The value of such services may be as much as 35 percent of the value of services provided by the state sector.[15] In many ways, this is, of course, a limited sector, as individual activity in a large economy must be. Most of these activities are carried out by individuals who *individual'shchiki* (moonlight) while holding state sector jobs.

It is in the larger-scale cooperative sector that the growth of entrepreneurship can be expected to affect the economy in a new sense. As we have seen, that growth has been impressive, but, even over the short period being discussed, different types of cooperatives have experienced varying rates of growth. In 1988 *public-catering* cooperatives (essentially, cooperative restaurants and cafés) grew by 100 percent and *trade-procurement* cooperatives (retailing) grew fourteenfold.[16] In 1989, however, both these categories fell off dramatically—the number of trade-procurement cooperatives grew by only 38.0 percent from January 1 to June 30, while the number of public-catering cooperatives declined by 13.2 percent.[17] In contrast, in the first half of 1989, construction, design, and surveying cooperatives grew by 338.2 percent and research and development cooperatives by 123.1 percent. Thus, the slow growth categories of 1988 became the fast movers of January–June 1989, and vice versa. Trade-procurement and public-catering cooperatives may have reached, in many areas, a saturation level. Just as likely, though, is a slowdown in growth due to public concerns over speculation, price-gouging, and other perceived cooperative "abuses," as well as envy of the high incomes of the "privateers." The growth areas, especially construction, design, and survey services, as well as computer-based research and development activity, do not involve "street-level" retail contact with the public. The clients are mainly state organizations; contracts regulate a process that goes beyond individual instances of selling and buying; the whole business is less public and less controversial.

All in all, predictions of the further growth of the cooperative and individual enterprise sector must, at the end of 1989, remain very conditional. The variety of meanings the term *cooperative* can take on—from a truly new business to leasing arrangements that take, for instance, an old state café or repair shop from the state to the cooperative sector—further complicates projections. The likelihood is that near-term growth will take place mainly in leasing arrangements and start-up cooperatives that deal with institutions, enterprises, and organizations rather than the public—in other words, a continuation of 1989 patterns. In 1989 the reality and perceptions of the consumer market and living standards in the USSR worsened. The essentially middle-of-the-road conservative line taken by Gorbachev and then Prime Minister Nikolai Ryzhkov on December 12–13, 1989, in projecting plans for 1990–1992 showed a sensitivity to a public mood that is increasingly hostile to cooperatives and what they seem to represent. Thus, the most publicly visible types of cooperatives are likely to be under the greatest pressure and grow the least; pressure of this sort will continue as long as Soviet citizens show a preference for rationing by coupon over rationing by price.

Diversity and Regional Variation

Although the growth of private enterprise has been impressive, it has also been uneven. Entrepreneurs find parts of the USSR more fertile than others. The Baltic republics—Estonia, Latvia, and Lithuania—with their Western heritage and memories of both political independence and market economies, might be expected to generate more cooperative and individual enterprises than Russia itself or predominantly Moslem Central Asia. Large cities are more likely to breed entrepreneurship than rural areas; single-industry towns (such as mining areas and oil-drilling settlements) are more likely to produce different patterns than more traditional, mixed settlements.

The evidence of varying degrees of development and intensity of private activity is striking and runs in the direction expected. In the Baltic, especially the Nordic/Protestant Estonian and Latvian republics, entrepreneurship is relatively abundant. In October 1988, 94 out of 10,000 Estonians and 62 out of 10,000 Latvians worked in cooperatives. Southward and eastward, the situation was very different: in the predominantly Moslem republics of Tadzhikistan, Azerbaidzhan, and Turkmenia, the numbers were, respectively, 16, 15, and 10 per 10,000.[18] Per capita cooperative output varied as well: the USSR-wide average was 21 rubles (presumably for all of 1988)—roughly equal to a tenth of the average monthly state sector wage. Latvia and Estonia markedly exceeded the average, at 71 and 64 rubles, while Tadzhikistan and Turkmenia were far below, at 7 and 6 rubles.[19]

While such figures ignore the active underground economy in the Moslem republics, a second economy in which Slavic settlers have little part,[20] underground economic activity is symptomatic of the command-administrative economy in general. It is not, politically or economically, a substitute for the rationalized, legalized opening of such an economy to aboveground independent activity. And it does not, over the long run, offer much to the growing numbers of Central Asian youth, who can no longer be absorbed by the underground economies of the region.

Tax policy varies as well—the February 1989 policy guidelines on corporate taxation left republics free, within the limit of a 40 percent ceiling, to set their own rates and vary them by type of cooperative enterprise and so forth.[21] Later 1989 legislation eroded the ceiling, however, and left republics with options to tax revenues at a higher rate.[22] These options have been exercised, producing a somewhat bewildering variety of business climates across the USSR. Given that authorities are accustomed to the existence of legal (if small-scale) private agricultural production through the private subsidiary plots of collective and state farmers, cooperatives hewing close to agriculture seem less unusual and their taxes are relatively low: in Azerbaidzhan, 3 percent on livestock products and 10 percent on crops; and in Belorussia, a flat 5 percent on income from agricultural output.[23]

In the Russian republic, agricultural cooperatives are taxed at a 10 percent rate; goods production at 30–50 percent; scientific-technical cooperatives at 35–40 percent. Public-catering cooperatives are subject to a 40–50 percent rate, while what must be seen as true middlemen, those trading and purchasing at cooperatives, are taxed at 60 percent.[24] In the Central Asian Kirgiz republic, these middlemen are taxed at a rate of 80 percent.

These differences index varying degrees of state discomfort with anticipated profits and varying degrees of distance from traditional Soviet or Marxian notions of "productive" activities. Food and goods production is production. Restaurants offering roughly what is on their menus, a pleasant atmosphere, and good service (things absent from most state restaurants) are not, somehow, really productive—much less so those that buy and sell goods, even though the state has never contrived to run an adequate retail sector.

The exception is the Baltic. In Latvia cooperatives are taxed at 10–15 percent; in Estonia, 10–20 percent, but with a rate of only 5 percent on goods produced for export. Latvia and Lithuania allow the deduction of investment funds from total income to determine what is taxable. Such bottom line provisions vary across republics as well, but wage expenditures are generally included in the total corporate income tax.

The present range of rules reflects numerous compromises. During the earliest phase of the development of cooperatives, taxes on their incomes were set very low (about 5 percent) to encourage start-ups and reinvestment of profit. In itself controversial, this policy led to fears of rapid enrichment by the members and employees of cooperatives and resulted in differentiated individual income tax rates for state employees and cooperative members. When this arrangement was replaced by a uniform rate running up to 50 percent, pressure again developed to tax the cooperatives' income per se at higher rates. Those rates, obviously, were much higher in the less-entrepreneurial Russian Republic and in Central Asia than in the Baltic. In most of the USSR, though, the atmosphere in which cooperative entrepreneurs operate combines public resentment at the incomes earned and the prices charged (and, one suspects, the fact that some people can pay the prices that most cannot afford) with an official tendency to control, level, or contain the new businesses. Many reject the rough logic of the market forces finally set in motion after long prohibition, having witnessed worsening shortages and perceived a fall in living standards, at the same time that cooperatives, despite all obstacles, have expanded.

Public Opinion

Few indeed can be the Soviet citizens who remember Lenin's New Economic Policy (NEP) of 1921–1928—the last time a high level of private enterprise was tolerated in the USSR. Few of today's citizens can be totally untouched by the history and crude economics that were instilled until the Gorbachev period; the "NEPmen" were exploiters and speculators who unjustly enriched themselves and were thus justly banned as the country embarked on the "building of socialism" under Stalin.

The experience of the Soviet people since then—more than half a century separates the onset of the first Five Year Plan from the coming of Gorbachev in 1985—has been varied: quiet times, tumultuous times, poverty, relative affluence, rather pronounced inequalities in wages and salaries, and especially the long period under Brezhnev when these inequalities were moderated.

The Brezhnev period, while no doubt justly denounced by Gorbachev's reformers as the time of "stagnation" (*zastoi*), produced in most of the Soviet population a mind-set, which in two senses has complicated perestroika and the place of cooperative entrepreneurship within it. The first evokes a rather deep, if general, egalitarian reaction, intolerant of people within one's range of vision doing significantly better than oneself. The second reflects an incomprehension of the market, the dynamics of supply and demand, and how these will naturally—in the absence of state control or intervention—play themselves out.

Given that entrepreneurs will make large amounts of money and thus enhance visible inequality and that the dynamics of a nascent market allow them to do so, the massive growth of cooperatives in 1988–1989 in no way betokens a resolution of the moral ambiguity of cooperatives in the public mind.[25] Those in cooperatives—whether well-publicized restaurants with high-priced menus, small plants producing goods, or those that were really engaged in middlemen activities; those that were honest as opposed to those previously illegal operators who laundered rubles by declaring them cooperative income—all ran up against a public attitude criticized by *Izvestiia:* "Don't anybody dare live better than I do."[26] For many workers, disconnected from the market for their product and paid whether that product was consumed or not, it seemed unjust that others were given the opportunity to profit by meeting a demand sharpened by long-term shortages. Typical was the complaint of a tractor driver on a state farm: when his tractor was down, he made only 2–3 rubles a day compensation, while "someone making bra-fasteners" could earn 100 rubles in the same day.[27]

Deep-rooted feelings are at work here. The tractor driver, if he is typical, is paid by the furrow, by the acreage plowed, not by the food produced and marketed. He may earn more by plowing more but shallower furrows. This is normal, "the way it is." That the cooperative must produce the bra-fasteners, that it does so because there is a market and earns money from the market demand, is strange, not really normal or immediately self-justifying. To many, demand does not justify high prices or high incomes from those prices—not to people whose social studies lessons in Soviet schools never explained the functions of the market, save to condemn them.

To the degree that retail trade cooperatives (effectively, private stores) replace state outlets—charging higher prices but having available the goods the state stores lack—puzzlement and public anger over market operations in a situation of excess demand will grow. Much evidence, including that from research on recent Soviet émigrés to the United States who have seen the alternative,[28] indicates that many Soviet citizens do not realize that the state retail price of bread, meat, dairy, and other products was heavily subsidized, much lower than production costs. Even when they do realize, the idea that lines might be shortened, that it might be rational to raise prices, or that the artificially low prices guarantee shortages generally falls on deaf ears. People believe that they are due a full supply of these goods at the prices quoted in the near-empty state stores. That many goods are available only from entrepreneurs at higher prices is not "logical"; it is unjust, underlining the inequality among would-be consumers, those with cash aplenty and those without.

Even some convinced reformers have had trouble with the unleashing of new inequalities by entrepreneurs. In 1987, Tatiana Zaslavskaia allowed that incomes from private labor might reasonably rise to double or triple the average state sector rates but that nine times those rates would be excessive.[29] Workers and other ordinary citizens can hardly be expected then to applaud. Workers, especially those in heavy industry, "signed on" to the social contract: the state provided the job and the materials and set the pay. It rendered the workers protected, but dependent, as the logic of Soviet industrial organization dictated they were supposed to be. The system did not encourage initiative; it tolerated sloppy work, and it insulated workers from the consumers of their product. There certainly are abuses in the cooperatives: many benefit, after the long drought, from the effective monopolies they enjoy in their area of enterprise; some are run by "crooks"; some do sell, into the economy of shortage, goods as shoddy as unavailable state manufactures at several times the state price. Grievances against the cooperatives go deeper, however.

Entrepreneurial skills and their exercise, Soviet citizens were taught for a long time, are wrong, morally inferior; they are "capitalistic," "bourgeois." Many believe this. They believe that family-contract lease farming in the countryside will bring back the kulaks and that "cooperatives in cities will revive the bourgeoisie."[30] They do not like this. Many fail to make the connection between the hard work and the long hours that many coooperative workers put in and their earnings. The understanding of the relationship of work to reward is weak.

How much inequality of earnings can be tolerated under the Soviet type of socialism? How much is consistent with broad notions of social justice in workers' minds? Although one cannot be precise, a likely answer is not very much. Those who have relied on state sector employment for their security and rewards have also come to expect the state to ensure that, in their field of social vision, no ordinary people make a great deal more than they do. Economists who argue that justice requires differentiation of reward, that much state sector income is unearned, and that high cooperative earnings should be equated with the quality and quantity of result-producing efforts find that their words generally make no impression. Their moral and economic arguments, against ingrained popular convictions, count for little. As one put it, "apathy and indifference, theft, disrespect for honest labor coupled with the aggressive envy of those whose earnings are high even if they are acquired honestly" have taken on "mass proportions."[31]

An envious leveling-down egalitarianism surely complicates perestroika's rocky course. Whether one sees this egalitarianism as bad or accepts it as fair (and with it the legitimacy of people's desires not to have their mediocrity underlined by the greater rewards of others), it is a social and political fact. Economists dismiss it at their peril. Those who, like the sociologist V. Z. Rogovin, have egalitarian sympathies also understand how deep such feelings go and how difficult they are to reconcile with perestroika. He quotes the revealing words of a middle-aged woman, employed in the state sector presumably at a modest income, about a contemporary who earned more by "growing spring vegetables" for sale (a commentary in itself on perceptions of affluence and how it can be gained): "I don't want to live like her; I want her to live like me."[32] If many share this conviction, it is stony soil indeed on which cooperatives aim to grow and develop legitimacy.

In fact, more systematic studies indicate that these views are widespread. Surveys of opinion among Muscovites show that as many men believe cooperative entrepreneurs are "reprehensible" (25 percent) as believe they are worthy of "respect and support" (23 percent), with a remaining 47 percent seeing them as neither better nor worse than other people. Women, likely to do more of the shopping, express a harsher view (38 versus 4 percent, respectively), with 33 percent seeing them like other people in their moral qualities.[33] Asked to compare the quality of goods, the time spent shopping, and the prices charged in cooperatives with those in state sector providers of goods and services, Moscow men rated quality higher in 44 percent of the cases, the same in 9, and lower in only 6 percent, with plentiful "don't knows." But 78 percent of the men rated prices higher, as opposed to only 1 percent who said they were lower. Women, again, were generally harsher.[34]

Data, available only in fragmentary form, from a spring 1989 study of urbanites in the capitals of the fifteen Soviet republics, offer other evidence of how marginal cooperatives remain in the public mind:[35]

- Only 45 percent agree that the development of cooperatives is "necessary."

- 56.3 percent have never patronized cooperatives.

- 58.8 percent say the quality of cooperative products "does not suit" them.

- 91.9 percent say the *prices* charged "don't suit" them.

- 76.7 percent agree that it is "possible" that cooperatives can cause a deficit of cheap goods and a rise in prices.

Of the respondents, 34.4 percent would "under no circumstances" want to work in a cooperative, and 27.4 percent found it "hard to say," in contrast to 28.7 percent who indicated they would like to moonlight in one, 6.7 percent who would like to leave their state sector jobs and go into a cooperative, and 2.9 percent who already worked either full- or part-time in one.

The worsening Soviet economic situation of 1989 and 1990 may well encourage a more favorable view of the cooperative sector as a locus of employment. Feelings in principle are one thing; the pull of more money in accelerating inflation and the push of threatened shutdowns of many typically overstaffed state sector plants are something else.

Over the long run, though, the development or failure of entrepreneurship on Soviet/Russian soil will depend heavily on the broad culture—the supports it offers or withholds from entrepreneurial activity. Here, beyond egalitarian impulses and a weak understanding of market logic, we might add another thought on culture and its constraints: a "culture of work," as well as a culture of entrepreneurship, is rather poorly developed in both the historical tsarist Russian and the contemporary Soviet social contexts.

In its Russian variant, the Eastern Orthodox moral and ethical tradition put little emphasis on individual conscience, moral striving, or the development of the individual internal controls that would guide moral behavior relatively autonomously and focus effort. Methodical work, well done, as its own reward—in a sense, the Protestant ethic— did not figure so prominently in this culture as in others farther west. The serfdom of the agrarian majority, which extended well into the nineteenth century, and an emancipation that subjected the "free" peasants to taxes and other obligations created an effective external compulsion. Few, under such a regime, could develop the internal controls that are essential to the entrepreneur's organization of effort. (Within this value system, financial or material rewards were not motivators of independent work. Punishment for nonperformance, yes—but for the legally unfree majority of the population, recognition of extra performance in enhanced rewards played a minor role. The shape of the economy left little space for acquisition- as opposed to subsistence-oriented activity on one's own. The "natural state" of all save the few was to be poor.)

Various elements of the Soviet institutional and moral structure altered this pattern in some aspects, but far from totally. Compulsion and organization again played major roles in Soviet economic development, as a peasant mass was changed into a largely blue-collar one; independent economic activity, in large measure, was criminalized. The generally poor base from which industrialization was launched at the end of the 1920s and the high reinvestment rates lowered living standards: material motivation was again survival, not prosperity.

In contrast, both Soviet policy and the labor hunger of a wasteful economy guaranteed employment; the threat of losing a job as an incentive to develop good work habits did not exist, effectively, from 1931 until just recently. And even though the Soviet economy has presumed to pay according to the "results of work," these results have depended on so many people's actions besides a given individual's—a factory's suppliers, the other workers, piece-rate setters—that a linking of individual effort and results to pay has been anything but direct or reliable.

Finally, though much has rightly been made of the Soviet economy's bias toward quantity over quality in production, the culture of work has not actually focused on maximum production but on exceeding (only by a certain amount) the stated production target—for the individual worker, the division, and the whole plant—thus earning bonuses while avoiding an upward ratcheting of the plant's target. Building in slack in production goals has been as important as investing labor in meeting and exceeding them.

These practices and procedures common to the vast majority of the Soviet work force for more than two generations have created a rather specific work culture that links expected employment security with a low level of effort, along with modest material expectations (conditioned by perennial shortages) and egalitarian notions. Entrepreneurship, as we have already seen, is anything but integral to the social and cultural system built around the Soviet culture of work. No one should underestimate how deeply this culture is rooted in the USSR or the difficulty even an expanding entrepreneurial sector will have in fixing itself in, or displacing, that culture.

Cooperatives, Entrepreneurship, Economic Crisis

Beyond the tensions of culture, values, and a sense of social justice that finds it hard to accommodate entrepreneurial habits, practices, and results, the problem of fitting cooperative enterprise into an overwhelmingly state-run economy has proved very large. The state, as a ministerial and bureaucratic culture, has been tenacious in its hold on the grass roots—a tenacity encouraged by the ambiguity of the economic and moral justification of private enterprise.

The state administers prices and decrees that cooperatives, seeking to purchase imports, must pay much higher prices than state enterprises.[36] The same cooperatives then, aiming to recover the higher costs,[37] become targets of criticism for the prices they charge. Cooperatives pay a great deal more than state sector competitors. A standard truck, priced at 17,000 rubles for state customers, for example, can cost 70,000 rubles to a cooperative.[38] Other examples abound, but the real costs of acquiring inputs demand, as well, energetic, time-consuming legal, sometimes even quasi-legal, dealings to get what is needed—and the cooperatives understandably want to pass on all these costs to customers.

Cooperatives that need significant capital face the general problem that the USSR lacks a banking system to provide it: the economy, after all, has not accommodated such "venturing." Fledgling cooperatives may thus find start-up long delayed: in mid-1989, for instance, perhaps 100,000 cooperatives, already legally registered, were not operating, many because of a shortage of finance.[39] Small, short-term loans are the rule, which is not surprising given the novelty of the state bank's involvement in financing of this sort. Such practices, though, hardly provide the nurture needed to stabilize cooperatives.

The broader problem, however, is that the state bureaucracy is set in its prejudices and practices toward control over people's behavior and is reluctant to support the new types of economic activity now legitimated by central authority. The actions of local authorities in the early phases of the legalization of cooperatives reflected, to some degree, not only incomprehension—Why were "capitalists" being allowed to set up businesses? Could Moscow be serious?—but a fear or confidence that such license would soon be revoked. When policies thus changed back, what local party or state official would welcome his past encouragement of speculators and profiteers on his turf? Pleading that one's acts followed the policy line of a given time has frequently been an effective defense when the line changes.

Many officials were thus confident early on that permissive policies would be reversed. They certainly placed numerous obstacles in the way of would-be entrepreneurs. Arbitrary grounds for denial of licenses were established in many areas, essentially according to local whim, despite public statements from the USSR *Prokuratura* that what was not forbidden by way of cooperative or individual enterprise was to be permitted.[40] Licenses have been denied under various pretexts, with the authorities creating paper barriers of all sorts, not authorized in the national legislation, which aspiring entrepreneurs must cross before becoming legally registered. Paradoxically, as central control under Gorbachev has weakened, the center has less power to limit local authorities to a definite number of criteria, which, once satisfied, must result in a legal license. The criteria are multiple and variant; the outcome, region by region, is uncertain.[41]

Existing cooperatives have been closed down when local authorities have decided on a hard line. One, making plastic costume jewelry, earned nearly 500,000 rubles in its first four months and was closed by officials who declared its earnings "illegal."[42] Another, installing natural gas service, was closed even though it was managing to provide hookups about nine times faster than the state organization could.[43] In some cases, cooperatives with a very successful start-up period found it advisable to dissolve, in anticipation of unwelcome attention, even persecution, from the local state or party officialdom. One cooperative, manufacturing pantyhose, generated 200,000 rubles for its four members over a four-month period. It closed down on its own, in anticipation of police attention to returns that were immense by Soviet pay scales.[44]

Even now, many broad bureaucratic restrictions are imposed on cooperatives, which remain, despite their numbers, marginal, alien to official habit and custom and conceptually odd and difficult to include in what is still a statist economy. Entrepreneurial achievement, even when all the customers are happy, is no sure defense in these circumstances. In a much publicized case, the Moscow cooperative Tekhnika successfully acquired recyclable scrap materials, sold these for hard currency to foreign customers, and set about filling the computer gap that bedevils Soviet institutions as much as individuals. Some of the computers purchased went gratis to the foreign trade ministry and the state material and technical supply agency (*Gossnab*) as compensation for their roles in facilitating the deal. Tekhnika then sold other computers to an Academy of Sciences institute and to the Justice Ministry at a healthy profit; so healthy, in fact, that press coverage of the whole exercise was largely negative. Thus, a performance that linked entrepreneurship with the earning of hard currency and supplying of deficit goods to Soviet institutions was lost sight of in accusations of profiteering.[45] Lack of computers is normal; the sorts of profits earned in altering this normality, necessarily large ones, are readily regarded as abnormal and excessive.

All in all, this is a formidable list. Bureaucratic interference, a liability to predation by "protection" racketeers who flourish in the larger cities, the advisability of bribes to local officials, "voluntary" contributions above the taxes paid on corporate income to local government, cultural institutions, and the like—all indicate the continuing marginality of the new entrepreneurs in political, legal, and cultural senses.

Added to this, however—and likely to test sorely the prospects for a broadening and deepening of the private sector in the Soviet economy—is the growing conviction of the Soviet public and Soviet leaders that their economy is falling into an unprecedented crisis This conviction is backed by no small amount of evidence. Wage increases unbacked by goods to give them the quality of real earnings press harder on supplies. While shortages of a wide range of goods result in rationing in many areas, multiple problems plague the railroad system over which most goods move, keeping any increased production from reaching consumers.

This is a portrait of the Soviet economy at the end of 1989—one in which the chase after goods grows more desperate and the convertibility of the ruble into goods ever more questionable; one in which massive suppressed inflation is beginning to break through in official price increases, though without any general price reform, and in the withdrawal of goods from state outlets.

To much of the public, the cooperative entrepreneurs are among the major villains in the scenario. Some retail trade cooperatives probably are guilty: they have the cash in hand to buy up state goods in short supply and then sell them at significantly higher prices than the ones set for them in the empty-shelved state stores.[46] This sort of speculation or "profiteering" would not typically earn praise in market economies, but it would not be regarded as abnormal. In the USSR, given the popular habituation to other standards and the lack of understanding or legitimacy accorded to the market at its rawest, it is regarded as a massive violation of justice.

But cooperative entrepreneurs in general are tarred with this brush. In the hard times now experienced, they seem, after all, to be the only ones doing well, the only real beneficiaries of perestroika: an obvious target for popular frustration. In many areas hit by the wave of miners' strikes in the summer of 1989, one of the demands was to close the cooperatives. In the wake of the strikes, top officials of the management-oriented All-Union Central Council of Trade Unions, seeking to find common ground with workers who had clearly rejected the unions' long passivity, have been very critical of cooperative "abuses,"[47] even urging a freeze through 1991 in the prices cooperatives may charge.[48] Among the bugbears of the generally conservative United Front of the Workers of Russia—founded in Sverdlovsk in September 1989, an organization combining populist appeals by discredited antireform politicians, blue-collar economic resentment, and nationalist feelings of Russian workers in the non-Russian republics—are the cooperatives and what they represent.[49]

In the face of growing tensions, even principled defenders of perestroika and the private sector's role in it, such as Leonid Abalkin, the deputy prime minister responsible for implementing the reform, have trimmed their sails somewhat. In late September 1989, Abalkin again backed the cooperatives but allowed that abuses might require more local control, including some control on prices.[50] In acknowledgment of continuing discomfort with the logic of the market, of economic levers, and of the temptation to rely again on command-administrative methods, such tactical moves demonstrate how uncertain the state's, and the society's, receptiveness to entrepreneurship remains.

Afterword: May 1991

Since this chapter was completed at the end of 1989, Soviet cooperatives, the "private" sector, and the numbers employed therein have continued to expand. But the broad economic context has changed: what looked like a drift toward nationwide economic crisis a year and a half ago has now become a full-blown crisis. Spotty evidence from opinion polls would seem to indicate increasing public acceptance of cooperatives—but this is less a product of any moral/ethical conversion to positive views of entrepreneurship than a component of a general loss of confidence in the rules and arrangements of the "old" Soviet economy. Until the announcement of a still-unclear "crisis program" in April 1991, the Gorbachev leadership lost valuable time by failing to launch economic "shock therapy" of the sort that Poland commenced, with harsh but positive results, at the beginning of 1990.

The Soviet government, having weathered—barely—the miners' strike of March–April 1991 and having imposed massive retail price increases (by decree, rather than through market forces), is now ostensibly committed to the privatization of virtually all small-to-medium–scale service and retail operations, and later to privatization, through the issuance of stock, of much larger state-sector enterprise. Certainly this is a concession to "entrepreneurship," but a desperate one. If the crisis program is actually implemented, many unprofitable enterprises will close. Unemployment must come; it will take cooperative and "private" sector growth to absorb those laid off. All in all, it is a tall order for an economy largely out of control in mid-1991—GNP down; a massive state budget deficit that exceeded, in the first quarter of 1991, the deficit projection for the whole of the year; the threat of hyperinflation looming. It is perhaps most accurate to say that if the time of entrepreneurship and a market culture has not yet arrived in the USSR, then the time of the old economy is already past. The people of the USSR—of nine republics that seem committed to remaining within some federation and six more that have signaled an intent to secede—are living in a period of uncertain transition.

Notes

Chapter 1: Brigitte Berger

1. Nathan Rosenberg and L. E. Birdzell, Jr., *How the West Grew Rich: The Economic Transformation of the Industrial World* (New York: Basic Books, 1986).

2. See David Birch, *Entrepreneurship and Employment* (New York: Basic Books, 1986), and George Gilder, *The Spirit of Enterprise* (New York: Simon and Schuster, 1984).

3. Alan Woods, *Development and the National Interest: U.S. Economic Assistance in the 21st Century* (Washington, D.C.: Agency for International Development, 1989).

4. See, for example, Gillian Godsell, "Black Entrepreneurs in South Africa" (Ph.D. diss., Boston University, 1990) (see also Chapter 6 in this volume); Cecilia Mariz, "The Religious Factor in Economic Advancement among the Brazilian Poor" (Ph.D. diss., Boston University, 1988); David Martin, *Tongues of Fire* (Oxford: Basil Blackwell, 1990); and Hernando de Soto, *The Other Path* (New York: Harper and Row, 1988).

5. Peter Berger, *The Capitalist Revolution* (New York: Basic Books, 1986).

6. Robert F. Hebert and Albert N. Link, *The Entrepreneur: Mainstream Views and Radical Critiques* (New York: Praeger, 1984).

7. Redding's findings are reported in S. Gordon Redding, *The Spirit of Chinese Capitalism* (New York: Walter de Gruyter, 1990).

Chapter 2: Brigitte Berger

1. Albert Hirschman, *The Strategy of Economic Development* (New York: Free Press, 1965).

2. Alexander Gerschenkron, "The Modernization of Entrepreneurship," in Myron Weiner, ed., *Modernization and the Dynamics of Growth* (New York: Basic Books, 1966).

3. Myron Weiner, ed., *Modernization and the Dynamics of Growth;* and Marion Levy, *Modernization: Latecomers and Survivors* (New York: Basic Books, 1972).

4. Emanuel Todd, *The Causes of Progress* (Oxford and Cambridge: Basil Blackwell, 1987).

5. Rudolf Braun, "The Demographic Transition of the Canton of Zurich in the 18th and 19th Century," in Charles Tilly, ed., *Historical Studies of Changing Fertility* (Princeton: Princeton University Press, 1978).

6. Douglass North and Robert Thomas, *The Rise of the Western World: A New Economic History* (Cambridge: Cambridge University Press, 1973).

7. Braun, "The Demographic Transition of the Canton of Zurich."

8. Gianfranco Poggi, *Calvinism and the Calvinist Spirit: Max Weber's Protestant Ethic* (Amherst: University of Massachusetts Press, 1983).

9. Jean-Francois Bergiere, "The Industrial Bourgeoisie," in P. Kilby, ed., *Entrepreneurship and Economic Development* (New York: Free Press, 1971).

10. Pierre Jeannin, *Merchants of the Sixteenth Century* (New York: Harper and Row, 1972), p. 68.

11. Karl Helleiner, "The Moral Conditions of Economic Growth," *Journal of Economic History* 11 (1951): 97–116.

12. Max Weber, *The Protestant Ethic and the Spirit of Capitalism* (London: Unwin, [1905] 1958).

13. Gordon Marshall, *In Search of the Spirit of Capitalism* (New York: Columbia University Press, 1982); Poggi, *Calvinism and the Calvinist Spirit;* Alan MacFarlane, *The Culture of Capitalism* (Oxford and Cambridge: Blackwell, 1987).

14. Norbert Elias, *The History of Manners: The Civilization Process* (New York: Pantheon, 1982).

15. David McClelland and David Winter, *Motivating Economic Achievement* (New York: Free Press, 1964).

16. Joseph Schumpeter, *A Theory of Economic Development* (Oxford and Cambridge: Oxford University Press, 1961); P. Kilby, ed., *Entrepreneurship and Economic Development* (New York: Free Press, 1979); Peter Morris and Anthony Somerset, *African Businessman: A Study of Entrepreneurship and Development* (London: Routledge and Kegan Paul, 1971).

17. Talcott Parsons and Neil Smelser, *Economy and Society* (New York: Free Press, 1956); Fred W. Riggs, *Administration in Developing Societies* (Boston: Houghton Mifflin, 1964); and Everett F. Hagen, *The Economics of Development* (Homewood, Ill.: Dorsey, 1968).

18. Hansfried Kellner and Frank Henberger, *Hidden Technocrats* (New Brunswick, N.J.: Transaction Press, 1991).

19. Peter Berger, Brigitte Berger, and Hansfried Kellner, *The Homeless Mind: Modernization and Consciousness* (New York: Random House, 1973).

20. Clark Kerr et al., *Industrialization and Industrial Man* (Cambridge: Cambridge University Press, 1960).

21. Edward Banfield, *The Moral Basis of a Backward Society* (Cambridge, Mass.: Harvard University Press, 1953).

22. Maurice Freedman, "The Family in China, Past and Present" in Harold Skinner, ed., *The Study of Chinese Society: Essays by Maurice Freedman* (Stanford: Stanford University Press, 1979).

23. Gilbert (Sin-Lun) Wong, School of Management, Hong Kong, "The Chinese Family Firm: A Model," *The British Journal of Sociology,*

Vol. XXXVI (November 1, 1985); S.K. Lau, *Society and Politics in Hong Kong,* (Hong Kong: The Chinese University Press, 1988); S. Gordon Redding, *The Spirit of Chinese Capitalism* (Berlin & New York: Walter de Gruyter, 1990).

24. Janet Salaff, *The Working Daughters of Hong Kong* (Cambridge and New York: Cambridge University Press, 1982).

25. Hugh Baker, *Chinese Family and Kinship* (New York: Columbia University Press, 1979).

26. Hernando de Soto, *The Other Path* (New York: Harper and Row, 1988).

27. Peter Lloyd, *Slums of Hope? Shanty Towns of the Third World* (New York: St. Martin's Press, 1979).

28. Lisa Peattie, "The Concept of Marginality as Applied to Squatter Settlements," MIT Department of Urban Planning, unpublished, n.d.

29. Cecilia Mariz, "The Religious Factor in Economic Development among the Urban Poor in Brazil," (Ph.D. diss., Boston University, 1988); and David Martin, *Tongues of Fire* (Oxford: Blackwell, 1990).

30. Bryand Roberts, *Cities of Peasants* (Hollywood, Calif.: Sage Publications, 1979).

31. Arthur H. Cole, "1946 Presidential Address to the Economic History Association," in Hugh G. J. Aitken, ed. *Explorations in Enterprise* (Cambridge, Mass.: Harvard University Press, 1965).

32. Bernard Rosen, *The Industrial Connection* (New York: Aldine, 1982).

33. W. J. Goode, *World Revolution and Family Patterns* (New York: Free Press, 1963).

Chapter 3: Don Lavoie

I would like to thank Arjo Klamer for steering my thoughts in this direction and the participants in the "Culture of Entrepreneurship" conference and Karen Vaughn for helpful comments on an earlier draft.

1. I am deliberately confining the idea of entrepreneurship to the creative actions that contribute to economic development in market contexts and will not address entrepreneurial actions in government contexts.

2. In most of the social sciences, however, there are encouraging signs that culture is being taken more seriously, for example, in the studies on political culture, and in the management literature's attention to corporate culture. Yet mainstream social science still treats human society as if it were a cultureless mechanism, and economics remains almost completely oblivious to cultural aspects of economic institutions and processes.

3. This chapter proceeds using a still-incomplete theory, which I would call an "interpretive" approach to economics. It has been influenced not

only by the classic works of the market-process school of economists and by my teachers in that school, Israel Kirzner and Ludwig Lachmann, but also by a school of contemporary philosophy, hermeneutics, especially the work of Gadamer. See Hans-Georg Gadamer, *Truth and Method,* 2d rev. ed. (New York: Crossroad, [1960] 1989). This study is part of a larger effort to clarify how economics could be strengthened by an infusion of hermeneutics. I have started to spell out the implications I believe hermeneutics has for economics in other related studies; see Don Lavoie, "Euclideanism versus Hermeneutics: A Reinterpretation of Misesian Apriorism," in Israel Kirzner, ed., *Subjectivism, Intelligibility, and Economic Understanding: Essays in Honor of Ludwig M. Lachmann on his Eightieth Birthday* (New York: NYU Press, 1986); idem, "The Accounting of Interpretations and the Interpretation of Accounts: The Communicative Function of 'The Language of Business'," *Accounting, Organizations and Society* 12:579–604; idem, "Hermeneutics, Subjectivity, and the Lester/Machlup Debate: Toward a More Anthropological Approach to Empirical Economics," in Warren Samuels, ed., *Economics As Discourse* (Boston: Kluwer Academic Publishing, 1990); and idem, "Understanding Differently: Hermeneutics and the Spontaneous Order of Communicative Processes," *History of Political Economy,* 22 (annual supplement): 359–77.

4. The exception that proves the rule is a new journal called *Cultural Dynamics,* which is aimed specifically at addressing this problem. See especially the journal's opening editorial by Pinxten et al.: R. Pinxten, E. Balu, D. Soberon, D. Verboven, and K. Snoeck, "Cultural Dynamics: A Vision and a Perspective," *Cultural Dynamics* 1, no.1:1–28.

5. This chapter does not attempt to offer a full-blown theory of the entrepreneurial process, or of the role of culture in that process. It focuses on the more deliberate aspects of entrepreneurship, while a fuller theory would also have to deal with unintended consequences. Moreover, it emphasizes only what happens when entrepreneurs *notice* opportunities, while a fuller theory would also have to deal with the exploitation of those opportunities. Klamer's work, for example, on the ability of entrepreneurs to form coalitions and persuade others to follow them illuminates this practical side. See Arjo Klamer, unpublished paper on entrepreneurship and rhetoric presented at the Austrian Economic Colloquium, Center for the Study of Market Processes, George Mason University, Fairfax, Va., Spring 1989. This chapter does not take up the questions of the differential strengths and weaknesses of cultures in their degree of "entrepreneurialness." Some cultures, no doubt, encourage entrepreneurship more effectively than others. My question here is, I think, a more fundamental one: How does any entrepreneurial act depend on a cultural context?

6. I will argue, however, that the Austrian school's overly individualistic way of thinking about subjective meaning limits its ability to grapple with culture.

7. F. A. Hayek, *The Fatal Conceit: The Errors of Socialism* (Chicago: University of Chicago Press, 1988).

8. Von Mises's main methodological contributions are contained in Ludwig von Mises, *Epistemological Problems of Economics*, trans. George Reisman (New York: NYU Press, [1933] 1981); idem, *Human Action* (Chicago: Henry Regnery Company, [1949] 1966); and idem, *Theory and History: An Interpretation of Social and Economic Evolution* (New Rochelle, N.Y.: Arlington House, 1969).

9. Hayek's exposition of the theory of spontaneous order can be found in many of Hayek's works. See, for example, F. A. Hayek, *Individualism and Economic Order* (Chicago: University of Chicago Press, 1948); idem, *The Counter-Revolution of Science* (London: Free Press, 1955); idem, *Studies in Philosophy, Politics, and Economics* (Chicago: University of Chicago Press, 1967); and idem, "Competition as a Discovery Procedure," in *New Studies in Philosophy, Politics, Economics and the History of Ideas* (Chicago: University of Chicago Press, 1978). My own interpretation of Hayek's argument appears in Don Lavoie, *Rivalry and Central Planning: The Socialist Calculation Debate Reconsidered* (New York: Cambridge University Press, 1985).

10. A classic exposition of the standard methodology of individual and market mental experiments can be found in Don Patinkin, *Money, Interest, and Prices: An Integration of Monetary and Value Theory* (New York: Harper and Row, 1965), pp. 11–12.

11. Economists are so fond of the maximizing and equilibrium ideas that they sometimes carry their application beyond economics to cases many noneconomists would consider absurd. Describing a parent's expenditures on a child's education as a form of capital investment, a matter of deploying resources toward the maximization of the present value of the child's future income stream, may not be a particularly helpful contribution to the sociology of the family. And describing a pattern of balance in special interest politics as an equilibrium may not be the best way to interpret political processes. But whether the economists' uses of the concept of maximizing and its partner concept of equilibrium are always appropriate, they certainly have aided enormously in the clarification of many problems in economics.

12. In an essay entitled "Alertness, Luck, and Entrepreneurial Profit," Kirzner elaborates on what he finds to be a "remarkable parallelism" between the entrepreneurial role on the strictly individual level and the market entrepreneur, identifying twelve propositions that pertain to each. See Israel Kirzner, *Perception, Opportunity, and Profit: Studies in the Theory of Entrepreneurship* (Chicago: University of Chicago Press, 1979), pp. 154–81.

13. Israel Kirzner, *Discovery and the Capitalist Process* (Chicago: University of Chicago Press, 1985), pp. 21–22.

14. For the distinction between control, in the sense of social engineering, and cultivation, in the sense of legitimate policy making, see Hayek, *The Counter-Revolution of Science,* p. 19.

15. Kirzner, *Discovery and the Capitalist Process,* pp. 8–9.

16. See for example the comments by Robert Lucas and others in Arjo Klamer's revealing book, *Conversations With Economists: New Classical Economists and Opponents Speak Out on the Current Controversy in Macroeconomics* (Totowa, N.J.: Rowman Allenheld, 1983).

17. In Hayek's work on business cycle theory, for example, all systematic market forces are said to be equilibrating, with the exception of trade cycles themselves, which is why he thought they deserved special treatment.

18. See, especially, F. A. Hayek, *Law, Legislation, and Liberty, Volume 1, Rules and Order* (Chicago: University of Chicago Press, 1973); idem, *Law, Legislation, and Liberty, Volume 2, The Mirage of Social Justice* (Chicago: University of Chicago Press, 1976); idem, *Law, Legislation, and Liberty, Volume 3, The Political Order of a Free People* (Chicago: University of Chicago Press, 1979); and idem, *The Fatal Conceit.*

19. For critiques of the "equilibration approach, see Ulrich Fehl, "Spontaneous Order and the Subjectivity of Expectations: A Contribution to the Lachmann-O'Driscoll Problem," in Israel Kirzner, ed., *Subjectivism, Intelligibility and Economic Understanding: Essays in Honor of Ludwig M. Lachmann on His Eightieth Birthday* (New York: NYU Press, 1986); and Jack High, "Equilibration and Disequilibration in the Market Process," in ibid. For elaborations of an alternative approach to spontaneous order analysis that is not equilibrium-bound, see P. Boettke, S. Horwitz, and D. Prychitko, "Beyond Equilibrium Economics: Reflections on the Uniqueness of the Austrian Tradition," *Market Process* 4, no. 2 (Fall 1986); and Steve Horwitz, "The Private Basis of Monetary Order: An Evolutionary Approach to Money and the Market Process" (Ph.D. diss., George Mason University, 1989).

20. See High, "Alertness and Judgment."

21. And of course, beyond reading opportunities, entrepreneurship involves the ability to act on them and to persuade others to join in such action. Here I am following Kirzner in focusing on the more intellectual side of the entrepreneurial process, but neither he nor I intend to underestimate the extent to which the process is a practical one. For an elaboration of the practical aspects, see Klamer, unpublished manuscript on entrepreneurship and rhetoric.

22. Even Defoe's famous character was first a social participant and only later shipwrecked. All his actions were clearly stamped with his English cultural background. But the theoretical Crusoes of economic theorizing are treated as if they are devoid of culture altogether. They have goals and deploy means to achieve them, but they are not beneficiaries of, or participants in, a larger cultural process.

23. In my view the Austrian school's version of methodological individualism is far less guilty of the difficulties I am identifying than mainstream economics is. I do believe, however, that even Austrian economics has depended too much on the imaginary construction of a Crusoe world and has accordingly failed to address the cultural dimension as much as it should.

24. Israel M. Kirzner, *Market Theory and the Price System* (Princeton, N.J.: D. Van Nostrand, 1963). Ludwig von Mises, *Nation, State, and Economy* (New York: NYU Press [1919] 1983).

25. The version of contemporary philosophy whose critique of Cartesian thinking I find the most compelling is that of philosophical hermeneutics, but one could find similar challenges in the work of the later Wittgenstein and others.

26. Von Mises, *Nation, State, and Economy*, p. 13.

27. I have tried to develop this point about the similarities between language and market processes in Lavoie, *National Economic Planning: What Is Left?* (Cambridge, Mass.: Ballinger, 1985); idem, "The Market as a Procedure for Discovery and Conveyance of Inarticulate Knowledge," *Comparative Economic Studies* 28 (Spring 1986); idem, "The Accounting of Interpretations"; idem, "Computation, Incentives, and Discovery: The Cognitive Function of Markets in Market-Socialism," *The Annals of the American Academy of Political and Social Science* 507 (January 1990): 72–79; and idem, "Understanding Differently." A more extensive elaboration of the analogy between language and markets is provided in Horwitz, "The Private Basis of Monetary Order."

Chapter 4: Janet T. Landa

I wish to thank Scott H. Gordon and Philip Selznik for helpful discussions on this chapter.

1. For a fascinating study of numerous trading groups throughout human history that have engaged in cross-cultural trade, see Philip D. Curtin, *Cross-Cultural Trade in World History* (Cambridge: Cambridge University Press, 1984).

2. For a theory of why overseas Chinese are successful as middlemen-entrepreneurs in Southeast Asia, see Janet T. Landa, "The Economics of the Ethnically Homogeneous Chinese Middleman Group: A Property Rights–Public Choice Approach" (Unpublished Ph.D. diss., Virginia Polytechnic Institute and State University, 1978). For a generalized theory of middleman success (the Chinese in Southeast Asia, Indians in East and Central Africa, Lebanese in West Africa, Jews in medieval Europe and elsewhere), see Jack

Carr and J. T. Landa, "The Economics of Symbols, Clan Names and Religion," *Journal of Legal Studies* 13 (1983): 135–56; and J. T. Landa, "Underground Economies: Generic or Sui Generis?" in *Beyond the Informal Sector,* ed. Jerry Jenkins (San Francisco: ICS Press, 1988).

3. William A. Darity, Jr., and Rhonda M. Williams, "Peddlers Forever? Culture, Competition, and Discrimination," *The American Economic Review,* Papers and Proceedings of the Ninety-Seventh Annual Meetings of the American Economic Association, December 28–30, 1984; published in 1985.

4. Israel H. Kirzner, *Competition and Entrepreneurship* (Chicago: University of Chicago Press, 1973).

5. Darity and Williams, "Peddlers Forever?" p. 256.

6. Thomas Sowell, *American Ethnic Groups* (Washington, D.C.: The Urban Institute, 1978); *Ethnic America* (New York: Basic Books, 1981); *The Economics and Politics of Race* (New York: Morrow, 1983).

7. Barry R. Chiswick, "The Earnings and Human Capital of American Jews," *Journal of Human Resources* 18 (1983): 313–36.

8. Sowell, *Ethnic America.*

9. Chiswick, "Earnings and Human Capital," p. 258.

10. Kirzner, *Competition and Entrepreneurship,* pp. 131, 205.

11. Ibid., pp. 259–60.

12. Jack Hirshleifer, "Evolutionary Models in Economics and Law: Cooperation versus Conflict Strategies," in *Research in Law and Economics* 4 (1982): 1–60.

13. For an in-depth study of the social structures and cultural values of the overseas Chinese in Southeast Asia, based on my field work in Malaysia and Singapore, see J. T. Landa, "Economics of the Ethnically Homogeneous Chinese Middleman Group." See also Landa, "Underground Economies."

14. An individual is said to engage in rational choice when his preference structure is complete (in that in comparing any two commodities he is able to prefer one to the other, or he is indifferent), transitive, and convex.

15. Herbert A. Simon, "Organizations and Markets" (unpublished manuscript, Carnegie-Mellon University, February 4, 1989), p. 13.

16. Clifford Geertz, *The Interpretation of Cultures: Selected Essays* (New York: Basic Books, 1973), p. 49.

17. Fredrik Barth, ed., *Ethnic Groups and Boundaries* (Boston: Little, Brown, 1969), p. 9.

18. Anya Peterson Royce, *Ethnic Identity* (Bloomington: Indiana University Press, 1982), p. 24.

19. Barth, *Ethnic Groups and Boundaries,* p. 13.

20. Ibid., p. 20.

21. Lewis Thomas, *The Lives of a Cell: Notes of a Biology Watcher* (New York: Penguin, 1978).

22. Philip Selznick and Gertrude Jaeger, "A Normative Theory of Culture," *American Sociological Review* 29, no. 5 (October 1964): 653–69.

23. Marshall D. Sahlins, "On the Sociology of Primitive Exchange," in *The Relevance of Models for Social Anthropology,* ed. Michael Banton, A.S.A. Monographs, no. 1 (London: Tavistock Publications, 1965).

24. Alvin Gouldner, "The Norm of Reciprocity: A Preliminary Statement," *American Sociological Review* 25 (1960): 161–78.

25. Pierre L. Van den Berghe, *The Ethnic Phenomenon* (New York: Elsevier Science Publishing Co., 1981), p. 25.

26. Barth, *Ethnic Groups and Boundaries,* p. 10.

27. Royce, *Ethnic Identity,* p. 26.

28. Ibid.

29. Robert Boyd and Peter J. Richerson, *Culture and the Evolutionary Process* (Chicago: University of Chicago Press, 1985), p. 2.

30. Elinor Ostrom, "An Agenda for the Study of Institutions," *Public Choice* 48 (1986): 5.

31. Elinor Ostrom, *Governing the Commons: The Evolution of Institutions for Collective Action* (New York: Cambridge University Press, 1990).

32. Landa, "Underground Economies."

33. Transaction cost economics began with Ronald Coase's seminal paper, "The Nature of the Firm," *Economica* 4 (1937): 386–405; reprinted in G. J. Stigler and K. E. Boulding, *Readings in Price Theory* (Homewood, Ill.: Richard D. Irwin, 1960). Coase argues that the institution of the firm emerges in a specialized exchange economy in order to economize on certain kinds of transaction costs, chief of which are contract-negotiation costs. If the price mechanism is used, input owners would be required to enter into a number of contracts with other factors with whom they cooperate. By organizing a firm, however, the costs of contract negotiation are reduced because, in place of several contracts, one employer-employee contract is substituted. The essence of the contract is that the employees agree to obey the directions and orders of the entrepreneur-coordinator within certain limits; and within these limits, the entrepreneur-coordinator directs and coordinates economic activities within the firm. To Coase, then, the distinguishing characteristic of the firm is the supersession of the price mechanism because of the transaction costs of using the latter. Today, transaction cost economics is most closely associated with Oliver E. Williamson's governance approach to the analysis of institutions of capitalism, in *Markets and Hierarchies* (New York: Free Press, 1975) and *The Economic Institutions of Capitalism* (New York: Free Press, 1985). The body of transaction cost economics most familiar to sociologists is Williamson's work, which extends the work of Coase and explicitly combines the disciplines of law, economics, and organization.

34. Williamson, *Economic Institutions,* p. 64.

35. Kenneth J. Arrow, "Political and Economic Evaluation of Social Effects and Externalities," in *The Analysis of Public Output,* ed. J. Margolis (New York: National Bureau of Economic Research, 1970).

36. Frank H. Knight, *Risk, Uncertainty, and Profit* (New York: Harper and Row, [1925] 1965); Joseph A. Schumpeter, *The Theory of Economic Development* (New York: Oxford University Press, [1934] 1961); Israel H. Kirzner, *Competition and Entrepreneurship* (Chicago: University of Chicago Press, 1973).

37. Peter Kilby, "Hunting the Heffalump," in *Entrepreneurship and Economic Development,* ed. Kilby (New York: Free Press, 1971).

38. William P. Glade, "Approaches to a Theory of Entrepreneurial Formation," *Explorations in Entrepreneurial History,* 2nd series, vol. 4, no. 3: 245–59.

39. Harvey Leibenstein, "Entrepreneurship and Development," *American Economic Review* 58 (1968): 72–83.

40. Nathaniel Leff, "Entrepreneurship and Economic Development: The Problem Revisited," *Journal of Economic Literature* 17 (1979): 48–49.

41. Ibid., p. 52.

42. Janet T. Landa, "Economics of the Ethnically Homogeneous Chinese Middleman Group"; idem, "A Theory of the Ethnically Homogeneous Middleman Group: An Institutional Alternative to Contract Law," *The Journal of Legal Studies* 10 (1981): 349–62; and idem, "Underground Economies."

43. Carr and Landa, "Economics of Symbols"; Robert Carter and Janet T. Landa, "Personal versus Impersonal Trade: The Size of Trading Groups and Contract Law," *International Review of Law and Economics* 4 1984: 15–22.

44. James M. Buchanan, *The Limits of Liberty* (Chicago: University of Chicago Press, 1975), chaps. 3, 7.

45. James S. Coleman, "Norms as Social Capital," in *Economic Imperialism,* ed. G. Radnitzky and P. Bernholz (New York: Paragon House Publishers, 1987).

46. Carr and Landa, "Economics of Symbols."

47. Royce, "Ethnic Identity," p. 202.

48. Cristina Blanc Sanzton, "Thai and Sino-Thai in Small Town Thailand: Changing Patterns of Interethnic Relations," in *Identity, Culture and Politics,* vol. 2 of *The Chinese in Southeast Asia,* ed. Linda Y. C. Lim and L. A. Peter Gosling (Singapore: Maruzen Pte. Ltd., 1983), pp. 92–125.

49. Abraham L. Udovitch and Lucette Valensi, *The Last Arab Jews: The Communities of Jerba, Tunisia* (New York: Harwood Academic Publishers, 1984).

50. Jacques Gurwith, "Antwerp Jewry Today," *Jewish Journal of Sociology* 10 (1968): 121–37.

51. Floyd Dotson and Lillian O. Dotson, *The Indian Minority of Zambia, Rhodesia, and Malawi* (New Haven: Yale University Press, 1968).

52. Royce, *Ethnic Identity,* p. 189.

53. Ibid., p. 208.

54. Mancur Olson, *The Logic of Collective Action* (Cambridge: Harvard University Press, 1965).

55. William E. Willmot, *The Chinese in Cambodia* (Vancouver: University of British Columbia, 1967); Clifton A. Barton, "Trust and Credit: Some Observations Regarding Business Strategies of Overseas Chinese Traders in South Vietnam," in *Ethnicity and Economic Activity,* vol. 1 of *The Chinese in Southeast Asia,* ed. Linda Y. C. Lim and L. A. Peter Gosling (Singapore: Maruzen Pte. Ltd., 1983).

56. Boyd and Richerson, "Sociobiology, Culture and Economic Theory," *Journal of Economic Behavior and Organization* 1 (1980): 97–121; and idem, *Culture and the Evolutionary Process.*

57. Boyd and Richerson, "Sociobiology, Culture and Economic Theory," pp. 101–2.

58. Boyd and Richerson, *Culture and the Evolutionary Process,* p. 6.

59. Ibid., pp. 14–15.

60. Ibid., p. 285.

61. Simon, "Organizations and Markets," p. 13.

62. Hirshleifer, "Evolutionary Models," p. 50.

63. Simon, "Organizations and Markets."

64. Kirzner, *Competition and Entrepreneurship.*

65. For a theory of how contract law deters breach of contract, and hence protects a trader's profit expectations, see Landa, *"Hadley v. Baxendale* and the Expansion of the Middleman Economy," *Journal of Legal Studies* 16 (1987): 455–70.

66. My theory of ethnic middleman success differs from Sowell's cultural theory of ethnic success in two ways. First, I incorporate the importance of transaction costs for explaining the institution of EHMGs in economizing on those costs in LDCs where the legal framework is not well developed. Second, whereas ingroup cooperation and group competition are central concepts in my theory of the success and persistence of EHMGs, Sowell does not appear to have such concepts in mind. Referring to the Chinese in Southeast Asia, for example, he speaks of the "Chinese aptitude for arduous and painstaking work" as an example of the cultural advantages that enable Chinese to be successful in Southeast Asia (*Economics and Politics of Race,* p. 139). By incorporating the concepts of ingroup cooperation and group competition, my theory takes account of Darity and Williams's criticism of Sowell's work by showing why and how cultural barriers to entry are erected and preserved by the successful EHMGs. My theory is also consistent with sociological theory of ethnic middleman success associated with the work of sociologist Edna Bonacich, but goes beyond it by incorporating transaction cost economics. Bonacich explains the success of minority middleman groups by referring to their ethnocentrism, attachment to their homeland, their status

as sojourners and the effects of sojourning on their attitudes toward thrift, their ability to accumulate liquid capital, and a high degree of internal solidarity. "Communal solidarity plays an important role in the economic position of the middleman group. Family, regional, dialect, and ultimately ethnic ties are used as preferential economic treatment. The 'primordial tie' of blood provides a basis of trust, and is reinforced by multi-purpose formal and informal associations" (Edna Bonacich, "A Theory of Middleman Minorities," *American Sociological Review* 38:5 (October 1973): 583–94).

Chapter 5: David Martin

1. Cecilia Mariz, "Religion and Coping with Poverty in Brazil" (Ph.D. diss. Boston University, 1989); and Cornelia Butler Flora, *Pentecostalism in Colombia: Baptism by Fire and Spirit* (Cranbury, N. J.: Fairleigh Dickinson University Press, 1976).

2. David L. Clawson, "Religious Allegiance and Development in Rural Latin America," *Journal of Interamerican Studies and World Affairs* 26 (1984): 499–524.

3. Jean-Pierre Bastian, *Protestantismo y Sociedad en México* (Mexico City: CUPSA, 1983).

4. Norman B. Schwartz and Rubem E. Reina, "The Structural Context of Religious Conversion in El Péten, Guatemala," *American Ethnologist* 1 (1974): 157–91.

5. Emilio Willems, *Followers of the New Faith* (Nashville, Tenn.: Vanderbilt University Press, 1967).

6. Schwartz and Reina, "The Structural Context of Religious Conversion in El Péten."

Chapter 6: Gillian Godsell

1. S. G. Redding, "Culture and Entrepreneurial Behavior among the Overseas Chinese" in Brigitte Berger, ed., *The Culture of Entrepreneurship* (San Francisco: ICS Press, 1991).

2. Gillian Godsell and Van Dijk, eds., *The Social Context of Small-Scale Business Development: Report of a Workshop* (Johannesburg: Centre for Policy Studies, University of the Witwatersrand, 1988).

3. Gillian Godsell, "The Social Networks of South African Entrepreneurs" (Unpublished Ph.D. diss., Boston University, 1990).

4. Jill Nattrass, *The South African Economy* (Cape Town: Oxford University Press, 1988).

5. World Bank, *World Development Report* (New York: Oxford University Press, 1990).

6. Brigitte Berger, ed., *The Culture of Entrepreneurship* (San Francisco: ICS Press, 1991).

7. Godsell, "Social Networks."

8. Redding, "Culture and Entrepreneurial Behavior."

9. Suzanne Model, "A Comparative Perspective on the Ethnic Enclave: Blacks, Italians, and Jews in New York City," *International Migration Review* 19 (1985): 64–81.

10. Ebrahim E. Kharsany, "A Profile of the South African Indian Business Community: Reasons for Success and Failure" (Unpublished M.B.A. thesis, University of the Witwatersrand, Johannesburg, 1971).

11. Godsell, "Social Networks."

12. Ibid.

13. Ibid.

14. Walter D. Connor, "The Rocky Road: Entrepreneurship in the Soviet Economy, 1986–1989," in Brigitte Berger, ed., *The Culture of Entrepreneurship.*

15. D. Bagwandeen, "Historical Perspectives," in *The Indian South Africans,* A. J. Arkin, K. P. Mahyar, G. J. Pillay, eds. (Durban: Owen Burgess, 1989).

16. B. N. Mokoatle, "The Black Entrepreneur in South Africa," in *South Africa's Urban Blacks,* G. Marais and R. Van Der Kooy, eds. (Pretoria: Unisa School of Business Leadership, 1978).

17. Connor, "The Rocky Road."

18. Khaba Mkhize, "The Stick That Beats the Baas," *Frontline* (Feb. 1980): 31–32.

19. Colin Bundy, *The Rise and Fall of the South African Peasantry* (London: Heineman, 1979), p. 42.

20. Gillian Godsell, "Work Values in Organisations," in *Behaviour in Organisations: South African Perspectives,* 2nd ed., Julian Barling, Clive Fullagar, Stephen Bluen, eds. (Johannesburg: McGraw-Hill, 1986).

21. Godsell, "Social Networks."

22. Dan O'Meara, *Volkskapitalisme: Class, Capital and Ideology in the Development of Afrikaner Nationalism, 1934–1948* (Johannesburg: Ravan Press, 1983).

23. Francis Wilson and Mamphela Ramphele, *Uprooting Poverty: The South African Challenge* (Cape Town: David Philip, 1989).

24. E. P. Du Plessis, *'n Volk staan op: die Ekonomiese Volkskongres en daarna* (Cape Town: Human en Rousseau, 1964).

25. Steven Black, personal communication, based on Ph.D. dissertation in progress, on the provision of small-business training to white and black schoolchildren in South Africa.

26. O'Meara, *Volkskapitalisme.*

Chapter 7: Ashis Gupta

This chapter is based on a study made possible by a grant from the Institute for the Study of Economic Culture, Boston University. The author wishes to express his gratitude to Subroto Sengupta, Visiting Faculty, Indian Institute of Management, Calcutta, for his invaluable help in implementing this study.

1. See Thomas A. Timberg, *The Marwaris: From Traders to Industrialists* (New Delhi: Vikas Publishing House, 1978); also, Milton Singer, *When a Great Tradition Modernizes* (New York: Praeger Publishers, 1972). A more recent work is Gita Piramal and Margaret Hardek, *India's Industrialists, Volume One* (Washington, D.C.: Three Continents Press, Inc., 1985).

2. Quoted from Ketaki Kushari Dyson, *A Various Universe: A Study of the Journals and Memoirs of British Men and Women in the Indian Subcontinent, 1756–1856* (Delhi: Oxford University Press, 1978), p. 130.

3. From John Mooney, "Trade Families Move with the Times," in *Beverly Times,* Beverly, Massachusetts, June 3, 1986.

4. Susan S. Bean, "Yankee Traders and Indian Merchants, 1785–1865," in *Festival of India* (New York: Abrams, 1985).

5. N. K. Sinha, *The Economic History of Bengal, Vol. I* (Calcutta: Firma K. L. Mukhopadhyay, 1965), pp. 35–36.

6. The French, however, extracted a revenge of sorts in the period between 1764 and 1778. According to Sinha, *Economic History of Bengal, Vol. I,* pp. 36–37: "They traded on the capital of the servants of the English East India Company who wanted to remit their fortune to England and keep their remittance concealed from their masters. There was no parliamentary provision at this stage against such transactions and the French private traders did brisk business in French bills of exchange. The court of Directors in England naturally complained in 1772, 'We cannot but enquire how the French without money or influence fill their ships with the prime and valuable manufactures of Bengal and from whom they draw such large and to us ruinous resources.'"

7. N. K. Sinha, *The Economic History of Bengal, Vol. II* (Calcutta: Firma K. L. Mukhopadhyay, 1965), p. 148.

8. Ibid., p. 179.

9. Sinha, *Economic History of Bengal, Vol. I,* p. 181.

10. Rajat Kanta Ray, *Social Conflict and Political Unrest in Bengal 1875–1927* (Delhi: Oxford University Press, 1984), pp. 150–151.

11. Ibid., p. 226.

12. Ibid., p. 227.

13. See *Aspects of the Black Economy in India,* Government of India, Ministry of Finance, New Delhi, March 1985, p. 52.

14. J. H. Broomfield, *Elite Conflict in a Plural Society: Twentieth-Century Bengal* (Berkeley: University of California Press, 1968), pp. 12–13, "A socially privileged and consciously superior group, economically dependent upon landed rents and professional and clerical employment; keeping its distance from the masses by its acceptance of high-caste proscriptions and its command of education, sharing a pride in its language, its literate culture, and its history; and maintaining its communal integration through a fairly complex institutional structure that it had proved remarkably ready to adapt and augment to extend its social power and political opportunities."

15. Singer, *When a Great Tradition Modernizes,* p. 350.

16. Singer, pp. 351–352.

17. Max Weber, *The Religion of India* (Glencoe, Illinois: Free Press, 1960), p. 200.

Chapter 8: S. G. Redding

1. Peter L. Berger, "An East Asian Development Model?" in *In Search of an East Asian Development Model,* eds. Berger and M. H. H. Hsiao (New Brunswick: Transaction Books, 1988), p. 6.

2. Lex Donaldson, *In Defence of Organization Theory* (Cambridge: Cambridge University Press, 1985).

3. Henry Mintzberg, *The Structuring of Organization* (Englewood Cliffs, N.J.: Prentice-Hall, 1979).

4. Stewart R. Clegg and S. G. Redding, *Capitalism in Contrasting Cultures* (New York: Walter De Gruyter, 1990).

5. This project is being conducted from the University of Hong Kong, under the sponsorship of Boston University's Institute for the Study of Economic Culture. For details, see R. D. Whitley, "Taking Firms Seriously as Economic Actors: Towards a Sociology of Firm Behaviour," *Organization Studies* 1987; Whitley, "The Social Structuring of East Asian Business Recipes: Towards a Comparative Analysis of Dominant Enterprise Structures," working paper no. 179, Manchester Business School, 1989; Redding and Whitley, "Beyond Bureaucracy: Towards a Comparative Analysis of Forms of Economic Resource Co-ordination and Control," in Clegg and Redding, *Capitalism in Contrasting Cultures.*

6. Berger, "An East Asian Development Model?" p. 10.

7. S. M. Greenfield and A. Strickon, "A New Paradigm for the Study of Entrepreneurship and Social Change," *Economic Development and Cultural Change* 29, no. 3 (1981): 467–99; J. A. Schumpeter, *The Theory of Economic Development* (Cambridge, Mass.: Harvard University Press, 1934).

8. Hugh G. J. Aitkin, "Entrepreneurial Research," in *Exploration in Enterprise,* ed. Aitkin (Cambridge: Cambridge University Press, 1965).

9. David C. McClelland, *The Achieving Society* (Princeton, N.J.: Van Nostrand, 1961); Everett E. Hagen, *On the Theory of Social Change* (Homewood, Ill.: Dorsey Press, 1962).

10. Greenfield and Strickon, "A New Paradigm," p. 471.

11. Ibid., p. 474.

12. Ibid., p. 484.

13. Ibid., p. 496.

14. C. C. Ragin, *The Comparative Method* (Berkeley: University of California Press, 1987).

15. Interviews were conducted by the author in Hong Kong, by Dr. Michael Hsiao in Taiwan, Dr. Theodora Ting Chau in Singapore, and the late Mr. Lie Han Hwa in Indonesia. For details see Redding, *The Spirit of Chinese Capitalism* (New York: Walter de Gruyter, 1990).

16. Experience of Communist China is perhaps not so critical for most overseas Chinese, since they left before its effects. In addition, although the Communist state has attempted welfare, its problems are those of having simply produced an equalization of poverty, and not having alleviated despotism.

17. G. G. Hamilton, "Patriarchalism in Imperial China and Western Europe: A Revision of Weber's Sociology of Domination," *Theory and Society* 13 (1984): 393–425.

18. S. K. Lau, *Society and Politics in Hong Kong* (Hong Kong: Chinese University Press, 1982).

19. Janet T. Landa, "A Theory of the Ethnically Homogeneous Middleman Group: An Institutional Alternative to Contract Law," *The Journal of Legal Studies* 10 (1981): 349–62.

20. G. L. Hicks and S. G. Redding, "Culture and Corporate Performance in the Philippines: The Chinese Puzzle," in *Essays in Development Economics in Honor of Harry T. Oshima* (Manila: Philippines Institute for Developmental Studies, 1982), pp. 199–215.

21. Simon Tam, "Centrifugal versus Centripetal Growth Processes: Contrasting Ideal Types for Conceptualizing the Developmental Patterns of Chinese and Japanese Firms," in Clegg and Redding, *Capitalism in Contrasting Cultures.*

22. N. Dannhaeuser, "Evolution and Devolution of Downward Channel Integration in the Philippines," *Economic Development and Cultural Change* 29, no. 3 (1981): 577–95.

23. K. Hewison, "The Structure of Banking Capital in Thailand," contribution to symposium on "Changing Identities of the Southeast Asian Chinese Since World War II," (Canberra: Australian National University: 1985).

24. Robert F. Silin, *Leadership and Values* (Cambridge, Mass.: Harvard University Press, 1976).

25. S. G. Redding and S. Tam, "Networks and Molecular Organizations: An Exploratory View of Chinese Business Firms in Hong Kong," in *Proceedings: Academy of International Business Hong Kong Conference,* 1985.

26. S. G. Redding, "Developing Managers without 'Management Development': The Overseas Chinese Solution," *Management Education and Development* 17, no. 3 (1986): 271–81; V. S. Limlingan, "The Chinese Walkabout: A Case Study in Entrepreneurial Education," working paper, Asian Institute of Management, Manila, 1980.

27. G. Poggi, *Calvinism and the Capitalist Spirit: Max Weber's Protestant Ethic* (London: Macmillan, 1983), p. 83.

28. Claes Hallgren, "Morally United and Politically Divided: The Chinese Community of Penang," *Stockholm Studies in Social Anthropology* 16 (1986), University of Stockholm.

29. Details of this literature are given in Redding, *The Spirit of Chinese Capitalism.*

30. Lucian Pye, *Asian Power and Politics* (Cambridge, Mass.: Harvard University Press, 1985).

31. Mark Granovetter, "Economic Action and Social Structure: The Problem of Embeddedness," *American Journal of Sociology* 19, no. 3 (1985): 481–510.

Chapter 9: Richard Whitley

1. John Child, "Culture, Contingency and Capitalism in the Cross-National Study of Organization," in *Research in Organizational Behavior 3,* eds. L. L. Cummings and B. L. Staw (Greenwich, Conn.: JAI Press, 1981); K. H. Roberts, "On Looking at an Elephant: An Evaluation of Cross-Cultural Research Related to Organizations," *Psychological Bulletin* 74 (1970): 327–50.

2. For example, see G. Hofstede, *Culture's Consequences* (London: Sage, 1980).

3. E. B. Ayal, "Value Systems and Economic Development in Japan and Thailand," in *Man, State and Society in Contemporary Southeast Asia,* ed. R. O. Tilman (New York: Praeger, 1969).

4. C. Johnson, *MITI and the Japanese Miracle* (Cambridge, Mass.: MIT Press, 1982).

5. Alice H. Amsden, "The State and Taiwan's Economic Development," in *Bringing the State Back In,* ed. P. B. Evans et al. (Cambridge: Cambridge University Press, 1985); F. C. Deyo, ed., *The Social Economy of the New Asian Industrialism* (Ithaca: Cornell University Press, 1987).

6. Gordon Redding, "The Role of the Entrepreneur in the New Asian Capitalism," in *In Search of an East Asian Development Model,* ed. P. Berger and H.H.M. Hsiao (New Brunswick, N.J.: Transaction Books, 1988).

7. P. Johnson, *New Firms: An Economic Perspective* (London: Allen and Unwin, 1986), pp. 16–19; G. P. Sweeney, *Innovation, Entrepreneurs and Regional Development* (London: Frances Pinter, 1987), pp. 8–21.

8. D. J. Storey and S. Johnson, *Job Generation and Labour Market Change* (London: Macmillan, 1987).

9. J. Shutt and R. Whittington, "Fragmentation Strategies and the Rise of Small Units: Cases from the North West," *Regional Studies* 21 (1987: 13–23).

10. D. Keeble and E. Wever, "Introduction," in *New Firms and Regional Development,* ed. Keeble and Wever (London: Croom Helm, 1986).

11. Storey and Johnson, *Job Generation.*

12. P. Aydalot, "The Location of New Firm Creation: The French Case," in *New Firms and Regional Development,* ed. Keeble and Wever; D. J. Storey, *Entrepreneurship and the New Firm* (London: Croom Helm, 1982). Sweeney, *Innovation;* Richard Whittington, "Regional Bias in New Firm Formation in the United Kingdom," *Regional Studies* 18 (1984): 253–56.

13. Pom Ganguly, *UK Small Business Statistics and International Comparisons* (London: Harper and Row, 1985); Storey, *Entrepreneurship and the New Firm,* pp. 6–13.

14. OECD, "Employment in Small and Large Firms: Where Have the Jobs Come From?" *OECD Employment Outlook,* September 1985: 64–82.

15. Storey and Johnson, *Job Generation,* p. 18.

16. Storey and Johnson, "Small- and Medium-Sized Enterprises and Employment Creation in the EEC Countries," in *Job Creation in Small- and Medium-Sized Enterprises,* ed. Storey and Johnson (Luxembourg: EEC, 1987), p. 10.

17. L. Lindmark, "Sweden," in *The Small Firm: An International Survey,* ed. Storey (London: Croom Helm, 1983).

18. Johnson and Storey, "Employment Creation in the EEC Countries," p. 11.

19. "VAT Registrations and Deregistrations of UK Businesses, 1980–88," *British Business,* August 25, 1989, pp. 10–12.

20. Ganguly, *UK Small Business Statistics.*

21. C. Hull, "Job Generation in the Federal Republic of Germany," in Storey and Johnson, eds., *Job Creation.*

22. Egbert Wever, "New Firm Formation in the Netherlands," in Keeble and Wever, eds., *New Firms and Regional Development.*

23. Storey and Johnson, *Job Generation.*

24. J. I. Gershuny and I. D. Miles, *The New Service Economy: The Transformation of Employment in Industrial Societies* (London: Frances Pinter, 1983).

25. John Allen, "Towards a Post-Industrial Economy?" in *The Economy in Question,* ed. J. Allen and D. Massey (London: Sage, 1988).

26. Johnson and Storey, "Employment Creation in the EEC Countries."

27. OECD, "Where Have the Jobs Come From?"; Storey and Johnson, *Job Generation,* p. 124.

28. Keeble and Wever, "Introduction."

29. Johnson, *New Firms,* pp. 74–81.

30. Hull, "Job Generation in the Federal Republic of Germany."

31. M. Cross, *New Firm Formation and Regional Development* (Farnborough, Hampshire: Gower, 1981), pp. 204–9; Johnson, *New Firms,* pp. 121–34; Storey and Johnson, *Job Generation.*

32. M. Binks and A. Jennings, "Small Firms as a Source of Economic Rejuvenation," in *The Survival of the Small Firm 1,* ed. J. Curran, J. Stanworth, D. Watkins (Aldershot: Gower, 1986); A. Gould and D. Keeble, "New Firms and Industrialisation in East Anglia," *Regional Studies* 18 (1983): 189–201.

33. R. Donckels and B. Dupont, "New Entrepreneurship and Labour Market Conditions," *International Small Business Journal* 5 (1989): 45–58; Storey, "The Case of Cleveland County."

34. Storey, *Entrepreneurship and the New Firm;* see also M. J. Piore and C. F. Sabel, *The Second Industrial Divide* (New York: Basic Books, 1984).

35. A. Amin, "A Model of the Small Firm in Italy," in *Small Firms and Industrial Districts in Italy,* ed. E. Goodman and J. Bamford (London: Routledge, 1989); S. Brusco, "Small Firms and Industrial Districts: The Experience of Italy," in Keeble and Wever, *New Firms and Regional Development;* M. H. Lazerson, "Organizational Growth of Small Firms: An Outcome of Markets and Hierarchies," *American Sociological Review* 53 (1988): 330–342.

36. Keeble and Wever, "Introduction."

37. Storey and Johnson, *Job Generation,* pp. 20–21.

38. Piore and Sabel, *The Second Industrial Divide,* pp. 208–20.

39. Julia Bamford, "The Development of Small Firms, the Traditional Family and Agrarian Families in Italy," in *Entrepreneurship in Europe,* ed. R. Goffee and R. Scase (London: Croom Helm, 1987); Brusco, "Small Firms and Industrial Districts."

40. Johnson and Storey, "Employment Creation in the EEC Countries."

41. Shutt and Whittington, "Fragmentation Strategies"; Whittington, "Regional Bias."

42. Guido Rey, "Small Firms: Profile and Analysis, 1981–85," in *Small Firms and Industrial Districts in Italy,* ed. E. Goodman and J. Bamford (London: Routledge, 1989).

43. George Richardson, "The Organisation of Industry," *Economic Journal* 82 (1972): 883–96.

44. Brusco, "Small Firms and Industrial Districts."

45. Keeble and Wever, "Introduction."

46. Aydalot, "The French Case"; Storey, "The Case of Cleveland County."

47. For example, see Keeble and Wever, *New Firms and Regional Development.*

48. Ganguly, *UK Small Business Statistics;* Johnson and Storey, "Employment Creation in the EEC Countries"; Storey and Johnson, *Job Generation.*

49. OECD, "Where Have the Jobs Come From?"; W. Korte, "Small- and Medium-Sized Establishments in Western Europe" in D. Keeble and E. Wever, eds., *New Firms and Regional Development* (London: Croom Helm, 1986).

50. Korte, "Small- and Medium-Sized Establishments in Western Europe."

51. Marco Bellandi, "The Role of Small Firms in the Development of Italian Manufacturing Industry," in *Small Firms and Industrial Districts in Italy,* ed. E. Goodman and J. Bamford (London: Routledge, 1989); Brusco, "Small Firms and Industrial Districts."

52. J. Bamford, "The Development of Small Firms."

53. Sven Illeris, "New Firm Creation in Denmark: The Importance of the Cultural Background," in *New Firms and Regional Development,* ed. Keeble and Wever.

54. S. J. Prais, *The Evolution of Giant Firms in Britain* (Cambridge: Cambridge University Press, 1976); Storey, "The Case of Cleveland County."

55. Prais, *The Evolution of Giant Firms,* pp. 115–24.

56. Ibid., p. 161.

57. Ibid., p. 156.

58. G. Ingham, *Capitalism Divided? The City and Industry in British Social Development* (London: Macmillan, 1984).

59. Prais, *The Evolution of Giant Firms,* p. 10.

60. Ibid., p. 160; Storey, *Entrepreneurship and the New Firm.*

61. John Child, M. Fores, I. Glover, P. Lawrence, "A Price to Pay? Professionalism and Work Organisation in Britain and West Germany," *Sociology* 17 (1985): 63–78; Ingham, *Capitalism Divided?*

62. M. Savage, P. Dickens, T. Fielding, "Some Social and Political Implications of the Contemporary Fragmentation of the 'Service Class' in Britain," *International Journal of Urban and Regional Research* 12 (1988): 455–75.

63. Keeble and Wever, *New Firms and Regional Development.*

64. Storey, "The Case of Cleveland County"; and idem, *Entrepreneurship and the New Firm.*

65. Wever, "New Firm Formation in the Netherlands."

66. J. M. Pennings, "Organisational Birth Frequencies: An Empirical Investigation," *Administrative Science Quarterly* 27 (1982): 120–44.

67. Ganguly, *UK Small Business Statistics.*

68. Aydalot, "The French Case"; Keeble and T. Kelley, "New Firms and High Technology Industry in the United Kingdom: The Case of Computer Electronics," in *New Firms and Regional Development,* ed. Keeble and Wever.

69. Evangelina Dokopoulo, "Small Manufacturing Firms and Regional Development in Greece: Patterns and Changes, " in *New Firms and Regional Development,* ed. Keeble and Wever; Korte, "Small- and Medium-Sized Establishments in Western Europe"; Wever, "New Firm Formation in the Netherlands."

70. A. Del Monte and A. Giannola, "Relevance and Nature of Small and Medium Sized Firms in Southern Italy," *Regional Studies* 23 (1989): 219–30; A. Del Monte and R. de Luzenberger, "The Effect of Regional Policy on New Firm Formation in Southern Italy," *Regional Studies* 23: 219–30.

71. Storey, *Entrepreneurship and the New Firm;* Whittington, "Regional Bias."

72. Aydalot, "The French Case."

73. Storey and Johnson, *Job Generation,* pp. 122–55.

74. Amin, "A Model of the Small Firm in Italy"; Bamford, "The Development of Small Firms"; Brusco, "Small Firms and Industrial Districts"; Lazerson, "Organizational Growth of Small Firms."

75. E. Goodman, "Introduction: The Political Economy of the Small Firm in Italy, " in *Small Firms and Industrial Districts in Italy,* ed. Goodman and Bamford.

76. Amin, "A Model of the Small Firm in Italy."

77. G. Redding and Simon Tam, "Networks and Molecular Organisations: An Exploratory View of Chinese Firms in Hong Kong," in *Perspectives in International Business,* ed. K. C. Mun and T. S. Chan (Hong Kong: Chinese University of Hong Kong Press, 1985).

78. A. Del Monte, "Job Generation in Small and Medium Sized Enterprises: Italy," in *Job Creation,* ed. Storey and Johnson.

79. Bamford, "The Development of Small Firms"; Bellandi, "The Role of Small Firms."

80. Lazerson, "Organizational Growth of Small Firms."

81. For example, Amin, "A Model of the Small Firm in Italy"; Piore and Sabel, *The Second Industrial Divide.*

82. Carlo Trigilia, "Small Firm Development and Political Subcultures in Italy," in *Small Firms and Industrial Districts in Italy,* ed. Goodman and Bamford.

83. Linda Weiss, "The Italian State and Small Business," *European Journal of Sociology* 25 (1984): 214–41.

84. Brusco, "Small Firms and Industrial Districts."

85. Simon Tam, "Centrifugal versus Centripetal Growth Processes: Contrasting Ideal Types for Conceptualising the Developmental Patterns of Chinese and Japanese Firms," in *Capitalism in Contrasting Cultures,* ed. S. Clegg and G. Redding (Berlin: de Gruyter, 1990).

86. Anna Pollert, "The 'Flexible Firm': Fixation or Fact?" *Work, Employment and Society* 2 (1988): 281–316.

87. Cristel Lane, "Industrial Change in Europe: The Pursuit of Flexible Specialisation in Britain and West Germany," *Work, Employment and Society* 2 (1988): 141–68.

88. Keeble and Kelley, "New Firms and High Technology Industry in the United Kingdom."

89. G. P. Sweeney, *Innovation, Entrepreneurs, and Regional Development* (New York: St. Martin's Press, 1987), pp. 108–20.

90. A. C. Cooper, "Technological Entrepreneurship: What Do We Know?" in *The Survival of the Small Firm 2,* ed. Curran, Stanworth, Watkins.

91. For example, Brusco, "Small Firms and Industrial Districts"; Roy Rothwell, "The Role of Small Firms in Technological Innovation," in *The Survival of the Small Firm 2,* ed. Curran, Stanworth, Watkins.

92. Brusco, "Small Firms and Industrial Districts."

93. Rothwell, "The Role of Small Firms in Technological Innovation."

94. Illeris, "New Firm Creation in Denmark."

95. Rodney Clark, *The Japanese Company* (New Haven: Yale University Press, 1979); Ronald Dore, *Flexible Rigidities* (Stanford: Stanford University Press, 1986).

96. J. Curran and J. Stanworth, "Franchising in the Modern Economy: Towards a Theoretical Understanding," *International Small Business Journal* 2 (1983): 8–26.

97. Rothwell, "The Role of Small Firms in Technological Innovation."

98. D. Friedman, *The Misunderstood Miracle* (Ithaca, N.Y.: Cornell University Press, 1988), pp. 166–75.

99. Linda Weiss, *Creating Capitalism: The State and Small Business since 1945* (Oxford: Blackwell, 1988).

100. P. Bourdieu and J. C. Passeron, *Reproduction in Education, Society and Culture* (London: Sage, 1977), pp. 72–79; Bourdieu, L. Boltanski, and M. de Saint Martin, "Les stratégies de reconversion," *Social Science Information* 12 (1973): 61–113.

101. Savage, Dickens, Fielding, "Some Social and Political Implications."

102. E. Auster and H. Aldrich, "Small Business Vulnerability, Ethnic Enclaves and Ethnic Enterprise," in *Ethnic Communities in Business,* ed. R. Ward and R. Jenkins (Cambridge: Cambridge University Press, 1984); J. Boissevain and H. Grotenberg, "Ethnic Enterprise in the Netherlands: The Surinamese of Amsterdam," in *Entrepreneurship in Europe,* ed. Goffee and Scase; T. Jones

and D. McEvoy, "Ethnic Enterprise: The Popular Image," in *The Survival of the Small Firm 1,* ed. Stanworth and Watkins; Susan Nowikowski, "Snakes and Ladders: Asian Business in Britain," in *Ethnic Communities in Business,* ed. Ward and Jenkins; Frank Reeves and Robin Ward, "West Indian Business in Britain," ibid.

103. N. Mayer, "Small Business and Social Mobility in France," in *Entrepreneurship in Europe,* ed. Goffee and Scase.

104. Illeris, "New Firm Creation in Denmark"; see also A. Lafuente and V. Salas, "Types of Entrepreneurs and Firms: The Case of New Spanish Firms," *Strategic Management Journal* 10 (1989): 17–30.

105. Goodman, "Introduction: The Political Economy of the Small Firm in Italy."

106. Robin Palmer, "The Rise of the Britalian Culture Entrepreneur," in *Ethnic Communities in Business,* ed. Ward and Jenkins; Reeves and Ward, "West Indian Business in Britain," ibid.

107. Dore, *Flexible Rigidities;* Lazerson, "Organizational Growth of Small Firms."

108. Giacomo Becattini, "Sectors and/or Districts: Some Remarks on the Conceptual Foundation of Industrial Economics," in *Small Firms and Industrial Districts in Italy,* ed. Goodman and Bamford.

109. Marco Bellandi, "The Industrial District in Marshall," ibid.

110. R. Whitley, "East Asian Enterprise Structures and the Comparative Analysis of Forms of Business Organisation," *Organisation Studies* 11 (1990): 47–74.

Chapter 10: Walter D. Connor

This chapter draws heavily on two broad treatments of the emergence of private enterprise: Carla Kruger, "Early Swallows of Transformation: Alternative Property Forms in the Soviet Union under Perestroika" (Department of Political Science, Massachusetts Institute of Technology, September 1989); and Anthony Jones and William Moskoff, "New Cooperatives in the USSR," Problems of Communism, *Nov.–Dec. 1989: 27–39.*

1. *Pravda,* March 28, 1986, 1.

2. N. Shmelev, "Avansy i dolgi," *Novyi mir,* no. 6, 1987, 142–158. Also in *Problems of Economics* 30, no. 10: 7–43.

3. On cooperatives, see *Ekonomicheskaia gazeta,* no. 43 (October), 1986, pp. 15–16. On individual labor, see *Pravda,* November 1, 1986, 1 and 3.

4. For examples on bureaucratic resistance, see *Izvestiia,* December 12, 1987, 5; *Izvestiia,* May 16, 1987, 2. On legal support, see *Izvestiia,* September 10, 1987, 3. On enabling rules, see *Pravda,* December 20, 1986, 3.

5. Anthony Jones and William Moskoff, "Private Enterprise," citing *Current Digest of the Soviet Press,* no. 30, 1988, 26. In addition, however, cooperatives were to pay approximately 12 percent of their income into the state's social insurance fund and 10 percent to a fund for the "development of cooperatives."

6. See John Tedstrom, "New Draft Law on Income Taxes," *Report on the USSR* (Radio Liberty), no. 24 (June 16, 1989), 8–10.

7. *Sotsialisticheskaia industriia,* February 21, 1989, 2.

8. *Pravda,* June 8, 1986, 2–5.

9. Jones and Moskoff, "Private Enterprise," citing *Current Digest of the Soviet Press,* no. 1, 1989, 1–10.

10. John Tedstrom, "New Regulations for Soviet Cooperatives," Report on the USSR, no. 5: 31.

11. *Argumenty i fakty,* no. 18, 1989, 6; *Ekonomicheskaia gazeta,* no. 37, 1989, 10.

12. John Tedstrom, "The Status of Soviet Cooperatives," *Report on the USSR,* no. 34: 13.

13. Ibid.

14. See Kruger, "Early Swallows," 40.

15. A. Glushchetskii, "Novye kooperativy: pliusy i minusy," *Ekonomicheskie nauki,* no. 12, 1988, 28.

16. Tedstrom, "Status of Cooperatives," 13.

17. Tedstrom, "The Soviet Cooperative Movement: An Update," *Report on the USSR,* no. 41, 1989, 4–5.

18. See Jones and Moskoff, "Private Enterprise," 30–31, and sources cited therein.

19. *Argumenty i fakty,* no. 18, 1989, 6; see also Kruger, "Early Swallows," 1–53.

20. For an overview, see Nancy Lubin, *Labour and Nationality in Soviet Central Asia: An Uneasy Compromise* (Princeton, N.J.: Princeton University Press, 1984).

21. *Sotsialisticheskaia industriia,* Februrary 21, 1989, 2.

22. See A. Luk'ianov in *Pravda,* July 25, 1989.

23. See *Sotsialisticheskaia industriia,* July 28, 1989, 3.

24. *Moscow News,* no. 28 (July 16–23, 1989), 8–9.

25. The pages that follow draw heavily on the current author's *The Accidental Proletariat: Workers, Politics, and Crisis in Gorbachev's Russia* (Princeton, N.J.: Princeton University Press, 1991, forthcoming) chap. 7.

26. *Izvestiia,* July 27, 1988, 1. Also in *Foreign Broadcast Information Service—Soviet Union,* August 4, 1988, 63.

27. *Izvestiia,* February 27, 1988, 3. (Also in *FBIS,* March 11, 1988, 42).

28. James R. Millar and Elizabeth Clayton, "Quality of Life: Subjective Measures of Relative Satisfaction," Soviet Interview Project Working Paper, No. 9 (Urbana, Ill: 1986, mimeo), 10.

29. *Argumenty i fakty,* no. 13, 1987, 4–5.

30. *Izvestiia,* February 27, 1988, 3.

31. Shmelev, "Avansy i dolgi," 13.

32. V. Z. Rogovin, "Sotsial'naia spravedlivost' i sotsialisticheskoe raspredelenie zhiznennykh blag," *Voprosy filosofii,* no. 9, 1986, 17.

33. Kruger, "Early Swallows," 75, citing data from the "Sociological Service" of *Moscow News.*

34. Ibid., 77.

35. Data from a survey by the recently established All-Union Institute for the Study of Public Opinion, which works under the auspices of the All-Union Central Council of Trade Unions and the State Committee on Labor and Social Problems.

36. *Moscow News,* no. 13, 1987, 14; and no. 47, 1987, 14.

37. Tedstrom "Cooperative Movement," 3.

38. *Moscow News,* no. 22, 1988, 11.

39. *Moscow News,* no. 28, 1989, 8.

40. *Izvestiia,* June 2, 1986.

41. *Sovetskaia Rossiia,* May 9, 1989, 2.

42. *Izvestiia,* December 12, 1987, 5.

43. *Current Digest of the Soviet Press,* no. 12, 1989, 27–28.

44. *Trud,* April 24, 1988, 1.

45. *Pravda,* April 20, 1989.

46. *Financial Times,* October 17, 1989, 20.

47. *Report on the USSR,* no. 41 (October 13, 1989), 38.

48. *Report on the USSR,* no. 37 (September 15, 1989), 32.

49. *Financial Times,* September 13, 1989, 3.

50. Tedstrom, "Cooperative Movement," 3.

Index